D1207468

The Doctor on the Stage

The Doctor
on the Stage

MEDICINE AND MEDICAL MEN

IN SEVENTEENTH-CENTURY ENGLAND

HERBERT SILVETTE

Edited by Francelia Butler

THE UNIVERSITY OF TENNESSEE PRESS · KNOXVILLE

822
558d

Copyright © 1967
All Rights Reserved
The University of Tennessee Press
Library of Congress Catalog Card Number 66–14775
Manufactured in the U. S. A.

TO
Paul Stanley Larson

SEP 25 '68

HUNT LIBRARY
CARNEGIE-MELLON UNIVERSITY

Editor's Foreword

The work of the editor of *Doctor on the Stage* has been made easier because Dr. Silvette's choice of texts was always careful; in many cases he had access to the first printed texts of the plays, some of which still remain as the authoritative ones recognized by scholars today. The quotations from these plays appear essentially as they are found in the sources consulted by Dr. Silvette. An exception was made in the case of Shakespearean works, which have been edited here to conform to the George Lyman Kittredge edition. As for the other playwrights, the work on modernization of their texts has been spotty and the scholarly interpretations not always unanimous; it seemed wise, therefore, to reproduce these quotations without substantive change. The editor also has refrained from commenting on some of the other scholarly questions about these plays (such as the exact authorship of plays attributed to Beaumont and Fletcher); hence, the works are cited as they appear in the sources consulted by Dr. Silvette. Authorship puzzles are not important to the author's theme or purpose. As a matter of typography, however, and especially to make the reading of these old plays more pleasant, the editor has normalized the persistent and sometimes obtrusive interior capitalization of nouns, as well as the interchangeable use of u and v, i and j. The flavor of antiquity is preserved by the old spellings and punctuation, retained in both text and titles. Those were the glorious days when a word could be spelled as many as three or four different ways on one page and when punctuation received scant attention.

Much of the source material on which this book is based was incorporated in a series of essays published by Dr. Silvette in the *Annals of Medical History*, which was founded and guided editorially for the twenty-five years of its existence by the distinguished medical historian, the late Francis R. Packard.

For their suggestions and help with the editing of this manuscript, I wish to express my deep gratitude to Professor Marjorie Hope Nicolson of the Institute for Advanced Study, Princeton University, and to Professor Ronald J. Wulf, Biochemical Pharmacist in the Pharmacy Research Institute of the University of Connecticut. I also wish to express my appreciation to Mr. Thomas McGovern of Fordham University Library for his effort to locate early editions of the plays; and to the library staffs of the University of Tennessee and the University of Connecticut, who contributed to the pleasantness as well as the fruitfulness of my research. Especially I wish to acknowledge the help of the Southeastern Institute of Medieval and Renaissance Studies, sponsored by Duke University and the University of North Carolina, under a grant from the Ford Foundation, for it was as a Fellow with the Institute that I was enabled to spend a summer period at Chapel Hill, during which most of the editing was accomplished.

FRANCELIA BUTLER

Storrs, Connecticut

Contents

Introduction

Learned he was, and cou'd take note,
Transcribe, collect, translate and quote.
　　　　　　　　　　　—Samuel Butler, *Hudibras*

Medicine consists of two separate bodies of knowledge: the technical information entombed in many-paged compendiums of mismated Latin and Greek roots, and that more popular medical lore handed down the centuries from the intuitive beliefs of primitive man. The first is the heritage of the physician; the second, that of the unlettered layman. The poet alone (and here I use the word in its old unrestricted sense) defies these categories, as such a troublesome fellow makes it his business to do. His mind covers the bare bones of ascetic truth with the superstition of a thousand irrational primitive imaginings, and thus unconsciously he synthesizes the divided aspects of medicine into a single cultural and social force.

Medicine, then, as it affects the broader intellectual life of any period, is revealed neither in the technical works of the scientist and physician nor in the primitive intuition of the illiterate. The synthesis of scientific truth and popular belief is the product of the literary man, who acts as the filter through which both truth and apocrypha flow. From the scientific textbooks alone it is impossible to predict which of the erudite conclusions of any given age is eventually to become a part of common knowledge or a social force, however well the scientist is able to recognize the data which represent his permanent conquest of truth. Medicine must pass through the lay mind rather than the professional one before it takes on a significance wider than that of mere technical knowledge designed to further a specific end. It is the unconscious task of the novelist, the dramatist, the journalist, and the poet to determine which part and how much of contemporary scientific belief will ultimately swell the cultural heritage of the human race.

Among the many ancient doctrines which the invention of printing invalidated was this from the Hippocratic Oath: "I will impart a knowledge of the art to my own sons, and those of my teachers, and to disciples bound by a stipulation and oath according to the law of medicine, *but to none others.*" [1] The italics are mine, though perhaps had Hippocrates owned our many fonts of type they would also have been his. For when "knowledge of the art" is available in editions of several thousand copies to anyone with the purchase price, it can no longer be restricted to initiates alone. One is familiar with the assertion (sometimes justified) that only true disciples of Aesculapius are able to understand the mystic texts, but it is obvious that the layman can read them; and if, as our professional conceit leads us to believe, the layman reads without understanding, he reads with only the more interest because of it. When the layman is an individual given to the writing of poems, plays, novels, or even letters, the result of his reading is apt to throw a fluorescent light on the mysteries of the healing art. That is to say, the literary man displays the phenomenon of fluorescence: the light he emits differs in wave length from the light he absorbs. And the conclusions he derives from his readings are quite different from those promulgated by the scientific authors.

Seventeenth-century England presents in this respect an unparalleled opportunity to the medical historian. From Elizabethan days to the eighteenth century many hundreds of plays were written and produced, for the theater served not only as an outlet for the creative impulses of the playwrights, but also as a daily gazette reflecting the interests and preoccupations of the playgoers. Many if not all of the plays were written solely for a public which never tired of seeing itself represented on the stage and which delighted in the details of actuality. On the whole, then, dramatic authors wrote in an idiom entirely familiar to their audiences, and that idiom is our prime concern here.

[1] *Genuine Works of Hippocrates*, trans. F. Adams (New York, 1929), II, 280.

It is chiefly in the dramatists' medical metaphors and allusions that the position of medicine in seventeenth-century life may be sought and found; and to do so is the purpose of this book. With such a Philistine aim it becomes pleasantly possible to ignore the literary standing of the individual dramatists. Some of our authors are bad poets, but they are excellent observers and truly permeable filters nevertheless. If within these pages Shadwell, for example, is exalted above Dryden, it is done with a spirit of enthusiasm for the fact rather than with a total insensibility to how the fact is presented. For, after all, it is facts that we are after, evidences within the old plays of the presence of a body of popular medical belief; if they are sometimes clothed in dull prose and halting verse rather than in impassioned lyricism or epic grandeur, let us simply consider them the droppings in Pegasus' stall!

Even as the literary exuberances of seventeenth-century England are formed as if predestined for the purposes of social study, so the age itself is peculiarly adapted by its scientific chronology to a record of changing medical notions. The last years of the preceding century had seen the still-unappreciated end of medievalism; but, for the previous fourteen hundred years a codification of medical knowledge had been going on, based upon Galen's great and enduring synthesis of the Greek tradition. By 1600 the Galenic system was well-nigh perfect. It had been polished by Muslim, Jewish, and Christian commentators until it shone with a luster which modern medical science does not entirely dim. But maturity contains the seeds of decay, and as the traditionalists of the sixteenth century worshiped at Galen's shrine, other hardy souls, headed by Leonardo da Vinci and the great anatomist Andreas Vesalius, had laid aside books for the scalpel and casuistic logic for the observation of nature. They were the fathers and stepfathers of modern science.

The seventeenth-century scientist was thus confronted with two distinct founts of medical information. On the one hand, he was intimately familiar with the Galenical system, which after so many centuries had gathered almost a religious force. On the other, new discoveries were almost daily occurrences, and some of them were so strange and irreconcilable with established convictions that they stirred the world of the layman as well as that of the physician. Hence one finds both ancient and modern opinion coexistent in some of the popular literature of the day, but with this distinction: the old is introduced with the deference usually paid to hereditary knowledge, while the new is treated as a fit subject for satire and farce. The layman was no less an enemy to a fluid world of knowledge than was the physician himself.

In the main the pigments with which these sketches have been painted are derived from seventeenth-century English plays. (I have omitted Shakespeare for the most part in my illustrations, because so many medical-historical studies have already been done on him.) I have read about five hundred plays with pencil in hand and perhaps a few additional ones when a pencil was not available. For curiosity's sake I would wish to have read many more, for the thrill of stumbling on a unique medical metaphor comes at last to have much of the fascination of a minor vice. But all too many of the plays of any age are hopelessly dull, and all too many editions of seventeenth-century remnants are a strain on spectacled eyes. In brief, then, I sacrificed my vice, which like most vices had its pleasures dolorously counterbalanced by its pains.

This examination is rather strictly limited to the popular literature of the time—to some novels and poems and to many plays. Few scientific works of seventeenth-century physicians (and this is true of later centuries as well) have any place in a discussion of social or literary life. To state the omissions more broadly, the works of any man with technical knowledge or training have been avoided unless helpful as a comment on purely popular works. For a true picture of the place of science in the life of a bygone day a scientist would be the last court of appeal, not the first.

In addition, there is another class of book, written by an unusual kind of writer, which deserves to be treated with suspicion in an examination of this sort. This type is well exemplified by *The Anatomy of Melancholy*; Robert Burton was not a popular writer, nor did he share the popular writers' preoccupations. He is the classic example of a bookworm; we other frequenters of the bookstalls should invariably mistrust the identification of his knowledge and sentiments with those of the crowd. The diarists, on the other hand, were in closer rapport with their fellows. Both Samuel Pepys and John Evelyn were laymen, in spite of the F.R.S. which ultimately followed their names.

Parallel allusions from some of the works of a few Continental writers—Rabelais, Cervantes, Molière and Le Sage—illustrate the universality of traditional medicine and the impulse to take satirical advantage of every vulnerable point. As Hazlitt once observed, Cervantes and Le Sage may be considered as having been naturalized among ourselves; and Molière, in the spirit of his writings, is almost as much an English author as French.

Not every sample of ore dug from the seventeenth-century mine turned out to contain pure gold. Many were lead, and not even the alchemy of history was able to transmute heavy Saturn into brilliant Sol. Such dull references deserve only permanent interment in the pages of manuscript notebooks, but many others have a fascination which is not altogether due to a quaint preoccupation with the past.

I have written about uroscopy, the favorite medieval diagnostic, which today has degenerated into a genuinely scientific examination beloved of life insurance companies; of phlebotomy, the cherished treatment for every disease; of madness; of ancient remedies and cures; of physicians whose names have been immortalized in the pages of old plays; of one remarkable play in detail, the position of which in medical history is probably unique; of the pox; and finally of the medical satire which abounded on the boards.

I hope that from these sketches a reasonably coherent and interesting picture of seventeenth-century art and practice will emerge. On the whole it will be a true one, at any rate. Norman Douglas in his *Birds and Beasts of the Greek Anthology* writes: "For rhetoric must approximate to reality, even as imagination must have its roots in fact. Rhetoric serves as a signpost to true sentiment; it corresponds to some underlying state of mind and dares not express what is palpably incongruous or inept." [2]

So in the century's rhetoric we shall discover the century's point of view.

[2] Norman Douglas, *Birds and Beasts of the Greek Anthology* (New York, 1929), p. 198.

1
The Urine Tells All

Whilst the urine is clear, let the physician beg.
—IAGO AB DEWI

BEHIND THE MEDIEVAL PHYSICIAN STOOD THE AUTHORITY OF Galen, and behind Galenism were marshaled the power and dogma of the Church. Medical practice was thus an official business, as formal and logical as Roman Catholicism itself. The medical system was, in fact, as perfect as any product of the human mind. Of course, it was based on metaphysics rather than on nature, but whosoever founded his medical practice on Galen's words built his professional career upon a rock. If the patient ignorantly died under the treatment, the doctor felt perhaps that a stupidly obstinate attitude toward authority had met with its just reward. A celebrated eighteenth-century physician, who really deserved better of posterity, has been immortalized in a quatrain, thus:

> *I, John Lettsom,*
> *Blisters, bleeds and sweats 'em;*
> *If after that they please to die,*
> *I, John, lets 'em.*[1]

[1] Many other variants of the epigram exist, as: "When patients comes to I,/I physics, bleeds, and sweats 'em;/Then—if they choose to die,/What's that to

One is reminded of M. Macroton's blithe remark to Sganarelle after having prescribed a murderous therapeutic course for
the latter's daughter: "Not but that your daughter may dye for
all this; but yet you will have done something, and you'll have
the consolation that she dyed according to form" (Molière, *Love
the Best Physician* [*L'Amour Médecin*], II, 5).

The ancient system of physic was based on the doctrine of the
four humors. Dr. George W. Corner has translated the twelfth-
century Salernitan *De quatuor humoribus ex quibus constat
humanum corpus* with the remark that he has never seen a
better concise statement of the old humoral theory. To borrow
the Englished exposition of the Salernitan author is perhaps to
do an injustice to Robert Burton, whose equally classic description of the four humors in *The Anatomy of Melancholy*
(I.i.2.3) might very well have been used. But Burton was not a
physician, and it seemed fitting in the first pages of these medical essays to pay tribute to medicine rather than erudition. In
any event, anyone comparing the twelfth-century treatise with
the seventeenth-century version will see at a glance that in five
hundred years medical theory remained essentially, and even
absolutely, unchanged.

> There are four humours in the human body, namely, blood,
> phlegm, yellow bile and black bile. They are mixed in such a way
> and in such quantities that normally man retains his health. If,
> however, they are diminished, or superabundant, or thickened, or
> retained, or if they escape, become bitter, leave their normal
> regions, or enter unusual situations, various diseases occur in
> mankind. Sometimes it is necessary to nourish the humours,
> sometimes to dilute them, sometimes to compensate, and some-
> times to moderate them.
>
> The four humours have their seats in four parts of the body:
> blood dwells in the arteries and veins; phlegm in the brain;
> yellow bile in the liver; black bile in the spleen. . . .
>
> Blood has a ruddy color, phlegm white, yellow bile is reddish;

I—I lets 'em." Dr. John Coakley Lettsom, by the way, has received his just
deserts at the hands of Sir St. Clair Thomson, "The Strenuous Life of a Physician
in the 18th Century," *Annals of Medical History*, n.s. I (1929), 1.

black bile is black and thick. Their qualities are as follows: blood is moist and warm; phlegm cold and moist; yellow bile warm and dry; black bile cold and dry. Therefore blood is bitter by nature; phlegm salt and sweet; yellow bile sharp; black bile strong and sharp. It is obvious that these humours rule differently in different ages. In infants yellow bile and blood are more important; in adolescents, black bile; in the mature, blood; in the old, phlegm. In spring, summer, autumn, and winter, different humours dominate. In the spring blood abounds; in the summer yellow bile; in the autumn black bile; in the winter phlegm.

We may add that the different humours act in the following way: blood makes the spirit wilder; yellow bile makes it bolder; black bile, firmer; phlegm, sluggish. . . .[2]

This basic theory of health and disease seems simple enough if we proceed no further into the refinements of terminology and Pythagorean numerology that bewilder and discourage the modern mind. There were not only four humors, but nine qualities, four members, three faculties, two operations, three spirits, four ages, five figures, three fevers, four inflammations, and so on. Fortunately it is not necessary here to go into these abundant details, or even to comprehend them, for few of the old dramatists concerned themselves with physiological subtleties.

According to the old humoral pathology, diseases passed through three stages. The first was a raw preliminary stage; the second, a ripening stage called the state of coction or pepsis, in which a cooking of the humors took place; the last, a stage of crisis in which elimination of the superfluous humor occurred. When the excremental humors formed in the process of coction were expelled, they appeared in and hence colored the patient's urine. Figures of urinoscopy or "urine rings" containing a score of urinary colors and a diagnosis appropriate to each are found in many medieval manuscripts.[3]

Naturally enough, visual inspection of the urine—uroscopy, or water-casting—became one of the foundation stones of me-

[2] G. W. Corner, "The Rise of Medicine at Salerno in the Twelfth Century," *Annals of Medical History*, n.s. III (1931), 6.

[3] Several of these "urine rings" have been reproduced in R. T. Gunther, *Early Medical and Biological Science* (London, 1926), pp. 27–29, 31.

dieval diagnosis and prognosis. Though not as ancient as sphyg-
mology, the study of the pulse, uroscopy was the more popular
procedure.[4] The plays illustrate this point in many ways. In
Beaumont and Fletcher's *The Captain*, when an old man has
given Lodovico a valuable ring as a love token from his daughter,
the young man cannot understand his good fortune and asks
incredulously: ". . . you are in health?" To which the father
replies:

> *I hope so,*
> *My water's well enough, and my pulse.*
>
>   V, 1

If the seventeenth-century physicians themselves had been
forced to choose, probably they would have dropped the patient's
wrist for his urinal in a moment.

SECOND DOCTOR. *But, sir, amongst all signs of sickness or health,*
    whereby the skilful physician is led into the knowledge of the
    state of the body; two above the rest are most certain, which are
    the pulse and the urin.
THIRD DOCTOR. *I, whereof the pulse shews the state of the heart and*
    arteries, and urin the state of the liver and veins.
SECOND DOCTOR. *Therefore the question is, whether of these two*
    severally considered, does give the most certain signification?
DOCTOR DRENCH. *Urin, urin, urin. . . .*

>   LACY, *The Dumb Lady,* V

A curious example of the popularity of water-casting during
the century occurs in Beaumont and Fletcher's *A Wife for a
Month*. Tony, the king's fool, appears on the stage with a urinal.
"How now Tony?" asks a courtier, "Whose water are you casting?" The fool replies in comic imitation of the court physicians:

---

[4] Besides the pulse and urine, other considerations influenced the doctor's
practice. Such were the patient's pain, fever, and physiognomic signs; and if the
physician or surgeon were learned enough, there was infinite knowledge to be
gained by the inspection of shed blood in the barber's basin. See "A Greek
Fourteenth Century Prognostic from the Blood, *Concerning safe and dangerous
bloods*" in Charles Singer's "Byzantine Medical Fragments," *Annals of Medical
History,* I (1917), 333.

A sick gentlemans,
Is very sick, much troubled with the stone,
He should not live above a month, by his urine,
About St. David's Day it will go hard with him,
He will then be troubled with a pain in his neck too.

II, 1

During the Middle Ages countless books were written on the art of uroscopy, one of the most famous and elaborate being that of the tenth-century Isaac Judaeus.[5] So numerous were they that James Atkinson in his rambling, Shandean *Medical Bibliography* genially remarked of another medieval physician, Constantinus Africanus, that "like others, he could not die contented without having written a *Libellus de Urinis* [little book about urine]."[6]

Throughout medieval days and, in fact, until the middle of the eighteenth century, the urinal was the symbol of the medical profession. All the pictorial examples of the "Dance of Death" show the physician accompanied by a flask of urine;[7] in the verses themselves Death apostrophizes the doctors in this manner:

Ye phisiciens/for money that loken so fast
In othir mennys watris/what thei eyle
Look weel to your self/. . . .[8]

And in another version:

Maister of phisik/whiche [o]n [y]owre uryne
So loke and gase/& stare a-[g]enne the sunne
For al [y]owre crafte/& studie of medicyne
Al the practik/& science that [y]e cunne

---

[5] The *Kitab al-baul;* Latin translation in *Omnia opera Isaaci* (Lyon, 1515). Also Joh. Peine, *Die Harnschrift des Isaac Judaeus* (Berlin, 1919).

[6] (London, 1834.)

[7] A. S. Warthin, *The Physician of the Dance of Death: A Historical Study of the Evolution of the Dance of Death Mythus in Art* (New York, 1931).

[8] *Incipit Macrobius* (Lansdowne MS 699) in *The Dance of Death*, ed. Florence Warren, E.E.T.S., o.s. 181 (London, 1931), p. 53.

[Y]owre lyves cours/so ferforthe ys I-runne
A[g]eyne my myght/[y]owre crafte mai not endure
For al the golde/that [y]e ther-bi have wonne
Good leche is he/that can hym self recure.

The Phecissian answereth

Ful longe a-gon/that I un-to phesicke
Sette my witte/and my diligence
In speculatif/also in practike
To gete a name/thurgh myn excellence
To fynde oute/a-[g]ens pestilence
Preservatifes/to staunche hit & to fyne
But I dar saie/shortli in sentence
A-[g]ens dethe/is worthe no medicyne.[9]

From solemnity to satire is a long step, but the urinal is found
at each end. One Barnes taunts Andrew Boorde, the famous
sixteenth-century physician, with: "For by castynge of a pys-
potte, ye have pollyd many a grote," [10] that is, "Oh, Andrew,
you've cheated men of many a groat by looking at their urine."
And Dr. Caius, the French quack in *The Merry Wives of Wind-
sor* (II. iii. 33, 57), is called "castallian king urinall" and "mon-
sire mockwater." Some years later, "To be a physician, a piss-pot
caster," exclaimed Robert Burton in *The Anatomy of Melancholy,* "'tis loathed" (I. ii. 3.10).

Rabelais lectured on medicine at Montpellier (which Dr.
Boorde called "the most nobilist universite of the world for
phisicions and surgions"), translated into Latin the aphorisms
of Hippocrates, and larded that polytechnical work *Gargantua
and Pantagruel* with such medical erudition as the following:

> If my wife at any time prove to be unwell and ill at ease—I will
> look upon the water which she shall have made in a urinal glass,
> quoth Rondibilis, grope her pulse, and see the disposition of her
> hipogaster, together with her umbilicary parts, according to the

[9] *The Daunce of Death* (Ellesmere MS 26/A.13) in *ibid.,* pp. 52 and 54.
[10] *Barnes in Defense of the Berde: a Treatyse made, answerynge the Treatyse of
Doctor Borde upon Berdes,* ed. F. J. Furnivall, E.E.T.S., e.s. 10 (London, 1870),
p. 311.

prescript rule of Hippocrates, 2 Aph. 35,[11] before I proceed any
further in the cure of her distemper.

Bk. III, Ch. 34

A few decades later in England John Lyly described the same
procedure:

My father no lesse sorrowefull for my disease, then ignorant of ye
cause, sent for divers phisitians, among the which ther came an
Italian, who feeling my pulses, casting my water, & marking my
lookes, commaunded the chamber to be voyded. . . .

Euphues and His England, II, 73

Thus the old Greek tradition transcended time, boundary
lines, and kings. No matter what language the patient spoke, his
physician was sure to diagnose his case in urine and Latin and
bleed him both figuratively and literally.

Nowadays the first thing a physician does when he visits your
bedside is to place his fingers on your pulse and pop a ther-
mometer into your mouth. In the seventeenth century he would
have fingered your radial artery just as promptly:

DRENCH. *Let me see how to behave my self like a doctor now; I will
first take your mistress by the pulse, and look up gravely at the
sieling all the while; then ask what she took last, and when she'd
a stool, and there's half a doctors work. . . .*[12]

LACY, *Dumb Lady*, I

But his eyes, instead of being on a watch, would have been fixed
intently on a flask of steaming urine. Here is evidence from the
popular literature of the time:

[11] The aphorism reads: "In all diseases it is better that the umbilical and
hypogastric regions preserve their fullness; and it is a bad sign when they are very
slender and emaciated; in the latter case it is dangerous to administer purgatives"
(*Genuine Works of Hippocrates*, trans. by Francis Adams [New York, 1929], II,
207).

[12] The reader may be interested to learn Dr. Drench's conception of the other
part of the physician's task: "then I'll prescribe something that will neither do
hurt nor good, so leave her to luck, and there's the other half of the doctor; then
(to amuse the people) I'll give her the powder of a dryed dock-leaf with
apothecaries hard name to it. . . ."

HUNT LIBRARY
CARNEGIE-MELLON UNIVERSITY

TAMBURLAINE. *Tel me, what think you of my sicknes now?*
PHYSICIAN. *I view'd your urine, and the hypostasis*
    Thick and obscure doth make your danger great,
    Your vaines are full of accidental heat,
    Whereby the moisture of your blood is dried.
                    MARLOWE, II *Tamburlaine*, V, 3

DOCTOR. *My Lord. These bodies are depriv'd of all*
    The radicall abilitie of nature.
    The heat of life is utterly extinguishe'd.
    Nothing remaines within the power of man
    That can restore them.
D'AMVILLE. *Take this gold; extract*
    The spirit of it, and inspire new life
    Into their bodies.
DOCTOR. *Nothing can my Lord.*
D'AMVILLE. *You ha' not yet examin'd the true state*
    And constitution of their bodies. Sure,
    You ha' not. I'le reserve their waters till
    The morning. Questionlesse, their urines will
    Informe you better.
                    TOURNEUR, *Atheist's Tragedie*, V, 1

PYANNET. *Shee's a young gentlewoman; may have many children yet,*
    let me note her eyes: I finde nothing there. When did you see her
    water Mr. Doctor?
                    BROME, *City Wit*, III, 1

The Pope . . . within two daies after fell sick, Doctor Zacharie
was sent for to minister unto him, who seeing a little danger in
his water, gave him a gentle comfortive for the stomach, and
desired those nere about him to persuade his holines to take some
rest, & he doubted not but he would be forthwith well.
               NASHE, *The Unfortunate Traveller*, p. 102

From some plays we learn that the languishing ladies of the court and their doctors formed a partnership which benefited both the delicate health of the beauties and the lean purses of the physicians. The court doctor was not, on the whole, an inviting character; the Hippocratic Oath was never signed by these combinations of panderer, poisoner, and physician. The doctor's first duty is to his patient; the court physician's first thought was usually the gratification of his royal master's lightest or most wicked wish.

When the King of Sicily divorced his queen for adultery, the suborned evidence was furnished by two cashiered lieutenants and (says Flavello)

> *Two dainty devils*
> *Birds, a doctor and a midwife, who accus'd*
> *Themselves for bawds i' th' action, and depos'd*
> *I know not how many, how many, how many times,*
> *They saw 'em linked in their unlawful pleasures.*
> BROME, Queen and Concubine, I, 9

Another apostate to the faith of Aesculapius was the Queen Mother's physician in Beaumont and Fletcher's *Thierry and Theodoret*. "I am your own," vows Dr. Lecure:

> *nor since I first*
> *Knew what it was to serve you, have remembred*
> *I had a soul, but such [a] one whose essence*
> *Depended wholy on your Highness pleasure. . . .*
> II, 1

This paragon of professional propriety agrees to delay the consummation of Thierry's marriage by mixing a drink

> *Which when given unto him on the bridall night*
> *Shall for five days so rob his faculties,*
> *Of all ability to pay that duty,*
> *Which new-made wives expect, that she shall swear*
> *She is not match'd to a man.*

Then, as if he had not done sufficient damage for one play, Lecure prepares a poisoned handkerchief with which the chagrined bridegroom wipes his tear-filled eyes. Thierry dies at the end of a tortured scene, and the physician, in greater fear of the vengeance of the courtiers than of the God of Medicine, kills himself.

The Hippocratic Oath promises:

> Into whatever houses I enter, I will go into them for the
> benefit of the sick, and will abstain from every voluntary act of
> mischief and corruption. . . . While I continue to keep this
> oath unviolated, may it be granted to me to enjoy life and the
> practice of the art, respected by all men, in all times! But should
> I trespass and violate this oath, may the reverse be my lot! [13]

The physician is not as fortunate as the politician: his oath
cannot be unilaterally abrogated with impunity.

Court physicians were also tempted to indulge in another less
mischievous but no less explicit breach of professional ethics.
Another sentence of the oath runs: "Whatever, in connection
with my professional practice, or not, in connection with it, I see
or hear, in the life of men, which ought not to be spoken of
abroad, I will not divulge, as reckoning that all such should be
kept secret." Ben Jonson describes an upright physician whose
duty to his patients takes precedence over the demands of his
king:

SEJANUS.   Goe to,
  Ye' are a subtill nation, you physitians!
  And growne the onely cabinets, in court,
  To ladies privacies. Faith which of these
  Is the most pleasant lady, in her physicke?
  Come, you are modest now.
EUDEMUS. 'Tis fit my lord.
SEJANUS. Why, sir, I doe not aske you of their urines,
  Whose smel's most violet? or whose seige is best?
  Or who makes hardest faces on her stool? . . .
                    These were questions
  That might, perhaps, have put your gravity
  To some defence of blush.

                                        Sejanus, I

As it was the physician's duty to keep a watchful eye on the
ladies' urines, it was one of the pleasures of the gentleman-usher
to spread abroad the report of their condition:

[13] *Genuine Works of Hippocrates*, trans. F. Adams, II, 280.

HOWDEE. *To be able to relate how this ladies tooth does, and tother ladies too. How this ladies milk does, and how tothers doctor lik'd her last water. How this ladies husband, and how tother ladies dog slept last night.*

BROME, *Northern Lasse, IV, 1*

The court was naturally interested in any scandal, but it was the patients themselves who most eagerly demanded the uroscopic tidings. The doctors' mornings were devoted to the inspection of the previous night's waters, as we learn from a merchant's gibe at a physician:

Indeed Mr. Doctor your comodities are rare,
A guard of urinals in the morning;
A plaguee fellow at midnight;
A fustie potticarie, ever at hand with his
Fustian drugges, attending your pispot worship.

The Wisdome of Doctor Dodypoll, I

With the rather exaggerated modesty which he affected, Sir Thomas Browne apologized for one of his most charming works in this manner:

And therefore surely in this work attempts will exceed performances; it being composed by snatches of time, as medical vacations, and the fruitless importunity of uroscopy would permit us.

Pseudodoxia Epidemica, To the Reader

John Aubrey, that indispensable gossip, tells the story of Will Butler, physician:

. . . he was of Clarehill, in Cambridge; never tooke the degree of Doctor, though he was the greatest physitian of his time. . . . A serving man brought his master's water to doctor Butler, being then in his studie (with turn'd barres) but would not bee spoken with. After much fruitlesse importunity, the man told the doctor he was resolved he should see his master's water; he would not be turned away—threw it on the Dr.'s head. This humour pleased the Dr. and he went to the gent. and cured him—

Brief Lives, I, 140

Dekker has a similar tale. One Angelo is masquerading as a doctor and asks a friend's opinion of his disguise.

BAPTISTA.   *Friend I protest,*
  So rarely counterfeit, as if a painter
  Should draw a doctour: were I sicke my selfe,
  And met you with an urinall in my hand,
  I'de cast it at your head, unlesse you cast
  The water for me. . . .

                                        Wonder of a Kingdome, II

Uroscopy, it seems, was a hazardous profession.

In John Earle's character book *Micro-cosmographie* (1628) the sketch of "A meere dull Phisitian" begins thus: "His practice is some business at bed-sides, and his speculation an urinall. . . . Of al odors he likes best the smel of urine, and holds Vespatians rule, that no gaine is unsavory. If you send this once to him, you must resolve to be sicke howsoever, for he will never leave examining your water till hee have shakt it into a disease." Of course, the physicians were not permitted to monopolize this form of diagnosis. At the other pole of iatric practice is the "Quacksalver," whom John Webster characterizes with these words: "Lastly, he is such a juggler with urinals, so dangerously unskilfull, that if ever the citie will have recourse to him for diseases that neede purgation, let them imploy him in scouring Moore-ditch" [14]

Between the two extremes of doctor of physic and quack there were other medical hangers-on who found the procedure good. Such were the apothecaries.

The ancient feud between the doctors and druggists rose to its height in the seventeenth century, culminating in the following century in the famous "Dispensarian War." Wycherley wrote in 1671: "Pimp and bawd agree nowadays like doctor and apothecary" (*Love in a Wood,* I, 2). And for the same reason: each strove to undermine the other's trade.

Although the physicians could not prevent the apothecaries

[14] *New Characters (drawne to the life) of severall persons, in severall qualities,* thirty-two characters by John Webster which appeared in the sixth (1615) edition of Sir Thomas Overbury's *Characters.*

from making money, and sometimes a great deal of it,[15] they were able nevertheless to keep their rivals in proper professional and social subjection. William Bullein, the sixteenth-century physician, drew up a list of rules for the apothecaries' conduct. One cautioned "That he meddle only with his vocation," and another "That he do remember that his office is only to be ye physician's cooke." [16] But moral admonitions unbacked by the power of law restrain druggists no more than other people, and in the scene below we see an apothecary breaching Bullein's code and stealing a march on his more learned brethren as well:

PAGE. . . . *though my father bee a citizen.*
COUNTESSE. *Of what profession?*
PAGE. *Neither foole nor phisitian, but an ingenious Pothecarie.*
COUNTESSE. *And what resort?*
PAGE. *Verie civil and most quiet resort,—patients: the house is set round with patients twice or thrice a day, and (because theile be sure not to want drinke) everie one brings his owne water in a urinall with him.*
COUNTESSE. *Doth a use physicke too? that's beyond his warrant.*
PAGE. *O Lord, Madam, better men than hee straine curtesie with their warrants in this age.*

DAY, *Law-trickes*, II, 1

There were plenty of quacks in Old England who learned the secret of transmuting urine into gold. Such a one was the itinerant mountebank Forobosco, who had never as much gold as when he was in England and called himself "Dr. Lambstones." There his closet was continually beset with women wanting their fortunes told, and to his clownish assistant he expressed amazement that, in spite of "this frequent resort of women and thy handling of their urinalls and their cases, thou art not given to lechery" (Beaumont and Fletcher, *Faire Maide of the Inne*, V, 1).

[15] Aubrey, *Brief Lives*, I, 216, says of Gideon de Laune (1565?–1659) :"—he was apothecary to Mary the queen mother: came into England. . . . He was a very wise man, and as a signe of it left an estate of 80,000 *li*." Perhaps "astute" would have been the better word than "wise."

[16] C. J. S. Thompson, *The Mystery and Art of the Apothecary* (Philadelphia, 1929), p. 163.

They exceeded the apothecary in pretensions as they fell short of him in skill, these wise-women and cunning-men, these country-sharpers and strolling mountebanks, who took the same advantage of bucolic gullibility then that mail-order urinalysists do today. The scope of their revelations, like those of the pretended uroscopists not many years earlier, grew beyond all bounds. Thomas Heywood pivoted the action of *The Wise-woman of Hogsdon* around such a character:

Enter the Wise-woman and her clyents, a countreyman with an urinall, [foure women like citizens wives; Taber a Serving-man, and a Chamber-mayd.]

WISEWOMAN. *Fie, fie, what a toyle, and a moyle it is,*
    For a woman to bee wiser then all her neighbours?
    I pray good people, presse not too fast upon me;
    Though I have two eares, I can heare but one at once.
    You with the urine.

COUNTRYMAN. Here forsooth Mistresse.

WISEWOMAN. *And who distill'd this water?*

COUNTRYMAN. *My wives limbeck, if it please you.*

WISEWOMAN. *And where doth the paine hold her most?*

COUNTRYMAN. *Marry at her heart, forsooth.*

WISEWOMAN. *Ey, at her heart, shee hath a griping at her heart.*

COUNTRYMAN. *You have hit it right.*

WISEWOMAN. *Nay, I can see so much in the urine. . . .*
    Shee hath no paine in her head, hath shee?

COUNTRYMAN. *No, indeed, I never heard her complaine of her head.*

WISEWOMAN. *I told you so, her paine lyes all at her heart. Alas good*
    heart! but how feeles her stomacke?

COUNTRYMAN. *O queasier, and sicke at stomacke.*

WISEWOMAN. *Ey, I warrant you, I thinke I can see as farre into a*
    mill-stone as another: you have heard of Mother Nottingham,
    who for her time, was prettily well skill'd in casting of waters; and
    after her, Mother Bombye; and then there is one Hatfield in
    Pepper-Alley, hee doth prettie well for a thing that's lost. There's
    another in Coleharbour, that's skill'd in the planets. Mother
    Sturton in Goulden-lane, is for fore-speaking; Mother Phillips of
    the Banke-side, for the weaknesse of the backe; and then there's a
    very reverent matron on Clarkenwell-Green, good at many
    things. . . .

II, 1

The wisewoman's catalogue of quacks appears in other plays. "Fore-speaking" was evidently popular:

WIN LITTLEWIT. *Sir, my mother has had her nativity-water cast lately by the cunning men in Cow lane, and they ha' told her her fortune. . . .*

JONSON, *Bartholomew Fayre*, I, 2

Ills of the spirit also made themselves known:

MARIA. *. . . Pray God he be not bewitch'd!*
FABIAN. *Carry his water to th' wise woman.*
MARIA. *Marry, and it shall be done to-morrow morning if I live.*

SHAKESPEARE, *Twelfth Night*, III, 4

William Lilly, the seventeenth-century astrologer who wanders in and out of these pages pursued by Samuel Butler's satiric pen, also dabbled in uroscopy. Of him an admiring contemporary wrote, "that many people of the poorer sort frequented his lodging, many whereof were so civil, that when they brought waters from infected people, they would stand at a distance." But there is little civility in Butler's burlesque:

Quoth Ralph, Not far from hence doth dwell
A cunning man, hight [named] Sidrophel,
That deals in destinie's dark counsels,
And sage opinions of the moon sells;
To whom all people far and near,
On deep importances repair.
When brass and pewter hap to stray,
And linnen slinks out of the way;
When geese and pullen are seduc'd,
And sows of suckling pigs are chews'd,
When cattle feel indisposition,
And need th' opinion of physitian;
When murrain reigns in hogs, or sheep,
And chicken languish of the pip;
When yeast, and outward means do fail,
And have no pow'r to work on ale;
When butter does refuse to come,
And love proves cross and humoursome:
To him with questions, and with urine,
They for discov'ry flock, or curing.

Hudibras, Pt. II, 3

The urine revealed many interesting things, and these not only to quacks but to practicing physicians as well. Said Vindici in Tourneur's tragedy:

> I grant you this,
> Tell but some woman a secret over night,
> Your doctor may finde it in the urinall i' th' morning.
>
> Revengers Tragaedie, I, 3

Other secrets appeared there also. Pregnancy, chastity, and even the true sex of the patient revealed themselves to the uroscopist's infallible eye.

FAIREFIELD.   . . . come hither let me kisse thee,
Now I am confirm'd, he that shall marry thee
Shall take thee a virgin at my perill.
BONAVENT. Ha you such skill in maidenheads.
FAIREFIELD. Ile know't by a kisse,
Better then any doctor by her urine.

> SHIRLEY, Hide Parke, IV

And Sidrophel could

> Detect lost maiden-heads, by sneezing,
> Or breaking wind of dames, or pissing. . . .
>
> BUTLER, Hudibras, Pt. II, 3

In another play a madman who was once a doctor exclaims: "If I had my glasse here, I would shew a sight should make all the women here call me mad doctor" (Webster, *Dutchesse of Malfy*, IV, 2). In his urinal they would be revealed unchaste, the sardonic inference runs.

Nowadays to detect pregnancy we inject woman's urine into immature rabbits. In the seventeenth century the procedure was simpler. "I was once sicke," recollects a bawd, "and I tooke my water in a basket, and cary'd it to a doctors."

PHILLIP. In a basket.
BAUD. Yes sir: you arrant foole there was a urinall in it.
PHILLIP. I cry you mercy.
BAUD. The doctor told me I was with child. . . .

> DEKKER, North-ward Hoe, IV, 1

And again:

PUTANA.   . . . shee is quicke, 'tis worse, she is with childe,
  You know what you have done; Heaven forgive 'ee,
  'Tis too late to repent, now Heaven helpe us.
GIOUANNI. With child? how dost thou know't?
PUTANA. How doe I know't? am I at these yeeres ignorant, what the
  meaning's of quames, and waterpangs be? of changing of colours,
  quezinesse of stomacks, pukings, and another thing that I could
  name; doe not (for her and your credits sake) spend the time in
  asking how, and which way, 'tis so; shee is quick upon my word,
  if you let a phisitian see her water, y' are undone.
                              FORD, 'Tis Pitty Shee's a Whore, III

But even the uroscopists sometimes erred. "Doctor" Rut had
made a diagnosis of pregnancy, but when the time came for the
prospective mother to be brought to bed, it developed that she
was not going to have a child after all. Listen to the comments:

ITEM. What had she then?
NEEDLE. Only a fit o' the mother [hysterics]!
  They burnt old shoes, goose-feathers, assafoetida,
  A few horne shavings, with a bone, or two,
  And she is well againe, about the house.
ITEM. Is't possible?
NEEDLE. See it, and then report it.
ITEM. Our doctors urinall-judgement is halfe crack'd then.
                              JONSON, Magnetick Lady, V, 1

Among the famous water-casters of seventeenth-century litera-
ture was Sancho Panza himself. A steward has impersonated
Countess Trifaldi. Sancho suspects, and whispers to his master:
"But mum's the word: I say nothing, though I shall watch his
waters to find out whether I am right or wrong in my suspicions"
(Cervantes, Don Quixote, Pt. II, Bk. 4, Ch. 44).

And to a man who has almost married a page disguised as a
gentlewoman, La-poop scoffs:

  Thou shouldst have had her urin to the doctors,
  The foolishest physitian could have made plain
  The liquid epicaene. . . .
  BEAUMONT AND FLETCHER, The Honest Man's Fortune, V

But the height of the uroscopist's skill was reached in the comedian John Lacy's free adaptation of Molière's *Le Médecin Malgré Lui* called *The Dumb Lady; or The Farriar made Physician*.[17] Here "Doctor" Drench, in a scene (Act III) which owes nothing to the Frenchman, performs what we would term a miracle; but to a seventeenth-century Englishman who knew his world, the doctor's deduction might have been equally evident without the urine. Drench is holding a clinic on "a seaman's wife, a countryman with an urinal, and an apprentice with an urinal, with other patients." It is the apprentice's turn:

DOCTOR. . . . *What are you, sir?*

PRENTICE. *A prentice, sir, that has brought my Mrs. water, sir.*

DOCTOR. *Has your Mrs. ne'er a maid, but she must send her water by her prentice? a foolish custom, I cannot break 'em on't; let me see, but are you sure this is your Mrs. water?*

PRENTICE. *Yes, and it please your worship.*

DOCTOR. *How sure are you? did you see her make it?*

PRENTICE. *I did not see her make it, but, and it please you, I heard her make it.*

DOCTOR. *Why, I find by thy Mrs. water, friend, that thou art almost out of thy time.*

PRENTICE. *Yes, truly, within three months, and it please you.*

DOCTOR. *I knew it; why here is twenty visible things in this water; your master is out of town about a purchase, is he not?*

PRENTICE. *Yes, and it please your worship.*

DOCTOR. *And you are removed out o' th' garret to lye in the next room to your Mrs. to keep spirits from her, are you not?*

---

[17] Of this play, which has furnished so many pieces of interesting and valuable information, Father Summers writes: "But once Molière is transferred to the London stage how entirely native does he not become! There can hardly be any talk of French influence here; he is metamorphosed into a regular John Bull as he is crossing the Channel. One only has to compare Lacy's *The Dumb Lady* with *Le Médecin Malgré Lui* or Shadwell's *The Miser* with *L'Avare* to realize that the Frenchman has not merely changed his language but he is as thoroughly and substantially English as if he had never lived out of the hearing of the bells of Bow" (*The Playhouse of Pepys* [New York, 1935], p. 150). It is apparent even at first glance that it is English and not French medicine which Lacy's play reflects. An analysis of *The Dumb Lady* is found in J. E. Gillet's "Molière en Angleterre, 1660–1670," Mémoires of the Académie Royale de Belgique, deuxieme série, tome IX, fasc. III, Bruxelles, Hayez, 1913, ch. X.

PRENTICE. *By my troth, and so I am, and it please your worship.*

DOCTOR. *The water shows it plainly; hold, ha, I find your Mrs. is apt to dream much, and is frighted, and walks in her sleep, and comes to your chamber to be awakened, does she not?*

PRENTICE. *By my truly, she has been so troubled with these frights since my master's absence, that I have never had a good nights rest, since he went; for she'l come in her sleep, and throw her self upon my bed; and then I lye as still as can be, and then she rises like a mad woman, and throws all the clothes off, and makes such work with me, that I'm ashamed your worship should know it, then tell her on't the next day, and she runs away and laughs at me.*

DOCTOR. *I know her disease, commend me to thy Mrs; and tell her, because I'll make a perfect cure on't, I'll come and lye in the next room to her my self, and thou shalt go into the garret again.*

Sometimes, properly conservative medical men such as Sir Thomas Browne censured the too-extravagant claims of the water-casters:

Physitians (many at least that make profession thereof) beside divers less discoverable wayes of fraud, have made them believe, there is the book of fate, or the power of Aaron's brest plate, in urins. And therefore hereunto they have recourse, as unto the oracle of life, the great determinator of virginity, conception, fertility, and the inscrutable infirmities of the whole body.

Pseudodoxia Epidemica, Bk. I, Ch. 3

But what was a needy practitioner, however dubious of the omniscience of uroscopy, to do when a patient presented him with a flask of urine and waited in open-mouthed expectancy for his body's secrets to be laid bare? Certainly it would have been financially fatal to follow the lead of one of Shakespeare's physicians:

FALSTAFF. *Sirrah, you giant, what says the doctor to my water?*

PAGE. *He said, sir, the water itself was a good healthy water; but, for the party that owed it, he might have moe diseases than he knew for.*

Henry the Fourth, Pt. II, I, 2

I doubt that a physician so outspoken could have kept his practice for long in Elizabethan England.[18] Or today, for that matter.

It appears that uroscopy was not limited to human urine. Domestic animals also had the benefit of the art.

HORSE-COURSER. *Wel god buy sir, your boy wil deliver him* [a horse he has just bought] *me: but hark ye sir, if my horse be sick, or ill at ease, if I bring his water to you, youle tel me what it is?*

FAUSTUS. *Away you villaine: what, doest thinke I am a horsedoctor?*
                          MARLOWE, *Dr. Faustus*, 11. 1137–1142

Evidently Dr. Faustus's indignation arose not from the slight to his science, but from the affront to his professional dignity, for horses, of course, had the same four humors found in man. As Doctor Drench put it, "do you think a farrier inferiour to a physician? He is the son of a mare that thinks a horse has not as many diseases as a man." [19] To which Squire Softhead heatedly replied: "And he is the son of a whore that thinks a squire has not as many diseases as a horse" (Lacy, *Dumb Lady*, I).

Early in the next century (1709) Steele poked gentle fun at fashionable ladies who held their lapdogs in exaggerated esteem. A pert maid has brought Cupid, one such pampered puppy, to Mr. Bickerstaff for treatment. The amused veterinarian reports: "I then asked her, if she had brought any of his water to show me. Upon this, she stared me in the face, and said, I am afraid, Mr. Bickerstaff, you are not serious" (*The Tatler*, No. 121).

In the difference between Marlowe's horse-courser and Steele's lady's maid lies the story of the decline of a once-proud art.

Aside from its beneficent influence on the health of the na-

---

[18] There was, however, Dr. John Radcliffe, who was notorious for speaking his mind. His formula for success, as he told his successor, Richard Mead, was "use all mankind ill." In his later days he would probably have qualified that with "— except royalty," for his forthright language so offended the sensibilities of Queen Anne that he almost lost his practice, his prestige, and even his life. See J. C. Jeaffreson, *A Book about Doctors* (New York, 1861), p. 115 *passim*.

[19] Pliny confirms Dr. Drench: "A horse is subject to the same diseases in maner that man is" (*Natural Historie*, trans. Philemon Holland [London, 1634], Bk. VIII, Ch. 42).

tion, water-casting also contributed a most effective and popular metaphor to English literature. Here are some examples:

MACBETH.   *If thou couldst, doctor, cast*
> *The water of my land, find her disease,*
> *And purge it to a sound and pristine health,*
> *I would applaud thee to the very echo,*
> *That should applaud again.*
>
>   SHAKESPEARE, Macbeth, V, 3

SPEED.   . . . *these follies are within you and shine through you like the water in an urinall.* . . .
>   SHAKESPEARE, Two Gentlemen of Verona, II, 1

SENILIS. *'Tis their owne faults, if they, 'fore springs or fals,*
> *Emptying wine glasses fill up urinals.*
>
>   DAY, Parliament of Bees, ix [20]

CARTER.   . . . *I that never cast away a fee upon*
> *Urinals, but am sound as an honest mans*
> *Conscience when hee's dying.* . . .
>
>   ROWLEY, DEKKER, AND FORD,
>   Witch of Edmonton, IV, 2

LOLLIO. *So, if you love my mistres so well as you have handled the matter here, you are like to be cur'd of your madness.*
FRANCISCUS. *And none but she can cure it.*
LOLLIO. *Well, Il'e give you over then, and she shall cast your water next.*
>   MIDDLETON, Changeling, IV

Tibaldo Neri, describing his first sight of a fair lady at a banquet, says:

> . . . *there I dranke*
> *My bane, the strongest poison that e're man*
> *Drew from a ladies eye, now swelling in me.*

---

[20] John Day contributed a few scenes to Dekker's *The Wonder of a Kingdome* (1636), and there the epigram appears in this form in Act IV:
> 'Tis their owne fault, if they feare springs or falls,
> Wine-glasses fill'd too fast, make urynalls.

ALPHONSINA. *By casting of thy water then, I guesse thou would'st*
    Have a medcine for the greene-sicknes.
TIBALDO. *'Tis a greene wound indeed.*

DEKKER, *Wonder of a Kingdome,* I

Tom Drum cries to the widow who refuses him admittance
while she is entertaining a medical suitor: ". . . what, must no
man but Doctor Burket cast your water? is his phisicke in most
request?" (Deloney, *Gentle Craft,* Pt. II, Ch. 8).

Uroscopy was responsible not only for a metaphor, but for an
idiom as well. "To watch (or look to) one's waters" was to keep
a sharp eye on anyone's actions.[21] In the light of the discoveries
made by the early uroscopists, this idiom sometimes becomes
curiously expressive in the dramatists' hands. Thus, Gostanzo,
speaking to Cornelio of the latter's mother, who had evidently
tasted extramarital pleasures:

> . . . *she would tickle Dob now and then, as well as the best on
> 'em . . . your father knew it well enough, and would he do as
> you do thinke you? set rascalles to undermine her, or looke to her
> water (as they say)? No, when he saw twas but her humour (for
> his owne quietnesse sake) hee made a backe-doore to his house
> for convenience, gott a bell to his fore doore, and had an odd
> fashion in ringing, by which shee and her Mayde knew him; and
> would stand talking to his next neighbour to prolong time, that
> all thinges might be ridde clenly out a the way before he came,
> for the credite of his wife.*

CHAPMAN, *All Fooles,* V, 1

Isbel suspects her mistress of carrying on an intrigue and says,
"Well, well, little would any one think it were in her; but I'll
watch your water" ([Dryden], *Mistaken Husband,* I, 3).

When Tell-troth's sweetheart has been following a Royalist
captain disguised as his page, her lover has no fears that the
soldier has penetrated her masquerade:

TELL-TROTH. *I had spies upon you, and am well assur'd of your
    honesty. Ask Dol!*
DOL. *Yes, faith, I watch'd your water at every turn.*

LACY, *Old Troop,* V

[21] Grose's *Classical Dictionary of the Vulgar Tongue* . . . , revised and corrected by Pierce Egan (1823).

"Doctor" Drench takes advantage of his medical habit to explore a servingmaid's bosom. Her husband quite naturally objects:

JARVIS. *Oh, Devil take you, sir, let my wives breasts alone!*
DOCTOR. *Sweet sir, I must see her breasts, it is the doctor's duty to look to the nurse's milk.*
JARVIS. *You shall not look to her milk; I'll look to your water for that, sir.*

LACY, *Dumb Lady*, II

Truly, the urine tells all!

In the seventeenth century the art of water-casting was already on the decline, and the faint ammoniacal odor of putrefaction was occasionally detected by sensitive nostrils. At least one of the dramatists owned a pair of these. In *The Dutchesse of Malfy*, produced about 1612, John Webster cynically wrote:

BOSOLA. *Doth he study phisiognomie?*
　There's no more credit to be given to th' face,
　Then to a sicke mans urine, which some call
　The physitians whore, because she cozens him.

I, 1

Now Webster was no medical man, though it will appear on some of these pages that his stock of medical and surgical information was astonishingly large and well digested. He was, however, an inspired borrower and may have owed his uroscopical metaphor to old Andrew Boorde's similar animadversion on water-casting in *The Breviarie of Health*, the first edition of which appeared in 1547. Dr. Boorde writes:

> There is not the wisest phisician livynge, but that I, beynge an whole man, may deceyve him by my uryne; and they shall judge a sicknes that I have not nor never had, and all is therowe distemperaunce of the bodye used the day before that the uryne is made in the mornynge; and this I do saye, as for the colours of the urynes, [uryne] is a strumpet or a harlot, and in it many phisicians maye be deceyved, but as touchynge the contentes of urynes, experte phisicians maye knowe the infyrmyties of a pacient unfallybly.[22]

---

[22] *The second boke of the Breviarie of Heal[t]h named the Extravagantes* (London, 1575), p. 25v.

And again: "I do say that an uryne is a strumpet, or an harlot, for it wyl lye; and the best doctour of Phisicke of them all maye be deceyved in an uryne, and his cunnyng and learning not a jot the worse." [23] It should be emphasized that Dr. Boorde is skeptical only of the knowledge purporting to come from the *color* of urines, not that to be gathered from the various sediments.

Dr. Boorde was a merry old soul, and his memory is honored in his own gathering of *The first and best parts of Scoggins Jests: full of witty Mirth and pleasant Shifts done by him in France and other Places*. The first edition extant of this work was printed in London in 1626, although the book was licensed in 1566. There is said to have been an edition in 1613 and another earlier still in black letter, undated. The *Jests'* physician says: "Ah . . . a water or urine is but a strumpet; a man may be deceived in a water."[24]

But whether Webster discovered the deceitfulness of urine from *The Breviarie of Health* or from *Scoggins Jests* is immaterial. He knew a good phrase when he found one.

In the old plays urine cozened the characters right and left, for there were infinite comic possibilities in the procedure. Thus Beaumont and Fletcher use uroscopy as a peg on which to hang a trio of physicians who see three different diseases in a single flask of the fluid:

1 PHYSICIAN. *A pleurisie, I see it.*
2 PHYSICIAN. *I rather hold it*
    For tremor cordis.
3 PHYSICIAN.   *Do you mark the faeces?*
    'Tis a most pestilent contagious feaver,
    A surfeit, a plaguey surfeit; he must bleed.
1 PHYSICIAN. *By no means.*
3 PHYSICIAN.   *I say bleed.*
1 PHYSICIAN.   *I say 'tis dangerous;*
    The person being spent so much before-hand,
    And nature drawn so low, clysters [enemas], cool clysters.

---

[23] *Ibid.*, p. 21v.

[24] Quoted by Furnivall in his edition of Boorde's *The fyrst Boke of the Introduction of Knowledge: A Dyetary of Helth* (London, 1870), p. 32.

2 PHYSICIAN. *Now with your favours I should think a vomit:*
   For take away the cause, and the effect must follow,
   The stomach's foul and fur'd, the pot's unflam'd yet.
3 PHYSICIAN. *No, no, we'll rectifie that part by mild means,*
   Nature so sunk must find no violence.

Monsieur Thomas, II, 3

Now this is legitimate satire, but in Wilson's play *The Cheats* it becomes downright farce:

DOCTOR MOPUS.   . . . *Have you sav'd the alderman's water, as I or-der'd?*

MRS. WHITEBROTH. *Yes sir:—Cis. Cis; thy masters state.*

CIS. *O Tim, Tim, 'twas in the silver tankard, and the cat overthrew it.*
   [This, and the next, to be spoke aside.]

TIM. *There stands some dead ale upon the table, put that i' the urinal;—He'll tell as much by one, as t'other.*
   [Exeunt TIM and CIS. . . . Enter CIS with an urinal.]

MOPUS. *Oh—let me see't—High-colour'd—His blood's enflam'd:—Feaverish—Feaverish.*
   [At every step, he shakes the urinal.]

MRS. WHITEBROTH. *Indeed sir he burns like a fire.*

MOPUS. *Sick—sick—sick—he cannot rest.*

MRS. WHITEBROTH. *I indeed;—You are as right—*

MOPUS. *Sometimes up, and sometimes down.*

MRS. WHITEBROTH. *Truly he has not been out of his bed, since he first took his cold, till just now.*

MOPUS. *Huh—a cold!—*[Aside.]*—Pains in his limbs; coughing, and now and then, wind;—This froth, and feather in the water, is a certain token.*

MRS. WHITEBROTH. *Now bless me sir!—How is't possible you should hit things so right?*

MOPUS. *How do you hit your mouth in the dark?—One's as easie as tother:—That is to say; to a man of art;—I could tell you a thousand things—But time is precious with me:—May I not see the alderman?*

MRS. WHITEBROTH. *O by all means;—I hear him coming:—*
   [Enter WHITEBROTH.]
O my Dear—here's a gentleman has told me all your distemper, as right—
   [WHITEBROTH coughs.]

WHITEBROTH. *And what does he think of it?*

MOPUS. *Pray bend your wrist sir.*—[He feels his pulse.]
   All will do well again:—A purge, and a vomit—
   A purge and a vomit:—Gi' me a pen, and ink:—

[He writes.]

MRS. WHITEBROTH. *Would not some parma-citty do him good?*
   Truly I would be loth, he should want anything.

MOPUS. *You do well:—Let me see—what sayes the colledge:—Sperma*
   Cæti, Confectio quæ dam—Pox on't—I have forgot the rest:—
   Sperma Cæti! Sperma Cocks-comb—They're a company of
   quacking fools,—'Tis parmacitty, and takes its name, from the
   city of Parma: Hang this foisting:—I'll trust ne'er a doctor of
   them all:—[He tears the paper.] *Have a little patience Madam,*
   and I'll send you a preparation of my own. . . .

II, 1

This joke, the cheater cheated, was on an astrological physician, but in the fifth act of Lacy's *The Dumb Lady* the incorrigible Drench puts a trick on three learned Galenists who have gathered to consult with him regarding the cure of a girl who will not speak. Previously he has told his confederate, the nurse, "be sure Nurse, that you be in the room; and when I bid you fetch your mistresses water, be sure you go out and bring me your own; and then mark what work I'l make with your learned doctors." When the time comes the nurse brings in the urinal.

NURSE. *Gentlemen, my mistress presents her service to you, and*
   desires you to be civil to her water, and use it with as much
   modesty as you may; for I assure you her virgin-water was never
   exposed to publick view before.

3 DOCTOR. *Pray give it the stranger.*

DOCTOR DRENCH. *By no means, gentlemen, I must have your opinions*
   first. Nurse, art thou true to me?

[The Doctors take the water.]

NURSE. *By my little life it's my own water, Doctor.*

DOCTOR DRENCH. *By my great life I'll marry thee tomorrow then; but*
   Nurse, when I wink at you, you must own the water to be yours.

NURSE. *I'l do it, dear doctor!*

2 DOCTOR. *Here is dangerous water, it does not show the three regents;*
   neither is here colour, substance, perspicuity, darkness, contents,
   or smell.

3 DOCTOR. *Therefore the urine being obstructed, must needs flye back upon the parts, as to the stomach in vomitings, to the belly in dropsies.*

2 DOCTOR. *Or to the head in frensies. . . .*

DOCTOR DRENCH. *Come on, let me see the water; hum, ha, here is no madness, nor the least sign on't. Come hither, sir; is your daughter married?*

GERNETTE. *No, sir; why do you ask?*

DOCTOR DRENCH. *Then I say she is a baggage; she had a child lately, and counterfeits madness to keep the knowledge on't from you.*

GERNETTE. *Gentlemen, I beseech you believe not this scandalous doctor: Sir, I'l have you punisht for this defamation: my daughter had a child, you wretch?*

DOCTOR DRENCH. *Come, you'r a weak old man. I say again, that she that made this water has had a child lately; therefore let search be made to find it out.*

2 DOCTOR. *You will do well to examine it, for 'tis possible it may not be her water; for doctors have had such tricks put on 'em ere now. . . .*

DOCTOR DRENCH. *But they can put no such tricks upon me, for my judgement cannot fail me; therefore, I say look to't, for there's a child in the case.*

GERNETTE. *Call all my servants; where's my daughters women? Here must be treachery, and Nurse you must need know it.*

NURSE. *Sir, I do know it indeed, and I crave your pardon.*

GERNETTE. *What has my daughter had a child then?*

NURSE. *No, Sir, but you know I have had one.*

GERNETTE. *But, the doctor says, she that made the water has had a child.*

NURSE. *The doctor says very true, for 'tis my water, sir. . . . If you'l have the truth, I did it to find out which would prove the ablest doctor, and the stranger it seems is the doctor of doctors i' faith.*

The second doctor was no fool. He knew it was not the "sicke mans uryn" which was always the physician's whore, but sometimes the sick man's attendants. And probably he was right, for in the course of the seventeenth century more cozenage was due to people than to what Falstaffe's physician called "a good healthy water."

As the urinal symbolized the physician in literature, it also represented the doctor in art. The seventeenth-century Dutch

artists, particularly Jan Steen and Gerard Dou, painted many
velvet-gowned physicians, and uroscopy is a feature in nearly all
the pictures. What English portrait painters there were at the
time probably followed suit; Haunce, talking to one of them,
says:

> . . . as you painted the doctor eene now,
> With his nose in an urinal.
>   The Wisdome of Doctor Dodypoll, II

Medical books, graphic representations, and popular literature
all show the intimate connection of water-casting with seventeenth-century medicine, but only in the plays do we see the
close relationship between the urinal and everyday life. In them
we see men and women searching in the urine for sickness and
health, unchastity and children, good fortune, and secrets which
cannot be kept. Gentlemen send servants with brimming urinals
in osier baskets to gowned physicians; humble folk sit stolidly in
apothecaries' shops patiently holding their naked glasses until
their turn arrives; credulous countrymen visit quacks who offer
more information for smaller fees.

Scientifically speaking, uroscopy was based on the doctrine of
the four humors, and its life was indissolubly bound up with
Galenical medicine. But under the attacks of the iatrochemists
the four humors were dissipated into earth, air, fire, and water,
and these returned to the metaphysical mists from which the
Greeks had called them over two thousand years before. By the
time of Dr. John Radcliffe at the turn of the seventeenth century, the well-educated physician turned his urinal into a flower
vase for his wife, and the custom of water-casting made its last
stand with the wise-women, cunning-men, and itinerant quacks
before it finally disappeared.[25]

[25] Besides these medical quacks there was another class of uroscopists, exemplified by Foresight in Congreve's Love for Love (1695). Foresight was "an
illiterate old fellow, peevish and positive, superstitious, and pretending to understand astrology, palmistry, physiognomy, omens, dreams, &c." His uroscopical
practice, as the following quotation from Act III shows, has an astrological tinge
and no medical end in view; it is sheer decadence. "And d'ye hear—bring me, let
me see—within a quarter of twelve—hem—he, hem!—just upon the turning of
the tide, bring me the urinal;—And I hope neither the lord of my ascendant, nor
the moon will be combust; and then I may do well."

It was a long time disappearing. In 1778 Dr. Lettsom lamented in a footnote: "No modern imposters have been more successful than water conjurers, with which this nation still abounds." [26] But for the licensed practitioners the good old days of water-casting were over. It was related

> that a foolish woman came to Radcliffe [carrying a flask of urine], and, dropping a curtsey, told him that, having heard of his great fame, she made bold to bring him a fee, by which she hoped his worship would be prevailed upon to tell her the distemper her husband lay sick of, and to prescribe proper remedies for his relief.
>
> "Where is he?" cries the doctor.
>
> "Sick in bed, four miles off."
>
> Taking the vessel, and casting an eye on its contents, he enquired of the woman what trade the patient was of; and, learning that he was a bootmaker, "Very well," replied the doctor; and having retired for a moment to make the requisite substitution, "Take this home with you; and if your husband will undertake to fit me with a pair of boots by its inspection, I will make no question of prescribing for his distemper by a similar examination." [27]

But medicine's gain is literature's loss. Urinalysis will never make the fascinating appearance in the twentieth-century novels that uroscopy did in seventeenth-century plays. There is not much glamor in this sort of report:

5-Hydroxyindole-acetic acid	5.36 mg.
Epinephrine	6.48 mg.
Ascorbic acid	7.23 mg.
Methylmalonic acid	3.91 mg.

[26] *History of the Origin of Medicine* (London, 1778), p. 153.
[27] William Macmichael, *Lives of British Physicians* (London, 1830), p. 118.

2

Bleeding in Health, Disease, and Dilemmas

It is a mere vulgar error, that the blood is of any use in the system; the faster you draw it off the better.

—LE SAGE, *Gil Blas*

AS UROSCOPY WAS A FAVORITE METHOD OF DIAGNOSIS IN EARLIER days, bloodletting was a universal method of treatment. The origin of the procedure is lost in antiquity. Pliny, whose tales have more charm but less accuracy than modern science demands, ascribes the invention of phlebotomy to the hippopotamus. Dr. Philemon Holland, whose translation of the *Naturalis Historia* [1] is a most fascinating book, renders the story thus:

> The river-horse hath taught physitions one device in that part of their profession called surgerie: for he finding himself over-grosse & fat by reason of his high feeding so continually, gets forth of the water to the shore, having spied afore where the reeds and rushes have bin newly cut: and where he seeth the sharpest cane and best pointed, hee sets his body hard unto it, to pricke a certaine veine in one of his legs, and thus by letting himselfe blood maketh evacuation: whereby his body, otherwise inclining to diseases and maladies, is well eased of the superfluous humor: and having thus done, hee stoppeth the orifice againe with mud, and so stauncheth the blood, and healeth the wound.
>
> Bk. VIII, Ch. 26

[1] *The Historie of the World. Commonly called, The Natural Historie of C. Plinius Secundus,* trans. Philemon Holland, Doctor of Physicke (2 vols.; London, 1634). All quotations from Pliny have been taken from this edition (the second).

There is no mention of surgical bloodletting in Homer, although to one of the Homeric heroes, Podilarus, the son of Aesculapius, is attributed the first use of the procedure. This warrior and physician, while on his way home from the Trojan wars, bled King Damaethus's daughter from both arms after she had fallen from a horse. This cured her and Podilarus married her. As romantic as the episode is, the erudite Le Clerc refuses to allow the legend more than an apocryphal place in sober medical history. Certainly the far more ancient records of the Babylonians and Egyptians show that these peoples were well acquainted with bloodletting and that they even examined the fluid drawn from the veins.

It was not until the fifth century B.C. and the works of the great Hippocrates that we find the detailed scheme of treatment upon which medicine rested for well over two thousand years. According to the Father of Medicine, there were two main therapeutic means for reducing superfluities of the bodily humors: purgation and the letting of blood. Minor but nevertheless widely popular methods were the administration of emetics to induce vomiting and clysters, or enemas. Passing for the moment down the centuries to 1639, we see two amateur healers preparing to try all four on one miserable love-sick man:

ALICE. *He grows fainter.*
VALENTINE. *Come, lead him in, he shall to bed: a vomit,*
    I'll have a vomit for him.
ALICE.   *A purge first;*
    And if he breath'd a vein—
VALENTINE. *No, no, no bleeding;*
    A clyster will cool all.
            BEAUMONT AND FLETCHER, Monsieur Thomas, II, 1

Like venesection, these other "important principles of prudence and morality, have been learnt from irrational creatures; as, the use of clysters from the stork,[2] and the benefit of vomiting

[2] "The like device to this [i.e. phlebotomy], namely of clisters, we learned first of a fowle in the same Egypt, called ibis [or the blacke storke.] This bird having a crooked and hooked bill, useth it in stead of a syringe or pipe to squirt water into that part, whereby it is most kinde and wholsome to avoid the doung and excrements of meat, and so purgeth and clenseth her body" (*ibid.*, Bk. VIII, Ch. 27).

from the dog" [3] (Cervantes, *Don Quixote*, Pt. II, Bk. 3, Ch. 12).

Hippocrates himself used the lancet with true Greek modera-
tion. He bled according to the age and habit of the patient, the
country, the season, and the disease; he spared children and the
aged. This is a far cry from the seventeenth-century Gui Patin,
who had his eighty-year-old father-in-law bled "eight times from
the arms, and each time I made them take nine ounces from
him." [4] But perhaps this irascible Frenchman got on as badly
with his relatives as he did with his colleagues. It is curiously
revealing to learn that the old man was on the point of leaving
his son-in-law a legacy of twenty thousand crowns. Another time
Patin bled "an infant of three days for an erysipelas of the
throat. He is still living, aged thirty-five years, a captain at Dun-
kirk. . . ." [5] Like many another proponent of a therapeutic
regimen, the doctor does not mention those who died.

The Hippocratic school recognized three reasons for bleeding:
to evacuate the plethora of blood from the vessels; to stop or
turn aside the flow of blood to a disordered part; or to procure
free movement of blood and vital spirits throughout the body.
To rid the patient of pain caused by an excessive amount of
blood in an organ, Hippocrates bled from the vein nearest the
site of the pain. To prevent pain, he drew blood from the vessel
farthest away. In both cases, however, the blood was drawn from
the same side of the body in which the pain occurred. This was
known as derivative bleeding, as opposed to the later Arabian
doctrine of revulsive bleeding, in which venesection was performed on the opposite side. Favorite points for the lancet's
entrance were the vessels of the arms, the backs of the hands, the
ankles, the backs of the knees, the forehead, the back of the
neck, the temples, between the middle and ring fingers and the
index finger and the thumb; the jugular veins; and the veins
under the tongue and in the anus.

Not only had the various veins their obvious anatomical con-
nections with the various parts of the body, but they had mysti-

[3] "It seemeth also that this domesticall creature taught men first the manner of
discharging and purging the stomacke by vomit" (*ibid.*, Bk. XXIX, Ch. 4).

[4] F. R. Packard, *Gui Patin and the Medical Profession in Paris in the XVII
Century* (New York, 1925), p. 115.

[5] *Ibid.*, p. 162.

cal relationships as well, and it mattered a great deal from which part the blood was drawn. Calamitous results, according to the Pseudo-Aristotle, might arise from injudicious bleeding; one cause of barrenness in women "is the letting of virgins blood in the arm before their natural courses are come down . . . and by these means the blood is diverted from its proper channel, so that it comes not down to the womb . . . whereby the womb dries up, and the woman is for ever barren." [6]

Even more deplorable, however (for the author of these little treatises was no feminist [7]), was the fact that misuse of the lancet might also cause sterility in men:

> But amongst other causes of barrenness in men, this also is one that makes them barren and almost of the nature of eunuchs, and that is the incision, or cutting of the veins behind the ears; which, in case of distempers, is oftentimes done; for, according to the opinion of most physicians and anatomists, the seed flows from the brain by those veins behind the ears more than from any other part of the body; from whence it is very probable the transmission of the seed is hindered by the cutting of the veins behind the ears, so that it cannot descend at all to the testicles, or come thither very crude and raw. [8]

[6] *The Works of Aristotle, in Four Parts. . . . A new edition* (London, 1792), p. 458.

[7] As one may see from his instructions of "How to cut the Child's Navel-string," a discourse so curious that I offer it to the reader here:

> As to the cutting it short or long, authors can scarce agree about it, nor midwives neither; some prescribe it to be cut at four fingers breadth, which is at the best but an uncertain rule, unless all fingers were of one size. 'Tis a received opinion, that the parts adapted to generation are either contracted, or dilated, according to the cutting of the navel-string; which is the reason that mid-wives are generally so kind to their own sex, that they leave a longer part of the navel-string of a male than the female, because they would have the male well provided for the encounters of Venus. And the reason they give why they cut those more short is, because they believe it makes them modest, and their parts narrower, which makes them more acceptable to their husbands. But whether this be so or not, (which yet some of the greatest searchers into the secrets of nature affirm for a truth) yet certain it is that great care ought to be used about cutting of the navel-string; and especially, that after it is cut, it be not suffered to touch the ground, for if it be, the child will never be able to hold its water, but be subject all its lifetime to a diabetes, as experience often confirms . . . (*ibid.*, pp. 73–74).

[8] *Ibid.*, p. 461.

The world has not yet entirely discarded its old belief in sympathetic blood vessels, as the traditional placement of the wedding ring proves. From the ring finger of the left hand runs a magical vein directly to the heart, and as its blood sanctified the marriage contract, so it also hallowed another sort of diabolic bond: "The veyne in his left hand that is derived from the hart with no faint blow he pierst, & with the full blood that flowed from it, writ a full obligation of his soule to the devill . . ." (Nashe, *Unfortunate Traveller*, p. 121).

Significant in the history of venesection is a report by Galen of a woman suffering from amenorrhea from whom he drew on the first day eighteen ounces of blood; on the second day, twelve; on the third, eight. As Le Clerc says, this is the first instance in medical literature in which the physician measured the amount of blood taken from a patient. "*No Greek,*" he adds in italics, "*ever spoke of pints and ounces.*" [9] Our sciences become increasingly quantitative, and the first quantitative expression of any procedure or phenomenon deserves Le Clerc's italicized words of recognition.

The practice of phlebotomy was influenced not only by the patient's disease, but also by the time of year, the course of the moon, and even the day of the month. According to the tenets of astrological medicine—which in the seventeenth century was on the wane—the twelve signs of the zodiac controlled twelve regions of the human body: "The Ram claims the head; the Bull the neck; the Twins the arms; the Crab the breast; the Lion the thorax; the Virgin the bowells; the Scales the reins [kidneys]; the Scorpion the secrets; the Archer the thighs; the Goat the knees; the Water-Carrier the legs; and the Fishes the feet." [10] It was considered most perilous to let blood from a member during the sign of the moon governing that part. In "A Propheme to Chirurgeons" in his *Breviarie of Health*, Andrew Boorde cautioned

[9] Daniel Le Clerc, *Histoire de la Médecine* (new ed., Pt. I; La Haye, 1929), p. 702.
[10] Manilius, *Astronomicon*, lib. 1. Quoted by T. J. Pettigrew, *Superstitions Connected with the History and Practice of Medicine and Surgery* (Philadelphia, 1844), p. 49.

the Elizabethan phlebotomists on this very point: "Also every chirurgion ought to know the complexion of his pacient . . . and that they be circumspect in incisions and scarifications and flebothomy, and sure in anathomy, and in no wise to let blud in any particular place, ther wher the signe hath any dominion." [11]

Almost all of the allusions in the seventeenth century to zodiacal phlebotomy are facetious in nature, for astrology no longer had the power and prestige it owned in medieval days. When Sweetball the Barber in Middleton's *Any thing for a Quiet Life* finds that his plans have gone all awry, he exclaims: "I must phlebotomize sir, but my Almanack says the sign is in Taurus; I dare not cut my own throat, but if I finde any pre[ce]dent that ever barber hang'd himself, Ile be the second example" (III, 2). When the moon was in Taurus, which governs the neck, it was dangerous to let blood from the jugular vein. Indeed, the Barber thought it would have been fatal to commit suicide in this manner.

Such punning allusions are fairly common. Here is another: Martin and Onion are playing a bout at cudgels. Martin breaks his opponent's head and goes off to fetch a remedy:

MARTIN. *Here, fellow Onion, heres a cob-web.*[12]
ONION. *How? a cob-web Martino, I will have another bout with you! S'wounds do you first breake my head, and then give me a plaister in scorne?*

Juniper then tries his best to dissuade Onion from continuing. "S'bloud! why what," he cries:

thou art not lunaticke, art thou? and thou bee'st, avoide Mephistophiles. Say the signe should be in Aries now: or it may be for all

[11] (London, 1575), p. 3v and 4.

[12] This popular remedy goes back to antiquity. Pliny writes (*Natural Historie*, Bk. XXIX, Ch. 6): "If the head be hurt, or the crown crackt, lay to the wound a copweb with oile and vinegar, and so let it lie, it will not lightly goe off untill such time as it be perfectly healed: this cop-web is very good also to staunch the bloud of wounds in a barbers shop." Philemon Holland's note explains: "Either when the barber would stop the orifice of a vaine after bloud letting: or when one that is newly wounded, cometh fresh bleeding to be dressed: or if his own rasor chance to go away & shave to the quicke whiles he hath a man under his hand to trim."

us, where were your life? Answere me that. . . . Come, come,
you are a foolish naturalist, go, get a white of an egge,[13] *and a*
little flax, and close the breach of the head, it is the most
conducible thing that can be.

JONSON, *The Case is Alterd*, II, 7

With the sign in Aries a bloody head was apt to be serious,
whereas the moon in any other sign would exert no malign
influence. It behooved the prudent to watch their almanacs with
care.

Even farther afield we find a pair of allusions which will
perhaps interest the amateur astrologer. In Act V of Marston's
The Malcontent Malevole asks Macquerelle, "an old pan-
dresse," whether she thinks the duchess Maria can be seduced.

MACQUERELLE. *Let me see, where's the signe now? ha ye ere a calen-*
dar, where's the signe trow you?
MALEVOLE. *Signe! why is there any moment in that?*
MACQUERELLE. *O! beleeve me a most secret power, looke yee a Chal-*
dean or an Assyrian, I am sure t'was a most sweete Jew tolde me,
court any woman in the right signe, you shall not misse: but you
must take her in the right veine then: as when the signe is in
Pisces, a fishmongers wife is very sociable; in Cancer, a precisians
wife is very flexible; in Capricorne, a merchants wife hardly
holdes out; in Libra, a lawyers wife is very tractable, especially, if
her husband bee at the terme: onely in Scorpio t'is very danger-
ous medling: has the duke sent any jewel, any rich stones?
MALEVOLE. *I, I thinke those are the best signes to take a lady in.*

Macquerelle tempts the virtuous Maria with all the wiles in her
possession, but to no avail. Baffled, she retires mumbling to
Malevole: "Now a my conscience, now I thinke in my discretion, we did not take her in the right signe, the bloud was not in
the true veine, sure."

When Jacomo, the valet of the libertine Don John, falls into
the hands of a band of vengeful shepherds, one of them threat-
ens:

[13] "It is said moreover, that the white of an egg is very good to conglutinat or
sowder any wound . . ." (*ibid.*, Bk. XXIX, Ch. 3).

> *We will not kill you, we'll but geld you,*
> *Are you so hot, Sir?*
> JACOMO. *Oh bloudy villains! have a care, 'tis not a season for that; the*
> *sign's in Scorpio.*
> SHADWELL, *Libertine,* IV

Scorpio does indeed govern the organs of generation, and one cannot blame the unfortunate valet for believing that the operation performed at such a time would be as dangerous as regrettable. But in 1555 Leonard Digges wrote, "The best tyme of Gelding is in Cancer, Scorpio, or Pisces in the wane." [14] Since Jacomo finally escaped intact, the question of whether or not the sign was propitious recedes into one more academic mist.

To the layman in seventeenth-century England the lancet and basin were familiar objects, recalling our own early and distasteful acquaintance with the castor-oil bottle and spoon. The physician of three centuries ago often neglected to establish his diagnosis before wielding the scalpel. Whatever the disease, bleeding was the remedy. Indeed, complained one doctor: "the great studie of physick is come to nothing now but letting Bloud . . . 'tis Alamode Paris; if your corn does but ake against rain, what says the doctor? Let him bloud: Nay, if you be troubled in conscience, they'l let you bloud for that too." "They let not blood for the small-pox, I hope," cries Leander in horror at these revelations. "But they do," retorts Dr. Drench, "and 'tis the opinion of Padua, that 'tis as sure a way to kill, as an old woman and saffron is to cure." (Lacy, *Dumb Lady,* III).

But the old medicos themselves, or at least those who felt it a solemn duty to kill or cure according to rule, never bled a patient: they had him bled. The doctor himself was averse to blood-stained hands and stood aloof while a humble barber-surgeon lanced the vein and caught the blood in a basin. The Medicus in William Bullein's *A Dialogue against the Fever Pestilence* commands:

> . . . you, surgian, prepare your lace, staffe, and launce, with your unce [own] vesselles, that I may consider his blood in order and

[14] *A Prognostication* (London, 1555), quoted by R. T. Gunther, *Early Medical and Biological Science* (London, 1926), p. 18.

*due quantitie. . . . Let hym bloud by little and little, and al-
though he doe fall into lipothimion [a faint], it is no matter; let
hym bloudde untill it partly doe chaunge into a good colour.
. . . Stop up the vein a Gods name.*[15]

The procedure actually followed in phlebotomy is given ex-
plicitly in one of John Ford's plays:

ORGILUS.   *My selfe, no surgeon.
   I am well skill'd in letting blood: bind fast
   This arme, that so the pipes may from their conduits
   Convey a full streame: here's a skilful instrument. . . .*

At this point Orgilus shows his dagger:

Reach me a staffe in this hand.

They give him a staff:

                                   *. . . thus I shew cunning
       In opening of a veine too full, too lively.*
                                        Broken Heart, V, 2

And here he pierces his vein with his dagger and bleeds to death.
The description might very well have come from a manual for
embryonic barber-surgeons.

As one might suppose, the operation was not a painless one.
In 1694, Congreve, accused of representing some women as
vicious and affected in his plays, wrote in the Epistle Dedicatory
to *The Double Dealer*: "I should be very glad of an opportunity
to make my complement to those ladies who are offended; but
they can no more expect it in a comedy than to be tickled by a
surgeon when he's letting 'em blood."

However, the discomfort restrained neither physician nor patient, and the important place which bloodletting occupied in
the life of the time is well shown in many of the plays:

FLIPPANTA. *Why, then your uneasiness is only a Disease, sir, perhaps a
   little bleeding and purging wou'd relieve you.*
                                        VANBRUGH, Confederacy, IV

---

[15] M. W. and A. H. Bullen, E.E.T.S., e.s. 52 (London, 1888), p. 28.

YOUNG WOU'DBEE. . . . *but are you sure he's past all recovery? Did you send for no surgeon to bleed him?*

FARQUHAR, *Twin-Rivals*, V

DORINA. *At length we prevailed upon her to be blooded; and that soon eased her.*

MOLIÈRE, *Tartuffe*, I, 4

The *post hoc ergo propter hoc* fallacy was no stranger to the disciples of the lancet and basin. If the first bleeding did not relieve, they attacked the obstinate malady again in the same manner. The patient's relatives paid off the physician and called in the priest "when thy disease is so daungerous y^t[that] the third letting of blood is not able to recover thee" (Lyly, *Euphues and his England*, II, 86).

It had been Galen's practice to phlebotomize not more than three times in any one case, but that his moderating example was not always followed in the seventeenth century must have been apparent from old Patin's account of his father-in-law's illness. On the whole, the English physicians were far less bloodthirsty than their Continental colleagues. Le Sage's *Gil Blas* is one long diatribe against the buckets of blood spilled on the altar of medicine. The quotation which heads this chapter gives the foreign point of view, for in France, where the basins were deeper, the satire was keener. Here is an example of it drawn from Molière's *M. de Pourceaugnac*:

PHYSICIAN. *How many times has he been blooded?*
COUNTRYWOMAN. *Fifteen times, sir,—within this fortnight.*
PHYSICIAN. *Fifteen times blooded within this fortnight?*
COUNTRYWOMAN. *Yes.*
PHYSICIAN. *And does n't he mend?*
COUNTRYWOMAN. *No, sir.*
PHYSICIAN. *That's a sign his distemper is n't in his blood.*

I, 6

But both Molière's doctor and Gui Patin were paragons of restraint compared with the sanguinary surgeons who, between September 6, 1726, and December 1, 1729, bled a young French-woman the unbelievable total of 26,230 times! [16]

[16] *Mercure de France*, April, 1728, and December, 1729. Quoted by J. C. Jeaffreson, *A Book about Doctors* (New York, 1861), p. 233.

It is no wonder that the dramatists advised their characters to "flie phlebotomie, fresh pork, conger, and clarified whay; they are all dullers of the vital spirits" (Beaumont and Fletcher, *Philaster*, II). These same poets touch on the theme in still another play. Perhaps one of them had an unfortunate experience with a Continental barber-surgeon:

RAFE. *Now butter with a leaf of sage is good to purge the blood;*
   Fly Venus and phlebotomy for they are neither good.
                         BEAUMONT and FLETCHER, *Knight*
                                  of the Burning Pestle, IV

The wonder is that bloodletting as it was practiced was not more often an extinguisher of vital spirits. Gentlemen went "to be let blood in a barbars shop against the infection" (Nashe, *Unfortunate Traveller*, p. 91), when every drop of blood was needed by the body to resist the virus.[17] And when one recalls that in Elizabeth's reign the entire populace, or at least all those who could afford the fees, submitted to a yearly prophylactic bleeding, one begins to admire the stamina of our forefathers. "The folly of our forefathers," Nicholas Gyer put it at the time:

> There cometh to my minde a common opinion among the ignorant people, which do certainly beleeve that, if any person be let bloud one year, he must be let bloud every yere, or else he is (I cannot tell, nor they neither) in how great danger. Which fonde opinion of theirs, whereof soever the same sprong first, it is no more like to be true, then if I should say: when a man hath received a great wound by chaunce in any part of his body, whereby he loseth much bloud; yet after it is healed, he must needs have the like wounde againe there the next yeare, to avoid as much blood, or els he is in daunger of great sickness, yea, and also in hazard to lose his life.[18]

[17] Compare Doctor Bullein's preventative advice in *A Dialogue against the Fever Pestilence:* "And to bee letten bloud a little at once, and to take pilles *contra pestem:* that is a good preservative against the plague" (p. 40). As to the quantity taken, "Forsoth, fower unces, or little more, and must bee doen every moneth, sometyme in the *median* [vein], sometyme in the *Basilica*, &c. . . . (p. 41).

[18] *The English Phlebotomy* (London, 1592), quoted by Jeaffreson, *A Book about Doctors*, p. 229.

In special diseases venesection fulfilled a genuinely beneficial function. One such condition, according to widespread popular report, was pleurisy.

> *There is nothing can cure the king's evill, but a prince, nothing ease a plurisie but letting bloud.*
> LYLY, *Euphues and his England, II, 95*

> KING. . . . *a small daggers point*
> *Opens the vaines to cure our plurizy.*
> DEKKER, *If this be not Good, the Divel is in it* [19]

Apparently in this distemper bleeding was prophylactic as well as curative, for in an exchange of invective a physician has the last word:

> CORAX. *Have at thee; thou affect'st railing onely for thy health, thy miseries are so thicke and so lasting, that thou hast not one poore denier to bestow on opening a veine. Wherefore to avoide a plurisie, thou't be sure to prate thy selfe once a month into a whipping, and bleed in the breech in stead of the arme.*
> FORD, *Lovers Melancholy, I*

There is one interesting aspect of this bleeding for pleurisy. Dr. Bullein's rules for the apothecary's conduct seem to relax their stringency at one point: it was permissible "That he may open well a vein for to help pleuresy." The honest apothecary must have called many a disease a pleurisy in order to earn a ten-shilling fee.

Those poor unfortunate creatures who were touched with madness were the most pitiful victims of the century's urge to bleed. The two contemporary cures for insanity were whipping and bleeding, helped along by dark and solitary confinement and a bread and water-gruel diet, and between the two there was not much to choose. These therapeutics sound so cruel, heartless, and even sadistic that an apology must be entered in behalf of those masters of the seventeenth-century madhouses who have been so long traduced.

In 1547 the famous old hospital of St. Mary of Bethlehem, founded three hundred years before, was turned into an insane

[19] *Dramatic Works* (1873), III, 336.

asylum, and it promptly found an important place in the life and literature of the times. Its name was shortened to Bedlam, which signified both the institution and its inmates—and any row which partook of the nature of either. The Elizabethans loved to visit the hospital where, on the payment of a small fee, they were allowed to watch the antics of the mad Toms incarcerated there. "Let us meete," says the Duke to his companions:

> At Bethlem monasterie, some space of time
> Being spent betweene the arivall each of other,
> As if we came to see the Lunatickes.
>
> DEKKER, Honest Whore, Pt. I, V

And as late as 1698, in Farquhar's *Love and a Bottle*, young Mockmode, the country squire who has come down from the university to get a wife and see London, confesses: "Of all the rarities of the town, I long to see nothing more than the poets and Bedlam" (II).

This strange form of amusement is as responsible as any other factor for the opinion that the insane must have been treated like beasts, since they were exhibited for the delectation of a populace devoid of finer sensibilities. But if modern madhouse keepers ever let down the bars, our own institutions would be equally crowded with curious visitors. Circus sideshows draw well, and mental as well as physical deformity will always claim sufficient attention to pay the expenses of the show.

Bleeding for lunacy seems to have been a relatively rare procedure before the Restoration. In the early part of the century the psychiatrists depended largely on the cat-o'-nine-tails and a therapeutic fast. Thus, from *Jacke Drums Entertainement* (1601) come:

FLAWNE. *I'le even lay him up in Bedlame: commit him to the mercie of the whip, the entertainment of bread and water.*

III

JACKE DRUM. *Oh sir, M. Mamon is in a Citie of Jurie [Jewry], called Bethlem, Alias plaine Bedlame: The price of whips is mightily risen since his braine was pitifully overtumbled, they are so fast spent upon his shoulders.*

V

Returning once more to Dekker's *Honest Whore*, we discover a sweeper employed in Bedlam itself who says: "Yes, forsooth, I am one of the implements, I sweep the madmens roomes, and fetch straw for 'em, and buy chaines to tie 'em, and rods to whip 'em, I was a mad wag my selfe here once, but I thank Father Anselm, he lasht me into my wits agen" (Pt. I, v, 2). Two important facts emerge from this speech: sometimes the whips were not spent in vain, for cures seem to have been effected; and the inmates of infamous Bedlam did not wallow in filth but rolled in clean straw—in which they were sometimes doubtless better off than a good many of their saner fellows outside the madhouse walls.

But this picture has a darker side as well. As time passed Bedlam deteriorated, for in Lacy's *The Dumb Lady* (produced in 1669) we encounter in Act IV two officers of the asylum who are closer to the barbarity of a later century than to the simple kindliness of Dekker's keeper:

1 OFFICER. *And though the woman be not mad, we can make her mad, if you please.*
DOCTOR. *Prithee, how?*
2 OFFICER. *With these engines: why people are not so mad when they come to Bedlam, as they are when they'r in't, I assure you.*
DOCTOR. *How comes that I prethee?*
1 OFFICER. *Do you think that the food of bread and water, to lie naked in foul straw, and to be whipt twice a day, will not make any body mad? I'l warrant you faith.*
DOCTOR. *But do you give them no physick?*
1 OFFICER. *Something they have, but a whip is the main ingredient; for we whip 'em out of a phrenzy into stark madness, and then whip 'em on till they come round to their wits again.*

At the turn of the century the same procedures held sway. Sir Tunbelly Clumsey cries: "Bind him, I say, he's mad—bread and water, a dark room, and a whip, may bring him to his senses again" (Vanbrugh, *Relapse*, IV, 6).

These therapeutic measures—chaining, whipping, and dieting —were purposefully designed and were not simply the sadistic reactions of the attendants. If a benevolent thrashing did not calm the patient, he was bound so that his violence would no

longer endanger himself or others; or he was so weakened by
fasting that he was rendered equally powerless. The production
of bodily debility was also the aim of that other curative measure, bleeding. Here we see the lancet in fulsome use:

TICKET. *Alas, he has over-studied himself!*
    You were best let blood in time sir.
                              BROME, City Wit, III, 4

PEG. . . . *her uncle designs this morning to let out some of her hot*
    blood, as he calls it, and he has sent for a surgeon, and pretending
    she is mad, means to try conclusions by opening a vein, or two.
                         DOVER, The Mall, IV, 1

LOVEL. *Why this is downright madness.*
    Prethee send for a chirurgeon and open a veine,
    Try what that will do; for thou wilt be as
    Ripe for Bedlam else as a fanatick.
                    SHADWELL, Sullen Lovers, I

DON JOHN. *Let the young fool have a vein open'd, he's stark staring*
    mad.
                        SHADWELL, Libertine, IV

PEDRO. *Let me come; if he be mad, I have that shall cure him. There's*
    no surgeon in all Arragon has so much dexterity as I have at
    breathing of the temple-vein.
                    DRYDEN, Spanish Fryar, V

BRASS. *Madam, you see master's a little—touch'd, that's all. Twenty*
    ounces of blood let loose, wou'd set all right again.
                    VANBRUGH, Confederacy, V

It is fitting now, though it be a digression, to consider those to
whom care of the insane was a professional charge. The best
example is Father Anselmo, the friar in charge of Bethlem Mon-
astery in the first part of Dekker's *Honest Whore* (Act V), who
whipped the aforementioned sweeper into a cure. When the
good father is asked by the courtier Castruchio:

    Pray may we see some of those wretched soules,
    That heere are in your keeping?

He replies:

> Yes, you shall;
> But gentlemen, I must disarme you then,
> There are of mad-men, as there are of tame,
> All humourd not alike: we have here some,
> So apish and phantasticke, play with a feather,
> And tho twould grieve a soule to see Gods image
> So blemisht and defac'd, yet doe they act
> Such anticke and such pretty lunacies,
> That spite of sorrow they'l make you smile;
> Others agen we have like hungry lions,
> Fierce as wilde bulls, untameable as flies,
> And these have oftentimes from strangers sides
> Snatcht rapiers sodainely, and done much harme,
> Whom if you'l see, you must be weaponlesse.

Then several madmen come upon the stage and exhibit their various lunacies. The dramatist's attitude toward them is kindly and sympathetic, and it is doubtful that the apprentices, pages, and citizens in the audience laughed loudly or long at the scene. Even the courtiers in the play exclaim, "A very piteous sight," to which Father Anselmo replies:

> They must be usde like children, pleasd with toyes,
> And anon whipt for their unrulinesse.
>
> DEKKER, *Honest Whore*, Pt. I, V, 2

The reader may object at this point that Father Anselmo was perhaps a rare specimen. But listen to this conversation between two keepers of a madhouse, two subordinates who serve for love of money, not love of God, and judge whether it be filled with simple kindness or not:

> 1 KEEPER. *Carry mad Bess some meat, she roars like thunder. And tye the parson short; the moon's i'th' full,*[20] *he has a thousand pigs*

---

[20] It is unnecessary to remind the reader of the derivation of the word "lunatic." The fits of the insane were supposed to reach their height as the moon increased. Cuddy Banks in Rowley, Dekker, and Ford's *The Witch of Edmonton* says, "Let me see an almanack, midsummer-moon, let me see ye. When the moon's in the full, then's wit in the wane" (II, 1). So Hazzard's taunt: "What means that Orlando Furioso, is the moon at full that he raves thus? Your name is Tom [i.e. of Bedlam]" ([Dryden], *The Mistaken Husband*, IV, 4).

in's brain. Who looks to the prentice? Keep him from women, he
thinks he has lost his mistress: And talk of no silk stuffs; 'twil run
him horn mad.

2 KEEPER. *The justice keeps such a stir yonder with his charges, and*
such a coil with his warrants.

1 KEEPER. *Take away his statutes; the devil has possest him in the*
likeness of penal laws; keep him from aqua-vitae, for if that spirit
creep into his quorum, he'll commit us all. How is't with the
scholar?

2 KEEPER. *For any thing I see he is in's right wits.*

1 KEEPER. *Thou art an ass; his head's too full of other peoples wits, to*
leave room for his own.

VANBRUGH, Pilgrim, III, 3

Later in this same play (IV, 2) a practical joke is played on
old Alphonso. He is decoyed to Bedlam and brought before the
Master of the Madhouse, who tells him: "you are a little mad,
which you don't perceive; your friends have found it out, and
have deliver'd you over to me." Naturally Alphonso (an irascible
old gentleman anyway) is indignant. He spits in the Master's
face. "Say ye so, old boy?" returns the latter good-humoredly,
and calls to the keepers: "A hey! Seize him here, and fifty slaps
o' th' back presently. . . . In the morning we'll take 30 or 40
ounces of blood away; which with a watergrewel-dyet for a week
or ten days, may moderate things mightily.—Go carry him in,
I'll follow presently." [21]

Now this is fit subject for laughter, for the audience was in on
the secret and understood intuitively the difference between
testy old Alphonso and poor mad Bess.

---

[21] Vanbrugh's play is merely an adaptation of Beaumont and Fletcher's *The
Pilgrim*, produced in 1621. In the earlier piece when Alphonso is delivered over to
the authorities he demands, "Why, prethee why?"

> *Master.* Ye are dog mad: you perceive it not,
>   Very far mad: and whips will scant recover ye.
> *Alphonso.* Ha! whips?
> *Master.* I whips, and sore whips, and ye were a lord sir,
>   If ye be stubborn here.

(IV, 3)

The introduction of therapeutic bleeding is Vanbrugh's later contribution.

In time Alphonso's friends explain their prank, and as the Master delivers over the patient he explains:

> . . . *I believe he may be something weak, for we have dieted him low, and taken a good deal of blood from him.*
> CURIO. *Poor Alphonso.*
> > [Enter Keeper with ALPHONSO.]
> SEBERTO. *Poor Alphonso indeed! Was there ever such a skeleton! Sir, I'm glad once more to meet with you.* [To ALPHONSO.]
> CURIO. *I'm overjoy'd to find you.*
> ALPHONSO. *Soft, no flights: passions are all forbid here. Let your tongue go like a pendulum, steddy: or that gentleman there will regulate your motion, with fifty streaks o' the back presently.*[22]
> > V, 4

Besides bleeding and whipping, the pharmacopoeia was also brought into play in the treatment of madness. In Brome's *The Court Beggar* Strangelove, a lady who fancies herself well skilled in medicine, chatters on at a great rate to teach a doctor his profession:

> DOCTOR. *Madam, my purpose was not—*
> STRANGELOVE. *My purpose is to advise you though, that if his frenzie proceed from love as you conjecture, that you administer of the rootes of helleboro, destill'd together with salt-peter, and the flowers of blind netles. I'le give you the proportions, and the quantity is to take.*
> DOCTOR. *Mistake not me good madam—*
> STRANGELOVE. *But if his malady grow out of ambition, and his over weening hopes of greatnesse (as I conjecture) then he may take a top of cedar, or an oake-apple is very sovereigne with the spirit of hempseed.*
> > V

This dramatic material sheds other light on the subject of madness. Feelings of guilt and disgrace on the part of the patient and his relatives were notably absent in the seventeenth century. Madness may not always have been comic, off the stage or on, but it was no more disgraceful than the pox, which in turn was

---

[22] This dialogue is Vanbrugh's. Beaumont and Fletcher's Alphonso makes no comment on his sad experience.

considered in that heroic century no more shameful or tragic than any other serious disorder. Nevertheless, there were euphemisms then too for both lunacy and syphilis, but they were due to manners and not morals. When Brass said (above): "Madam, you see master's a little—touch'd, that's all" (Vanbrugh, *The Confederacy*, V, 2), his hesitant choice of an inoffensive word was dictated by natural good manners and not by affected squeamishness.

These many quotations from the old plays demonstrate that, although methods of treatment have improved since the seventeenth century, the underlying motives remain the same. The aims of both the seventeenth-century floggers and bleeders and the modern governors of psychiatric institutes are identical—the rehabilitation of the sufferer. Undoubtedly there were many brutal keepers in those days, and ignorant masters, and it is impossible to state categorically whether they were the exception or the rule. It appears, however, that conditions after the seventeenth century drew to a close became far worse before they began to improve under the influence of Philippe Pinel (1755–1826). We know now that it may be neither good morals nor good manners to laugh at the antics of the insane, but nevertheless such antics are sometimes comic enough,[23] and there is such a thing as compassionate laughter. We must also remember (and this will be borne out even more strongly in a later chapter) that many of our morals are rather recent inventions, that manners change only too rapidly, and that the Elizabethans and their immediate descendants were remarkable for their strong stomachs and strong minds, as well as for their strong therapeutic measures.

Now that we have nodded toward those much-maligned seventeenth-century precursors of psychiatrists, let us return to blood letting uncomplicated by whips and chains. Occasionally we hear of a minor heresy in the practice of phlebotomy: per-

[23] When I wrote this note, a group of schizophrenics had recently been exhibited before a class in pyschiatry. An old countryman, whose delusion that he was God had sent the students off into roars of laughter and had left the professor shorn for the moment of his professional seriousness.

haps unorthodoxy would be the better word. In the fourth century A.D., Caelius denounced bleeding from under the tongue as "superstitious, and based on a false principle; moreover it engorges the head, besides the fact that one can only with difficulty stop the flow of blood." Nevertheless, we hear of later doctors who felt, despite Caelius, that what veins were good enough for Hippocrates were good enough for the seventeenth century.

> TRUDGE. . . . *Roebuck was a doctor, that let me blood under the tongue for the quinsey, and made me hoarse ever since.*
> FARQUHAR, *Love and a Bottle*, IV

And in Chapman, Jonson, and Marston's *East-ward Hoe* Quicksilver warns Sir Petronell against marrying a rich wife by reciting a list of her probable demands:

> *Nay harke you sir; what nurses, what midwives, what fooles, what phisitions, what cunning women must be sought for (fearing sometimes she is bewitcht, some times in a consumption) to tell her tales, to talke bawdy to her, to make her laughe, to give her glisters, to let her bloud under the tongue, and betwixt the toes. . . .*
> II, 2

Bleeding from betwixt the toes was another superstitious practice, and we find Dr. Sangrado, a traditionalist to the core, inveighing against it in his old age: "Bleeding in the feet, for example, so rarely practised in better times, is now among the fashionable follies of the day. . . . In short, chaos is come again! (Le Sage, *Gil Blas*, Bk. X, Ch. 1).

Now let us take a page from real life and the *Diary* of John Evelyn. In 1646 Evelyn was taken sick at Beveretta.

> *I was constrained to keep my chamber, imagining that my very eyes would have dropped out; and this night I felt such a stinging about me, that I could not sleep. In the morning, I was very ill, but sending for a doctor, he persuaded me to be let blood. . . . He afterwards acknowledged that he should not have bled me, had he suspected the smallpox, which brake out a day after. He afterwards purged me, and applied leeches, and God knows what this would have produced, if the spots had not appeared, for*

*he was thinking of blooding me again. . . . My physician, to
excuse his letting me blood, told me it was so burnt and vicious
as it would have proved the plague, or spotted fever, had he
proceded by any other method.*

I, 236

The following year he was living in Paris and writes: "In May,
I fell sick, and had very weak eyes; for which I was four times let
blood" (I, 241). When in April, 1649, he was back in London,
even his own countrymen took their toll of his blood:

*17th. I fell dangerously ill of my head; was blistered and let blood
behind the ears and forehead: on the 23rd, began to have ease by
using the fumes of camomile on embers applied to my ears, after
all the physicians had done their best.*

I, 247

Evelyn would have agreed with Le Sage, who, in the Author's
Declaration in *Gil Blas*, averred that "Certain physicians of
Castille, as well as of France, are sometimes a little too fond of
trying the bleeding and lowering system on their patients."

Nevertheless, there were times in England when the effects of
such a system were very welcome, for rascally characters on the
stage found the surgical loss of blood a convenient alibi which
they did not hesitate to use. A valet named Lopez served Vanbrugh in two plays, and in each of them phlebotomy furnished
the prudent scoundrel with an excuse:

DON PEDRO. *How now, Lopez, where are you going?*

LOPEZ. *I'm going, sir, I—I'm going—if you please I'm going about my
business.*

DON PEDRO. *From whence do you come?*

LOPEZ. *Only, only sir, from—taking the air a little, I'm mightily
muddled with a whur—round about in my head for this day or
two, I'm going home to be let blood, as fast as I can, sir.*

DON PEDRO. *Hold sir, I'll let you blood here.*

False Friend, V

LOPEZ. *I don't like these nightly projects; a man can't see what he
does: we shall have some scurvy mistake or other happen: a brace
of bullets blunder through your head in the dark perhaps, and
spoil all your intrigue.*

DON LORENZO. Away, you trembling wretch, away.

LOPEZ. Nay, sir, what I say is purely for your safety; for as to my self
—Uds-death, I no more value the losing a quart of blood, than I
do drinking a quart of wine. Besides, my veins are too full; my
physician advis'd me but yesterday to let go twenty ounces for my
health. So you see, sir, there's nothing of that in the case.

Mistake, V, 1

In another case it was a bleeding already undergone which
exposed another timid soul. Cheatly, one of the knaves in Shadwell's *Squire of Alsatia,* is as full of brave words as empty of
courage. Belfond tickles his ears with a string of epithets, and as
a further test of his valor, kicks him heartily behind. Cheatly's
feelings are as hurt as his rump, and he complains: "I understand honour and breeding; besides, I have been let blood to
day" (III).

This same bleeding and lowering treatment gave one seventeenth-century husband a welcome rest, at least until his spouse's
hematopoietic organs had regenerated her lost blood. A ballad
entitled *A Caution for Scolds or a True Way of Taming a Shrew*
tells how the poor man

> . . . to a skilful doctor went,
> Promising that he would give him content,
> If he could cure the cause of a distracted wife
> Which almost made him a weary of his life;
> Yes, quoth the Doctor, I'le do it ne'r fear;
> Bring her, for now 'tis the spring of the year;
> I'le take the lunacy out of her brains,
> Or else I wont have a groat for my pains.
>
> Then home he went and sent her thither out of hand,
> Now when the shrew, she did well understand
> All their intent, she cal'd the doctor sneaking knave;
> Now when he see she began for to rave,
> Straightways the doctor did bind her in bed,
> Letting her blood, likewise shaving her head:
> Sirrah, said she, I would have you to know,
> That you shall suffer for serving me so.
>
> Madam, said he, I know you are beside your wits,
> But I will soon bring you out of those fits;

I'le cut your tongue, and when a gallon you have bled,
'Twil cure that violent noise in your head. . . .[24]

One of the unkind epithets—"pisspot caster," one of the more polite ones—hurled at the seventeenth-century physicians was the consequence of his familiarity with urine. Another, still more unkind, was derived from his propinquity to clysters. Rabelais must have been recalling his own student experiences when the youthful Pantagruel went to Montpellier "and thought to have set himself to the study of physic; but he considered that that calling was too troublesome and melancholy, and that physicians did smell of glisters like old devils" (*Gargantua and Pantagruel*, Bk. II, Ch. 5).

Perhaps the dramatists had the same thought, and the same olfactory impression!

MISTRESS BIRDLIME. . . . *and what meanes hath your husband to*
    allow sweet Doctor Glisterpipe, his pension.
                                    DEKKER, *West-ward Hoe*, I

BRUNHALT [to her physician]. *Ye doss, you powder'd pigsbones, ru-*
    barbe glister. . . .
                        BEAUMONT and FLETCHER, *Thierry and Theodoret*, I

And here are two valets masquerading *en médecin* who have run afoul of the blistering tongues of a bevy of servingmaids:

JOSINA. *Out you pispot-caster.*
BRIDGET. *You suppository.*
JOSINA. *You glister-pipe, thinkst to dishonest me?*
                                    BROME, *City Wit*, V, 1

But the honor of the profession is at stake, and this section cannot end on such a derogatory note. With Ben Jonson's aid the opprobrium can be shifted to the members of a lesser art. When Tucca asks one Minos his profession, the latter answers, "A pothecarie, sir." "I knew thou wast not a physician," retorts Tucca, "fough: out of my nostrils, thou stink'st of lotium, and the syringe: away, quack-salver" (*Poetaster*, III, 4).

---

[24] Quoted by J. Ashton, *Humour, Wit and Satire of the XVII Century* (New York, 1884), p. 82.

According to the old scheme of medicine each organ was supplied with blood by veins peculiar to that organ. Thus, the idea of drawing blood from the vessel nearest the diseased part in order to relieve the morbid symptoms was not at all far-fetched. Because the seat of madness lay in the brain, "breathing" of the temple vein followed in an attempt to draw off the peccant humors. To relieve a pleurisy, blood was drawn from the nearest vein, that of the arm. But with the discovery of the circulation of the blood, the theory which underlay the ancient practice of bloodletting was doomed. For if the same blood flowed through every vein and artery of the body in its circuit, the blood which gushed out of the cut vein of the arm was no different from that which emerged from the temple vein. Nor would bleeding at any one point of the body relieve that part to the exclusion of all others. After Harvey it soon became evident that phlebotomy merely reduced the total volume of blood and not its quantity in or flow through one organ.

The intelligent physician, of course, realized this long before the layman. Sir Thomas Browne wrote in 1646 in *Pseudodoxia Epidemica* concerning bleeding: "All which with many respective niceties, in order unto parts, sides, and veines, are now become of less consideration, by the new and noble doctrine of the circulation of the blood." (Bk. IV, Ch. 4).

We shall see, however, in a later chapter that Harvey's doctrine did not percolate through the inertia of popular thought until well along in the seventeenth century, and even then its true implications were not recognized. Consequently the dramatists were, perhaps, bleeding from "under the tongue, and betwixt the toes" for some time after the more enlightened surgeons had stopped.

3
Remedies – Animal, Vegetable, and Mineral

Our bodies we commit to the physicians, who never themselves take any physic.

—Rabelais, *Gargantua and Pantagruel*

The seventeenth-century man was more fortunate than his twentieth-century descendant. He had fewer diseases (or perhaps merely fewer names for diseases) and many more remedies for them. The first edition of the *Pharmacopoeia Londinensis* (1618) listed 1,960 drugs. Of course, most of them had only a psychological value, but it must have been comforting to think of such a well-stocked arsenal against disease.

Modern pharmacopoeias read like chemists' catalogues, the ancient ones like an interminable witch's song from *Macbeth*. Among the 1,960 remedies were 1,028 simples or herbs with medicinal virtues and 91 animal and 271 vegetable preparations.

> Worms, lozenges of dried vipers, foxes lungs, powders of precious stones, oil of bricks, oil of ants, oil of wolves, and butter made in May. . . . The blood, fat, bile, viscera, bones, bone-marrow, claws, teeth, hoofs, horns, sexual organs, eggs, and excreta of animals of all sorts; bee-glue, cock's-comb, cuttlefish, fur, feathers, hair, isinglass, human perspiration, saliva of a fasting man, human placenta, raw silk, spider-webs, sponge, sea-shell, cast-off snake's skin, scorpions, swallow's nests, wood-lice, and the

triangular Wormian bone from the skull of an executed criminal.[1]

Modern *littérateurs* would find the *Pharmacopoeia Londinensis* an appropriate means to excite the queasiness of their readers, but to the old dramatists such witch's brews occasioned neither astonishment nor satire. Too many of them had perhaps swallowed the crushed crabs' eyes of Gascoigne's powder or had been rubbed with album graecum to have found anything strange in mixtures which now seem to us far more revolting than, for example, the extracts of liver which our own scientific physicians inject into our flesh.

The apothecaries had no monopoly of the sale of drugs. The greater part of the business, even then tremendously lucrative, fell to the grocers; and it was not until 1617 that the druggists succeeded in ridding the trade of the grocers under a charter granted by James I. Beaumont and Fletcher's *The Knight of the Burning Pestle* was produced in 1610, before the proscription, and in this play we find Ralph, a grocer's boy, discontented with his lot:

> But what brave spirit could be content to sit in his shop with a flapet of wood, and a blew apron before him selling methridatum and dragons water to visited houses, that might pursue feats of arms, and through his noble atchievements, procure such a famous history to be written [of his] heroick prowesse.
>
>   I, 3

The "visited houses" refer to those infected with the plague, for England from the beginning of the century to the great epidemic of 1665 was periodically afflicted with this terrible malady. Along with mithridatium the juice of the plant called Dragon's Blood (*Pterocarpus draco*) was a popular remedy for it.

Dekker's plague pamphlet, *The Wonderfull Yeare* (1603), presents a stark picture of London during the severe visitation of 1602: "every house lockte like S. Bartholmewes-Hospitall, and every streete like Bucklersbury, for poore mithridatum and drag-

---

[1] F. H. Garrison, *Introduction to the History of Medicine* (4th ed.; Philadelphia, 1929), p. 289.

on-water (being both of them in all the world, scarce worth three-pence) were boxt in every corner, and yet were both drunke every houre at other mens cost" (*Plague Pamphlets*, p. 33). Bucklersbury was the street of the grocers and apothecaries. Probably Ralph sat in a shop there, impatiently selling the remedies which, though "scarce worth three-pence," must have sold for many times that amount.

The dramatists were only following the therapeutic lead of the physicians, for when in Dr. William Bullein's *Dialogue against the Fever Pestilence* a man is stricken with the plague, his wife exclaims: "I will sende for maister doctor Tocrub; in the meane tyme drinke dragon water and mithridatum mingled together, to put this passion from your harte." [2]

The plagues came so frequently, and calls for the remedies were made so often, that a metaphor was born. Says Mistress Birdlime in Dekker's *West-ward Hoe*: "Nay, but will you send her a box of mithridatum and dragon water, I meane some restorative words" (II, 2).

Mithridatium was the universal antidote of the age, considered equally effective against poisons, the bites of venomous animals, and the indiscretions of faulty diets. It was invented by the famous King of Pontus after whom it was named. Galen gives its history in his work *On Antidotes*:

> This Mithridates . . . in his eagerness to gain an acquaintance with almost all the simple herbs which antagonise poisonous substances, tested their powers on criminals who had been condemned to death. Some of them he found especially useful for the bites of venomous spiders, others of scorpios, others of vipers: then as regards poisonous drugs, some of his simples he found useful against aconite, others against sea-hare, and so forth. So Mithridates mixed these all together and made a single drug, hoping he would now have a resource against all poisons. . . . And if one takes the drug daily, as did Mithridates himself, he will be quite secure against deadly poisons and the drugs called deleteria. Thus it is said that when Mithridates preferred to die

---

[2] Ed. M. W. and A. H. Bullen, E.E.T.S., e.s. 52 (London, 1888), p. 120.

by poison rather than become subject to the Romans, he could not find anything capable of killing him.[3]

Later experimenters, amateur and professional alike, added their own ingredients to the original formula. Some, perhaps, were like Le Sage's Dr. Alvar Fanez, "an eminent member of the Faculty" who wanted a journeyman: "He boards his family very handsomely, has everything comfortable about him, and gives very high wages; but he is a little too fond of experiments. When he gets a parcel of bad drugs, which happens very often, there is a pretty quick succession of new servants" (*Gil Blas*, Bk. I, Ch. 17).

By the middle of the seventeenth century, mithridatium contained:

Myrrhae Arabicae [Myrrh]
Croci [Saffron]
Agarici [Agarie]
Zingiberis [Ginger]
Cinnamoni [Cinnamon]
Spicae Nardi [Spikenard]
Thuris [Frankincense]
Sem. Thlaspios [Mithridate Mustard], ana drachmas decem.
Seseleos [Hartwort]
Opobalsami [Balm of Gilead] seu Olei Nucis Moschatae per
     expressionem [Oil of Nutmegs]
Junci odorati [Camel's hay]
Stoechados Arabicae [Lavender]
Costi veri [Costus]
Galbani [Galbanum]
Terebinthinae Cypriae [Turpentine]
Piperis longi [Long pepper]
Castoroi [Russian castor]
Succi Hypocistidos [Rape of cistus]
Styracis Calamitae [Storax]
Opopanicis [Opoponax]
Fol. Malabathri recentium [Indian leaf], sey, ejus defectu

[3] A. J. Brock, *Greek Medicine, Being Extracts Illustrative of Medical Writers from Hippocrates to Galen* (London, 1929), p. 196.

Macis [Mace], ana unciam unam.
Casiae ligneae verae [Laurus cassia]
Polii montani [Poley mountain]
Piperis albi [White pepper]
Scordii [Water-germander]
Sem. Dauci Cretici [Carrot of Crete]
Carpobalsami [Fruit of balsum tree], vel Cubebarum [Cubebs]
Trochisch. Cypheos
Bdellii [Bdellium], ana drach. septum.
Nardi Celticae purgatae [Celtic nard]
Gummi Arabici [Gum arabic]
Sem. Petroselini Macedonici [Macedonian parsley]
Opii [Opium]
Cardamomi minoris [Lesser cardamom]
Sem. Foeniculi [Sweet fennel]
Gentianae [Gentian root]
Flo. rosar. rubrarum [Red roses]
Dictamni Cretensis [Dittany of Crete], ana drachmas quinque.
Sem. Anisi [Anise]
Asari [Asarabacca]
Acori, seu Calami Aromatici Sweet flag]
Ireos [Wild valerian]
Phu majoris [Raisins]
Sagapeni [Sagapenum], ana drachmas tres.
Mei Athmantici [Spignel]
Acaciae [Acacia]
Ventrium Scincorum [Bellies of Skinks]
Summitatum Hyperici [St. John's wort], ana drachmas duas
    semis.
Vini Canarini optimi quantum sufficit as solutionem gummi &
    succorum, nempe circiter uncias viginti sex.
Mellis deinde despumati triplum ad omnia, praeter vinum.
Fiat Electuarium secundum artem.[4]

[4] *Pharmacopoeia Regalis Londini* (London, 1677), p. 100. The English equivalents are from *The Dispensatory of the Royal College of Physicians, London*, trans. H. Pemberton (2nd ed.; London, 1748). Although the mithridatium was not deleted from the pharmacopoeia until the sixth edition of 1788, several minor changes were made after the 1677 revision. The laurus cassia was omitted as having been used by Galen only because of the scarcity of cinnamon; asarabacca was left out because it apparently crept in by an error in transcription of the

If each ingredient represented a condemned criminal or a new journeyman, the century's confidence in its universal remedy was dearly bought.

But mithridatium was not as infallible as its composition was imposing. It was no cure for lovesickness, and there were poisons which it could not invalidate.

CANOPE. *Where Ladie, doe you feele your most paine.*
SAPHO. *Where no bodie els can feele it Canope.*
CANOPE. *At the heart?*
SAPHO. *In the heart.*
CANOPE. *Will you have any mithrydate?*
SAPHO. *Yea, if for this disease there wer any mithridate.*
MILETA. *Why? what disease is it madame, that physick cannot cure?*
SAPHO. *Onely the disease, Mileta, that I have.*
LYLY, Sapho and Phao, III, 3

In Beaumont and Fletcher's *Valentinian* the Caesar has been poisoned by Aretus:

PHIDIAS. *It was not to be cur'd I hope.*
ARETUS. *No Phidias,*
   I dealt above his antidotes: physicians
   May find the cause, but where the cure?
V, 1

When Valentinian begins to feel the effects of the poison, he cries to his helpless physicians:

    . . . drink, drink, ye dunces;
What can your doses now do, and your scrapings,
Your eyles, and mithridates? if I do die,
You onely words of health, and names of sickness
Finding no true disease in man but mony,
That talk your selves into revenues, oh
And e're ye kill your patients, begger 'em,
I'le have ye flead, and dri'd.
V, 2

---

original description; the raisins were dropped because their quantity was trifling; and the trochisci Cypheos (composed of pulp of the grape, turpentine, cinnamon, cassia wood, aloes, bdellium, saffron, etc.) were omitted because most of the ingredients were also incorporated in the mithridatium itself.

Perhaps the oils which so often accompanied the administration
of the antidote were more effective against corrosive poisons
than the mithridatium itself.

THORELLO. *I feele me ill; give me some mithredate,*
    Some mithredate and oyle; good sister fetch me,
    O, I am sicke at hart: I burne, I burne;
    If you will save my life goe fetch it mee.
                JONSON, *Every Man in His Humour,* IV, 3

Mithridatium was not the only universal remedy, however.
Others promised even more far-reaching results and fulfilled
even fewer expectations. But these were quack remedies and had
no place on the official drug lists. The seventeenth-century Englishman was quite as gullible as his modern American cousin.
Mountebanks, charlatans, and quacksalvers flocked across the
Channel to purvey their remedies as today their descendants
cross the Atlantic to sell their cancer cures to an equally credulous public. A foreign name and a foreign accent, then as now,
often formed the basis of a successful and lucrative trade and an
inflated reputation.

It would be a fascinating study to trace in earlier days the path
of the quacks who found England such a happy hunting ground
for their knavery. The path is easily followed, for as signposts we
recognize both the jibes of the popular authors and the execra-
tions of the legitimate physicians. Back in 1552 a blast from the
learned John Caius in *A Boke, or Counseill against the Disease
Commonly called the Sweate, or Sweatyng Sicknesse* rocked
foreign and domestic quacks alike, but at the end left those
omnipresent ornaments of society firm on the foundations of
human credulity.[5]

It would be too much to expect, however, that Doctor Caius's
castigation touched the consciences of either the mountebanks
or their gulls. Yet in 1608, when Tom Coryat the traveler was in
Italy, he thought the folks at home would be interested to learn
that "The first mountebanke that ever I saw, was at Mantua the

---

[5] Caius' little treatise is reprinted as an appendix to B. G. Babington's
translation of Hecker's *The Epidemics of the Middle Ages* (London: Sydenham
Society, 1846).

eighteenth day of June, being Saturday, where he played his part
upon a scaffold. Of these mountebankes I will write more at
large in my observations of Venice" (*Crudities*, I, 267). And
when he came to that sink of iniquity he wrote:

> amongst many other thinges that doe much famouse this citie,
> these two sorts of people, namely the cortezans and the mounte-
> banks, are not the least. . . . [Of these last there were] a greater
> concurse of them in Venice than elsewhere, and that of the
> better sort and the most eloquent fellowes; . . . neither doe I
> much doubt but that this treatise of them will be acceptable to
> some readers, as being a meere novelty never before heard of (I
> thinke) by thousands of our English gallants.
>
> Crudities, I, 409–410

This statement seems incredible, even though Dr. Walter
Harris, some seventy years later, mentions a contemporary Restoration quack named Pontaeus as "the first mountebank who
ever appeared on a stage in England." If that was true, it was no
wonder that Coryat marveled at female mountebanks and at the
music which was a preamble and introduction to the ensuing
matter:

> in the meane time while the musicke playes, the principall
> mountebank which is the captaine and ring-leader of all the rest,
> opens his truncke, and sets abroach his wares; after the musicke
> hath ceased, he maketh an oration to the audience of halfe an
> hourse long, or almost an hourse. Wherein he doth most hyper-
> bolically extoll the vertue of his drugs and confections:
>
> Laudat venales qui vult extrudere merces.
>
> Though many of them are counterfeit and false. . . . The prin-
> cipall things that they sell are oyles, soveraigne waters, amorous
> songs printed, apothecary drugs, and a commonweale of other
> trifles.
>
> Crudities, I, 410–411

Tom also marveled to see the charlatans receive no hurt from
the stings of vipers or, hackled and gashed so that the blood
streamed from their naked arms, apply a certain "oyle" that
staunched the blood and healed the wound so thoroughly that

he could see no sign of it. He also observed "that after they have extolled their wares to the skies, and having set the price of tenne crownes upon some one of their commodities, they have at last descended so low, that they have taken for it foure gazets, which is something lesse than a groate." (*Crudities*, I, 409–412).

In spite of Tom Coryat and Dr. Harris, however, we are forced to conclude that even in Elizabethan days there were more quacks in England than snakes in Ireland. One authority for this conclusion is Ben Jonson and the second act of *Volpone, or The Foxe*, produced in 1605. In this scene (2) quackery is raised to the dignity of an art (as indeed it very often is), and it deserves to be transcribed in full. But it must suffice to remind the reader that Volpone therein masquerades as a mountebank, one Scoto Mantuano, in order to catch a glimpse of his beloved.

Now Scoto was by no means a creature of Ben's imagination. King James I in his *Daemonologie* (1597), writing of "The devilles contract with the magicians" (Bk. I, Ch. 6), says of Satan: "As in like maner he will learne them manie juglarie tricks at cardes, dice, & such like, to deceive mennes senses thereby: and such innumerable false practicques; which are proven by over-manie in this age: As they who ar acquainted with that Italian called Scoto yet living, can reporte." In *The Unfortunate Traveller*, Thomas Nashe also mentions "Scoto that dyd the juggling tricks before the Queene," and adds that he "never came neere that abundant scholler Cornelius Agrippa one quarter in magicke reputation" (p. 48).[6] And where Scoto found a ready audience, other charlatans very probably set up their banks.

If Jonson's *Volpone* offers us a fair basis for comparison, there was as much difference between Scoto and "These turdy-facy-nasty-paty-lousy-farticall rogues, with one poore groats-worth of un-prepar'd antimony, finely wrapt up in severall 'scartoccios,

[6] In *Thomaso, or The Wanderer* (London, 1663), Thomas Killigrew "has made use of Ben Johnson considerably, for not only the character of Lopus, but even the very words are copied from Johnson's *Fox*, where Volpone personates Scoto of Mantua: as the reader will see by comparing Act 4. Sc. 2. of this play with that of the *Fox*, Act 2. Sc. 2" (Langbaine, *An Account of the English Dramatick Poets* [Oxford, 1691], pp. 313–314).

[who] are able, very well, to kill their twentie a weeke" (II, 2) as there was between its author and the literary hacks who ground out the mountebanks' bills. But aside from the charm of his manner, Scoto Mantuano is the typical quack of the early seventeenth century.[7] As Caius complained, they all recited an imposing list of miraculous cures (always performed, happily, in distant climes) and a still more remarkable list of diseases which they stood ready to cure with the aid of their nostrums. With a flood of awe-inspiring Latin terms the mountebank first bewildered, then frightened his audience. To bring home the symptoms to the common understanding, he had his zany sing a popular ballad in which Anglo-Saxon replaced the learned tongues:

> You that would last long, list to my song,
> Make no more coyle, but buy of this oyle.
> Would you be ever faire? and yong?
> Stout of teeth? and strong of tongue?
> Tart of palat? quick of eare?
> Sharpe of sight? of nostrill cleare?
> Moist of hand? and light of foot?
> (Or I will come neerer to't)
> Would you live free from all diseases?
> Doe the act, your mistris pleases;
> Yet fright all aches from your bones?
> Here's a med'cine, for the nones.
>
> JONSON, *Volpone*, II, 2

Every mountebank, from that age to penicillin, has burned his annual candle on the feast day of Job Patriarch, patron saint of the pox.

---

[7] Other examples from the plays are to be found in Middleton's *The Widdow,* IV, 2; and in Beaumont and Fletcher's *The Faire Maide of the Inne,* where the quack Forobosco "does professe physicke, and counjuring; for his physicke; he has but two medicines for all manner of diseases; when he was i' th low countryes, he us'd nothing but butt'rd beere, colourd with allegant, for all kind of maladies, and that he called his catholick medcine; sure the Dutch smelt out it was butt'rd beere, else they would never have endur'd it for the names sake: then does he minister a grated dogs turd instead of rubarbe, many times of unicornes horne— which working strongly with the conceit of the patient, would make them bescummer to the height of a mighty purgation" (IV, 2).

The quack nostrums, like the *oglio del Scoto*, were, of course, secret in composition, the fruit of many years' labor and of countless nights spent with books. Money could not buy it, and yet Scoto, for example, was "a man may write ten thousand crownes, in banke, here" (*Volpone*, II, 2).

Once again during the century a mountebank's disguise served the turn of an enterprising lover. In the second part of Aphra Behn's play, *The Rover*, Willmore appears on the stage "like a mountebank, with a dagger in one hand, and a vial in the other" (II, 1). This gentleman, also with the aid of a zany, sells a divine elixir, twenty-four drops of which will recall to life a twenty-four-hour-old corpse. In addition, he offers for sale a beauty powder and a philter guaranteed to induce the most passionate love. Like that in *Volpone*, it is a scene drawn from life.

Quackery has always been a lucrative business, and always will be. Sir John Suckling compared religion and liberty, "most specious names," to

> the bills of subtle mountebanks,
> Fill'd with great promise of curing all,
> Though by the wise pass'd by as common cozenage,
> Yet by th' unknowing multitude they're still
> Admir'd and flock'd unto.
>
> Brennoralt, III, 2

Unfortunately, not only the "unknowing multitude," but also men who might have been expected to know better, often lent their praises (as well as purses) to the quacks. The list of famous men and physicians who have thus exposed their credulity to the amused historian is a long one and well deserving of a chapter of its own. (Indeed, one credulous contemporary physician has been the subject not only of articles, but of *books*.) The British government itself was a party to one of the outstanding quackeries of medical history. In the second quarter of the eighteenth century a certain Joanna Stephens discovered a cure for kidney stones, and after curing duchesses and bishops along with commoner clay for many years, she decided at last to part with her secret for a lump sum. A thousand pounds raised by public subscription did not tempt her, and Parliament took a hand. This august body appropriated five thousand pounds, and Joanna gladly sold—both her secret and Parliament. Dr. Richard Mead, the medical luminary of the day, wrote in retrospective chagrin in 1751:

> Nor can I avoid observing, though I am extremely sorry for the occasion, that some gentlemen of the faculty a few years since acted a part much beneath their character, first, in suffering themselves to be imposed on, and then, in encouraging the legislature to purchase an old woman's medicine at an exorbitant price; by vouching, that it was capable of breaking the stone in the bladder, and bringing away the fragments with the urine. This medicine is a composition of soap and lime made of different shells, which every body knows to be highly caustic.[8]

One wonders why a cure as ineffectual as Mrs. Stephen's eggshells did not bring the wrath of many an unrelieved sufferer down on her head years before. But not all pains in the back are due to kidney colic, and the *vis medicatrix naturae* has always been the staunchest ally of the quack. It is ruefully admitted in the council rooms of the physicians that when nature heals, the charlatan gets the credit; when the patient dies, the doctor gets the blame.

Physicians, however, have never been notable for their friendly feeling toward those medicines not sanctioned by the faculty. Aphra Behn turned the observation into an epigram:

> Wits, like physicians, never can agree,
> When of a different society;

[8] "Medical Precepts and Cautions," in *Medical Works* (London, 1762), p. 531. In Virginia, too, governmental cognizance was made of various nostrums. On December 22, 1739, £100 was paid to John Tennent for "his discovery of the use of the Seneca rattle snake root." On December 3, 1748, the House reported favorably on Mary Johnson's receipt for curing cancers, and she was subsequently paid £100. On March 19, 1752, the House agreed to pay £250 to Richard Bryan for his "medicine for curing the dry-gripes." On April 11, 1767, Constant Woodson also was awarded £100 for her cancer cure. Wyndham B. Blanton, M.D., *Medicine in Virginia in the Eighteenth Century* (Richmond, Va., 1931), pp. 213–215.

And Rabel's drops [9] were never more cry'd down
By all the learned doctors of the town,
Than a new play, whose author is unknown. . . .

The Rover, Pt. I, Prologue

And Dryden more soberly argued that a physician had no right to forbear an approved medicine merely because a mountebank had used it with success.[10]

A seventeenth-century preparation with a more modest history than Mrs. Stephens' nostrum was "Green Salve." [11] Along with several other ointments it turned up on the stage in the armamentarium of another Madam Strangelove:

LADY VAINE. *Madam, d'ye think, I that am a virtuosa understand no better than to leave you now you are not well? what's your distemper? no woman in England was more serviceable among her neighbours then I with my Flos Unguentorum, Paracelsian and Green-Salve.*
LOVEL. *And your Album Graecum, I warrant you.*
LADY VAINE. *That Album Graecum was a salve of my invention.*

SHADWELL, Sullen Lovers, II

Here the dramatist is taking a sly dig at the healing pretensions of Lady Vaine in claiming to be the originator of album graecum, a preparation made of the droppings of a dog.[12] This substance had both official standing and approbation. Taken internally, it was specific for quinsy and inflammations of the jaw, and Robert Boyle recommended it as a remedy for dysentery. This celebrated scientist, by the way, wrote a book called *The Skeptical Chymist*, but in medical matters he was a credulous mortal indeed. He recommended the livers of eels for easy

[9] Rabel's Drops, Aqua Rabelii, Eau de Rabelle: a mixture of one part of concentrated sulphuric acid and three parts of alcohol. Employed as an astringent in hemorrhages; R. Dunglison, *Medical Dictionary* (Boston, 1833), I, 332, col. 1.

[10] "Of Heroick Plays," prefixed to *The Conquest of Granada*, Pt. I.

[11] Recipe in J. Schroeder, *A Chymical Dispensatory* (London, 1669), Bk. II, Ch. 87, p. 146.

[12] Steele (*Tatler*, No. 121, January 17, 1709) turns the origin of this remedy to humorous account when Mr. Bickerstaff is asked to treat the lady's lap-dog: "In the mean time, to remove his hoarseness, it will be the most natural way to make Cupid his own druggist; for which reason, I shall prescribe to him, three mornings successively, as much powder as will lie on a groat, of that noble remedy which the Apothecaries call *Album Graecum*."

labor, and for certain diseases "a little bag hung about the neck, containing the powder made of a *live* toad, burnt in a *new* pot." [13]

According to the dramatists, Album Graecum had still other uses. Fetherfool has just been beaten and tossed naked out of a bawdy-house. "I am oblig'd to Seignior Harlequin too," he groans, "for bringing me hither to the mountebank's, where I shall . . . procure a little album graecum for my backside" (Aphra Behn, *The Rover*, Pt. II, v, 1). And in Ford's *The Fancies*, Secco the barber is lathering Spadone's face preparatory to shaving him. The shaving ball was composed, according to the barber, of "most odorous camphire, pure sope of Venice, oyle of sweet almonds, with the spirit of al lome." But as the lather is daubed under his nose Spadone complains:

> this water me thinks is none of the sweetest; camphire and soape of Venice say ye.
>
> SECCO. *With a little* grecum album *for mundification.*
>
> NITIDO. Grecum album *is a kinde of white perfum'd pouder, which plaine countrey people, I beleeve, call dog-muske.*
>
> SPADONE. *Dog-muske, poxe o' the dog-muske. . . .*

V

A very squeamish soul was Spadone.

The "Green Salve" dispensed by Lady Vaine was sold in the time of Charles II by a quack doctor called Pontaeus, that "first mountebank who ever appeared on a stage in England." [14] So quickly then was the illustrious Scoto Mantuano forgotten! This man mystified Restoration audiences with the same tricks which intrigued Tom Coryat in Venice many years before. One of Dr. Pontaeus' assistants washed his hands in a ladle of molten lead and in the presence of the horrified spectators withdrew them horribly burnt. Quickly the doctor anointed the discolored flesh with his Green Salve, applied bandages, and led the anguished patient off the stage. The next day, before the same expectant audience, Pontaeus removed the bandages, and behold! the hands were entirely well. How the audience must have gobbled

---

[13] Quoted by J. C. Lettsom, *History of the Origin of Medicine* (London, 1778), pp. 48 and 150.

[14] C. J. S. Thompson, *The Quacks of Old London* (Philadelphia, 1929), p. 54.

up the jars of the precious ointment! They did not know, of course, that its secret virtue lay in the fact that the molten lead was merely quicksilver in a ladle painted red.

Lady Vaine's other salves were less spectacular. Flos Unguentorum was listed in the *Pharmacopoeia Londinensis* of 1650 and consisted of resin, beeswax, suet, olibanum, turpentine, myrrh, mastich, camphor, and white wine. Paracelsus was responsible for an ointment made of human ordure which he called Zebethum occidentale, and a "Tincture of Flowers" was also manufactured under his name.

The aforementioned Dr. Pontaeus also popularized in England a salve called Orvietan, one of the notorious remedies of the time. This electuary was composed of theriac (an antidote similar in composition to mithridatium), dried vipers, scorzonera, carlina, imperitorium, angelica, bistort, rosemary, juniper, cinnamon, cloves, mace, honey, and a crowd of other substances. In 1647 a merchant of Orvieto paid liberally for the endorsement of this drug by twelve members of the Paris Faculté. When the rest of this solemn body had news of the deed, it expelled the erring dozen by decree. Later on, however, the brethren were reinstated, but Gui Patin wrote with grim enjoyment: "No matter what they have been able to do since, the stain remains on them." [15] Molière must have remembered all this when he later (1665) sang the praises of Orvietan with a satirical note directed toward the Faculté, for whose ineptness he had such contempt and scorn:

> All the silver and gold
>   That's contain'd in the earth,
> Of this famous secret,
>   Can ne'er pay the worth.
> My receipt, with its wondrous effect, will surmount
> More distempers than in an whole year you can count.
>   The scabs, the itch,
>   The gout, the stich,
>   The fistula in ano,
>   All this and ten times more is cur'd,
>   By my Orvietano.

[15] F. R. Packard, *Gui Patin* . . . (New York, 1925), p. 158.

Admire me then,
  Who for such a small pittance,
Do give you from death
  As it were an acquittance;
With this precious med'cin you may boldly despise
All the evils that heaven it self can devise:
    The scabs, &c.
All this and ten times more is cur'd
By my Orvietano.
                   Love the Best Physician [*L'amour Médecin*], II, 7

The origin of these secret medicines was made as mysterious as the verbal powers of their discoverers could render them. Then, as now, the secret of the nostrum's potency lay not so much in the ingredients as in the compounding of them. They were all mixed with a "science metaphysicall," like the one below:

OLYMPIA. *Stay good my lord, and wil you save my honor,*
  Ile give your grace a present of such price,
  As all the world cannot affoord the like.
THERIDAMUS. *What is it?*
OLYMPIA. *An ointment which a cunning alcumist*
  Distilled from the purest balsamum,
  And simplest extracts of all minerals,
  In which the essentiall fourme of marble stone,
  Tempered by science metaphysicall,
  And spels of magicke from the mouthes of spirits,
  With which, if you but noint your tender skin,
  Nor pistol, sword, nor lance can pierce your flesh.
                   MARLOWE, Tamburlaine, Pt. II, IV, 2

After the "patent medicines" we come to more orthodox specifics. Their multiplicity is discouraging to anyone who would reduce this therapeutic chaos to order. Three hundred years ago medical diagnosis was in a rudimentary state, and prognosis belonged as much in the province of the prophet as the physician. But if diagnosis and prognosis were alike uncertain in the doctor's hands, his therapeutics were invariably his strong point. The physician may not have known the disease or its outcome, but he was always ready with a treatment:

1 COURTIER. What cures has he?

BAWDBER. Armies of those we call physitians, some with glisters,
Some with lettice-caps, some posset-drinks, some pills,
Twenty consulting here about a drench,
As many here to blood him.
Then comes a Don of Spaine, and he prescribes
More cooling opium then would kill a Turke,
Or quench a whore ith dogdayes; after him
A wise Italian, and he cries, tie unto him
A woman of fourescore, whose bones are marble,
Whose blood snow water, not so much heate about her
As may conceive a prayer: after him
An English doctor, with a bunch of pot hearbes;
And he cries out endiffe and suckery,
With a few mallow rootes and butter milke,
And talkes of oyle made of a churchmans charity,
Yet still he wakes.
            BEAUMONT and FLETCHER, Thierry and Theodoret, V

Only a physician as wise and honest as John Radcliffe would
look back over the course of his medical practice and admit that
"when a young practitioner, he possessed twenty remedies for
every disease; and at the close of his career, he found twenty
diseases for which he had not one remedy." [16]

The pharmacopoeia has already borne witness to the century's
ample stock of remedies animal, vegetable, and mineral. The
origin of the use of simples for medicinal purposes belongs to
remote antiquity. Sir E. A. Wallis Budge writes:

Primitive peoples believed that the first beings who possessed a
knowledge of plants and their healing properties were the gods
themselves. They further thought that the substances of plants
were parts and parcels of the substances of which the persons of
the gods were composed, and that the juices of plants were
exudations or effluxes from them likewise. Some of the ancients
thought that certain curative plants and herbs contained portions
of the souls or spirits of the gods and spirits that were benevolent
to man, and that poisonous plants were the abodes of evil spirits

[16] J. C. Jeaffreson, A Book about Doctors (New York, 1861), p. 119.

that were hostile to the Creator—inasmuch as they destroyed His
handiwork, man—and to man and beast.[17]

The Apocrypha says, "The Lord hath created medicines out
of the earth, and he that is wise will not abhor them," [18] and the
Bible, "He causeth the grass to grow for the cattle, and herb for
the service of man. . . ." [19] The Lord did not say that herbs
grew for the service of the physician, and the omission is significant, for folk medicine has always been, in the main, botanic
medicine. The rustic inhabitants of the fields and forests were
naturally drawn closer to the plants they saw growing around
them as free gifts of Heaven than were the physicians who saw
merely the dried simples in a dingy apothecary's shop. Thus we
find that those best versed in the lore of medicinal plants were
shepherds and farmers, wise-women and white witches. It was
due to them as much as to the doctors that the old pharmacopoeias were overflowing with the names of herbs, for these country Aesculapians took literally the Psalmist's words. So, for that
matter, did the physicians themselves, for we find Andrew
Boorde writing with full conviction: "There is no herbe, nor
weede, but God have gyven vertue to them, to helpe man." [20]
This traditional bucolic knowledge appears in a scene in the
second act of Fletcher and Beaumont's pastoral, *The Faithfull
Shepheardesse*, in which Clorin, the shepherdess, is found sort-
ing herbs and telling the natures of them:

> Now let me know what my best art hath done,
> Helpt by the great power of the vertuous moon
> In her full light; O you sons of earth,
> You only brood, unto whose happy birth
> Vertue was given, holding more of nature
> Than man her first born and most perfect creature,
> Let me adore you; you that only can
> Help or kill nature, drawing out that span

[17] *The Divine Origin of the Craft of the Herbalist* (London, 1928), p. 1.
[18] Ecclesiasticus, xxxviii, 4.
[19] Psalms civ, 14.
[20] *The fyrst Boke of the Introduction of Knowledge: A Dyetary of Helth*, ed.
Furnivall (London, 1870), Ch. 20, "Of all herbes in generall," p. 282.

Of life and breath even to the end of time;
You that these hands did crop, long before prime
Of day; give me your names, and next your hidden power.
This is the clete bearing a yellow flower,
And this black horehound, both are very good
For sheep or shepherd, bitten by a wood-
Dogs venom'd tooth; these ramuns branches are,
Which stuck in entries, or about the bar
That holds the door fast, kill all inchantments, charms,
Were they Medeas verses that doe harms
To men or cattel; these for frenzy be
A speedy and a sovereign remedie,
The bitter wormwood, sage, and marigold,
Such sympathy with mans good they do hold;
This tormentil, whose vertue is to part
All deadly killing poyson from the heart;
And here narcissus roots for swellings be:
Yellow lysimacus, to give sweet rest
To the faint shepherd, killing where it comes
All busie gnats, and every fly that hums:
For leprosie, darnel, and sellondine,
With calamint, whose vertues do refine
The blood of man, making it free and fair
As the first hour it breath'd, or the best air.
Here other two, but your rebellious use
Is not for me, whose goodness is abuse;
Therefore foul standergrass, from me and mine
I banish thee, with lustful turpentine,
You that intice the veins and stir the heat
To civil mutiny, scaling the seat
Our reason moves in, and deluding it
With dreams and wanton fancies, till the fit
Of burning lust be quencht; by appetite,
Robbing the soul of blessedness and light:
And thou light varvin too, thou must go after,
Provoking easie souls to mirth and laughter;
No more shall I dip thee in water now,
And sprinkle every post, and every bough
With thy well pleasing juyce, to make the grooms
Swell with high mirth, as with joy all the rooms.

Gathering simples was a much more intricate affair than merely finding and plucking them. To have the proper virtue they must have been gathered at certain times of the day and year and in certain phases of the moon,

> *Helpt by the great power of the vertuous moon*
> *In her full light . . .*

or,

> *Root of hemlock, digg'd i' th' dark;*
> *Liver of blaspheming Jew,*
> *Gall of goat, and slips of yew*
> *Sliver'd in the moon's eclipse. . . .*
> SHAKESPEARE, Macbeth, IV, 1

Otherwise the plants were likely to be powerless to cure or even actively prone to injure instead of heal. The reader may recall Chapters 49 to 52 of the third book of *Gargantua and Pantagruel*, "How the Famous Pantagruelion Ought to be Prepared and Wrought," which constitute a fascinating disquisition on the names, history, and uses of various herbs.

The English physicians were as noted for their propensity to simples as were the French for their penchant for bleeding. The "English doctor, with a bunch of pot hearbes" may not have helped, but at least he did not seriously hinder nature, and he pleased his countrymen at the same time. "Is sicknesse come to thy doore!" asked Dekker in *London Looke Backe:*

> Make much of thy physitian: let not an emperick or mountibancking quacksalver peepe in at thy window, but set thy gates wide open to entertaine thy learned physitian: honour him, make much of him. Such a physitian is Gods second . . . for he has been in Gods garden, gathering herbes: and soveraine rootes to cure thee: a good physitian deales in simples, and will be simply honest with thee in thy preservatiō.
> *Plague Pamphlets, p. 188*

Of all the vegetable remedies the most frequently mentioned by the dramatists was rhubarb, and its literary popularity was matched by its medical use. "Shee is as common as rubarbe among Phisitians," [21] was Nashe's apt simile, for it was the purge *par excellence* of the century:

> BELLEUR. *This I'll promise ye.*
>   I will take rhubarb, and purge choler mainly;
>   Abundantly I'll purge.
>   BEAUMONT and FLETCHER, *Wild-Goose Chase*, IV, 2

> FLAMINEO.   Are you cholericke?
>   I'le purg't with rubarbe.
>   WEBSTER, *White Divel*, V, 1

> FERDINAND. Rubarbe, oh, for rubarbe
>   To purge this choller. . . .
>   WEBSTER, *Dutchesse of Malfy*, II, 5

> MACBETH. What rhubarb, senna, or what purgative drug,
>   Would scour these English hence?
>   SHAKESPEARE, *Macbeth*, V, 3

The French and Spanish were as fond of the drug:

> SGANARELLE. *Here's the handsome nurse. Ah nurse of my heart, I'm glad to meet you thus; your sight is rhubarb, casia, and sena, which purge all Melancholly from my heart.*
>   MOLIÈRE, *The Forced Physician*
>   [*Le Médecin Malgré Lui*], III, 3

> *Truly, cry'd the curate, he, with his second, third, and fourth parts, had need of a dose of rhubarb to purge his excessive choler.*
>   CERVANTES, *Don Quixote*, Bk. I, Ch. 6

Scattered here and there throughout the plays are references to other vegetable remedies, far more common, however, off the stage than on; for we shall be expecting too much to look for the *Pharmacopoeia* of 1650 divided into acts and scenes. Liquorice, for example, was perennially popular as a remedy for hoarseness:

> WIFE. *Now I pray you make my commendations unto him,*
>   *And withal, carry him this stick of licoras,*
>   *Tell him his mistriss sent it him,*

---

[21] *Have with you to Saffron-Walden* in *Works*, ed. R. B. McKerrow (London, 1905), III, 121.

> And bid him bite apiece,
> 'Twill open his pipes the better, say.
> BEAUMONT and FLETCHER, *Knight of the Burning Pestle*, I

When Roderigo in Rowley's *Alls Lost by Lust* gives money to a bawd, he accompanies it with these words:

> I see thou hast persuasive oratory.
> Here's juyce of liquorish, good for thy voyce.
>
> I

There are a great number of references to asafetida, the offensive smell of which was used to combat hysterical attacks:

> LADY VAINE. . . . *perhaps it may be a fit of the mother;*
> *If it be, we must burn some blow-inkle, and partridge*
> *Feathers under your nose; or she must smell to assa festida,*
> *And have some cold water with a little flower to drink.*[22]
> SHADWELL, *Sullen Lovers*, II

Asafetida thus furnished the poets with a derogatory comparison:

> MIRABELL. . . . *Is there a worse disease than the conversation of fools?*
> MRS. MILLAMANT. *Yes, the vapours; fools are physick for it, next to assa-foetida.*
> CONGREVE, *Way of the World*, II

> LADY DUNCE. *Then for his person 'tis incomparably odious; he has such a breath, one kiss of him were enough to cure the fits of the mother; 'tis worse than asa foetida.*
> OTWAY, *Souldiers Fortune*, I

Add one more vegetable remedy: opium, for curing a man of a disease called a wife. Of all the many allusions to the juice of the

[22] Shadwell must have had plenty of experience with vaporish women, for his characters invariably know how to handle a fainting fit: "Ah me, help, help my lady, cut her lace, get some arsa foetida, blew inkle, or patridge feathers, and burn under her nose" (*Amorous Bigotte*, V). Or hysterics: "Gad take me! hold the gentlewomen, bring some cold water, and flower, burn some blew inkle and partridge feathers, 'tis my ladies medicine" (*Scowrers*, I). Inkle was a linen thread or yarn which when set on fire smouldered with a strong smell. The odor of singeing fowl needs no explanation.

poppy, none possesses the interest of old Gripe's plan to poison
his flighty spouse:

> Hah—I have thought on the best way, if I can get her home with
> me, I'll give her opium in her drink, and that ne'r a doctor or
> chyrurgeon on 'em all can discover, when they open her.[23]
>
> SHADWELL, Woman-Captain, V

Turning from the vegetable to the animal kingdom, one's
interest heightens as the scientific respectability of the remedies
wanes. The fascination of the older therapeutics lies in the
fantastic uses to which animals were put in the cure of disease.
Books XXVIII, XXIX, and XXX of Pliny's Natural Historie are
taken up mainly with medicines derived from the parts of man
and animals. Most of these are magical in nature, and find their
seventeenth-century dramatic counterparts in such materia medica as the following:

> MALEVOLE. . . . Lady ha ye now no restoratives for your decayed
> Jasons, looke yee, crabs guts, bak't, distil'd oxe-pith, the pulver-
> ized haires of a lions upper lip, jelly of cock-sparrowes, hee-
> monkeis marrow, or powder of foxe-stones. . . .
>
> MARSTON, The Malcontent, II, 2

The basis for the use of many of these animal organs lay in the
ancient Greek conception of illness as a dyscrasia, or imperfect
balance of the humors. The physician attempted to restore the
normal balance by applying remedies contrary to the nature of
the disease; "Contraria contrariis curantur." Thus, continued
fevers called for bleeding and drafts of cold water, the first
removing the excess of hot blood and the second cooling the
intemperate heat of the heart. Bodily debility, on the other
hand, would by the same token be treated by heat, and prefer-
ably by the vital heat emitted by a living organism.

The body holds tenaciously to its normal temperature, and
when a sick man begins to grow cold it is a sign that death is not
far away. As a last measure to forestall the coming dissolution,

---

[23] Autopsies were not uncommon in the late seventeenth century, especially
when the cause of death was suspicious. The significant point in Gripe's speech is
that he says "when they open her," rather than "if."

the old physicians placed live pigeons against the feet of the dying man. When Katherine, Charles II's queen, was believed at the point of death, Pepys wrote:

> *Coming to St. James, I hear that the Queen did sleep five hours pretty well to-night, and that she waked and gargled her mouth, and to sleep again; but that her pulse beats fast, beating twenty to the King's or my Lady Suffolk's eleven; but not so strong as it was. It seems she was so ill as to be shaved and pidgeons put to her feet, and to have the extreme unction given her by the priests, who were so long about it that the doctors were angry.[24]*
>
> Diary, Oct. 19, 1663

The practice furnished the poets once more with a striking metaphor:

BOSOLA. *I would sooner eate a dead pidgeon, taken from the soles of the feete of one sicke of the plague,[25] than kisse one of you fasting. . . .*

WEBSTER, *Dutchesse of Malfy*, II, 1

LADY DUNCE. *. . . bless us to be yok'd in wedlock with a paralitick coughing decrepid dotrell, to be a dry nurse all one's life time to an old child of sixty-five, to lye by the image of death a whole night, a dull immoveable, that has no sense of life, but through its pains; the pidgeon's as happy that's laid to a sick man's feet, when the world has given him over. . . .*

OTWAY, *Souldiers Fortune*, I

[24] Another contemporary account tells of the illness of Sir John Perceval in April, 1686. On the eighteenth he treated himself with a Carduus posset, and from that date until the twenty-eighth he was clystered and bled and blistered until, his physician reported, "this day, we applied to his feet pigeons, after the application of them he seemed lethargic, upon which account we removed our blister plasters, etc." On the twenty-ninth: "We have this day applied pigeons to his feet a second time, but we do not find that he is so disposed to sleep after them as yesterday." The report ends with the promise to use cupping glasses next, but first to apply more gentle means. (Royal Commission on Historical MSS publications printed by H. M. Stationery Office, London. Mss. of the Earl of Egmont, 1909, 2, 183.)

[25] *The English Huswife* (London, 1615), recommends ". . . if you be infected with the plague" apply hot bricks to the feet, "then to the same apply a live pidgeon cut in two parts."

Sir John Suckling gives some advice to Jack Bond in a letter written about 1642: "Marrying . . . would certainly cure it [love]; but that is a kind of live pigeons laid to the soles of the feet, a last remedy, and (to say truth) worse than the disease." [26]

Mice too were medically useful. William Bullein prescribed for a nervous malady "a small young mouse rosted," and the good Wife in Beaumont and Fletcher's *The Knight of the Burning Pestle*, a priceless repository of unofficial curative secrets, mentions another use in Act I:

> Faith and those chilblaines are a foul trouble, Mistris Merrythought when your youth comes home, let him rub all the soles of his feet, and his heels, and his ankles, with a mouseskin; or if none of your [people] can catch a mouse, when he goes to bed, let him rowl his feet in the warm embers, and I warrant you he shall be well, and you may make him put his fingers between his toes, and smell to them, it's very soveraign for his head, if he be costive.

According to the old physiology the heart was the site of heat formation in the body. Aristotle knew that the mouse's heart was of large size compared to the small bulk of its body, and consequently for its weight the mouse was an extraordinary source of heat. This has been confirmed by modern experts on metabolism. Since chilblains are caused by excessive cold, application of the skin of this very warm-hearted little beast would, by its sympathetic virtue, supply heat to the affected limbs. Although one may suspect that warm embers would have proven more efficacious in the long run, one cannot but admire the logic of the sympathetic cure.

Still another animal—the human one—was used in medicine, but dead, powdered, or in the form of "mummia," or mummy. Webster's two great tragedies are overflowing with ghastly and sinister metaphor, and such "unnaturall and horrid Phisicke" as mummy fascinated his dreadful muse.

---

[26] Suckling, *Works*, ed. A. H. Thompson (London, 1910), p. 301 (*Letters to divers Eminent Personages* [London, 1646]).

GASPARO.   *Your followers*
Have swallowed you like mummia, and being sicke
With such unnaturall and horrid Phisicke
Vomit you up i'th kennell.

White Divel, I

In the second act Isabella, in an outburst of fury against the White Devil, cries:

To dig the strumpets eyes out, let her lye
Some twenty monethes a-dying, to cut off
Her nose and lippes, pull out her rotten teeth,
Preserve her flesh like mummia, for trophies
Of my just anger. . . .

The best mummia was Arabian, a liquor which exudes from carcasses embalmed with myrrh, aloes, and balsam. This drug was scarce, and very precious; so precious, indeed, that Albius in Jonson's *Poetaster* calls his wife "my deare mummia, my balsamm, my spermacete" (II) and Sir Sampson to gain the good will of old Foresight cries:

What, *I'll make thee a present of a mummy: Now I think on't, body o'me, I have a shoulder of an Egyptian king, that I purloyned from one of the pyramids, powder'd with hieroglyphicks, thou shalt have it sent home to thy house, and make an Entertainment for all the philomaths and students in physick and astrology in and about London.*

CONGREVE, Love for Love, II

Sir Sampson's shoulder of mummy was not the most valuable kind from a medicinal point of view. Egyptian mummies, which were embalmed with pissasphaltum, and the flesh of bodies "dried in the sun, in the country of the Hammonians between Cyrene and Alexandria, being pasengers buried in the quicksands," were both inferior to the Arabian product. The latter, however, was so rare that the other kinds were usually substituted for it. Like all precious substances, mummy was often adulterated or counterfeited outright. Bodies stolen from the gallows sometimes ended in seventeenth-century apothecaries' shops; [27] and the Moslems, ever on the lookout to turn a Christian into an honest penny, were credited by legend with:

4 SERVITOR. *The merchant, sure she will not be so base to have him*
    [to marry].
1 SERVITOR. *I hope so, Robin, he'll sell us all to the Moors to make*
    mummy. . . .
                    BEAUMONT and FLETCHER, *Honest Man's Fortune,* V

The process was repeated nearer home. A clown who has been beaten into a jelly laments:

> *. . . who ever lives to see me dead,*
> *Gentlemen, shall find me all mummie good to fill gallipots,*
> *And long dildo glasses.*
>   BEAUMONT and FLETCHER, *Nice Valour,* II

But this was all in fun: usually any simple resinous substance, such as bitumen and pitch-pissasphaltum, served the druggists' purpose. These gentlemen were not above substituting *quid pro quo*, with or without the prescribing physician's knowledge. Ambroise Paré shrugged his shoulders over this state of affairs, for there was far more shrewdness than imagination in his make-up, and he pointed out that mummia from whatever source was equally valueless. But Sir Thomas Browne, always sympathetic to the fate of long-dead worthies, wrote in sonorous prose: "Mummie is become merchandise, miszraim cures wounds, and pharaoh is sold for balsoms" (*Urne-Buriall*, Ch. 5).

Animal remedies were easily counterfeited. Thomas Nashe tells the tragic tale of Dr. Zacharie, the Pope's physician, whose parsimony led him to prepare medicines in stranger ways "than ever Paracelsus dream'd of."

---

[27] Here, according to W. Salmon, *The New London Dispensatory* (London, 1678), p. 194, is how they got there: "Take the carcase of a young man (some say red hair'd) not dying of a disease, but killed; let it lie 24 hours in clear water in the air; cut the flesh in pieces, to which add powder of myrrh and a little aloes; imbibe it 24 hours in the spirit of wine and turpentine, take it out, hang it up twelve hours; imbibe it again 24 hours in fresh spirit, then hang up the pieces in dry air and a shadowy place, so will they dry and not stink." Strangely enough, for one would have thought that age lent virtue, this modern mummy was second only to the excessively rare Arabian drug in its medicinal qualities.

Out of bones after the meate was eaten off, hee would alchu-
mize an oyle, that hee sold for a shilling a dram. His snot and
spittle a hundred times hee hath put over to his apothecarie for
snow water. Anie spider hee would temper to perfect mithridate.
His rumaticke eies when hee went in the winde, or rose early in a
morning, dropt as coole allome water as you would request. He
was dame Niggardize sole heire & executor. A number of old
books had he eaten with the moaths and wormes, now all day
would not he studie a dodkin, but picke those wormes and
moaths out of his librarrie, and of their mixture make a preservative against the plague. The licour out of his shooes hee would
wring to make a sacred balsamum against barrennes.

Unfortunate Traveller, p. 101

As succeeding editions of the pharmacopoeias dropped more
and more animal and vegetable remedies from their rolls, an
increasing number of chemical preparations took their place.
These rarely found their way into the plays, however, for the
dramatists were raised on animal parts and Galenicals, and what
was good enough for them served their characters on the stage.
Besides, chemical medicines had neither the intrinsic interest of
animal remedies nor the poetic charm of herbs and flowers.

Both Glauber's and Rochelle salts were introduced into the
materia medica in the seventeenth century, and then too hartshorn, or ammonia-water, started on its long path of popularity
as a remedy for faintness. Said Silvia in Farquhar's *The Recruit-
ing Officer:* "So far as to be troubled with neither spleen, cholick,
nor vapours, I need no salt for my stomach, no hart's-horn for
my head, no wash for my complexion . . ." (I). Other characters were not as healthy:

LADY ADDLEPLOT.   . . . the very thought of him gives me the
vapours; prithee give me my spirit of hartshorne.

D'URFEY, Love for Money, II, 1

LADY FROTH.—My dear, you're melancholly.
LORD FROTH. No, my dear, I'm but just awake—
LADY FROTH. Snuff some of my spirit of hartshorn.
LORD FROTH. I've some of my own, thank you, dear.

CONGREVE, Double Dealer, V

From this touching conjugal dialogue one would never suspect that Lord Froth had just been presented with a pair of horns. Perhaps the fops carried spirit of hartshorn, not out of affected elegance, but for domestic episodes of this sort.

In another tale of extramarital amour it was also the cuck-olded husband who offered his faithless wife a whiff of ammonia. Mrs. Hackwell and her friend Nickum have retired to a bedroom to lengthen old Colonel Hackwell's horns. The Colonel, tipped off by a revengeful servingmaid, surprises the pair in bed. "Ounds, we are undone!" wails Nickum. Then inspiration seizes him. "Counterfeit a sounding fit," he whispers, whereupon Mrs. Hackwell groans and falls back on the bed while Nickum suc-cessfully pulls the wool over the cuckold's eyes:

NICKUM. *Oh Heavens she's gone! she's gone! Nay, you are come to late, you'd no body hear me, when I knock't for help (as if I would have beaten the house down!) poor lady! I heard a noise in her chamber; and found her upon the floor, beating herself and knocking her head against the ground. She has kill'd herself, I believe.*

LETTICE. *Oh Devil. Thou father of lies!*

COLLONEL HACKWELL. *Oh my Lamb,—my poor Lamb—take my keys! run, run for some spirit of heartshorn, run—run.*

SHADWELL, *Volunteers, IV*

Even more popular than ammonia for fainting spells was alcohol. There were many alcoholic cordials in use, particularly two called Rosa solis and Aqua mirabilis, and including of course Aqua vitae.[28] The use of these panaceas overflowed the bounds

[28] Others were named after their patrons or discoverers, like Hungary water (aqua Hungarica), first prepared for the Queen of Hungary. This was made of oil of rosemary or rosemary leaves infused in alcohol and distilled; the dose was 1–4 ounces, a quite sufficient tipple. Bellinda says: "Your ladyship seems disorder'd; a breeding qualm, perhaps, Mr. Heartfree: your bottle of Hungary water to your lady" (Vanbrugh, *Provok'd Wife*, V, 5). And Pindress cries: "Pray give me my Hungary-bottle.—As I hope to be sav'd I will have my Hungary-bottle" (Farqu-har, *Love and a Bottle*, IV).

Another famous cordial was named after a Dr. Stephen. Says Isabel in Brome's *City Wit*: "Reach the bottle againe of Doctor Stephens water" (III, 1).

of medical propriety,[29] and even the easygoing dramatists were scandalized at the amount of tippling that went on under the guise of taking a little nip for the stomach's sake. It was not drunkenness to which they objected, one gathers, but hypocrisy. The ladies were the greatest offenders and paid for their sins by frequent castigation on the stage. The affinity between bawd and brandy was especially notorious; Samuel Butler wrote:

> 'Tis strange how some mens tempers suit
> (Like bawd and brandy) with dispute.
>
> Hudibras, Pt. II, Canto 2

The one dramatic example, however, of Mistress Birdlime's tribulations and her mode of relief will suffice:

> Oh my sides ake in my loines, in my bones? I ha more need of a posset of sacke, and lie in my bed and sweate, then to talke in musick: no honest woman would run hurrying up & down thus and undoe her selfe for a man of honour, without reason? I am so lame, every foot that I set to the ground went to my hart. I thoght I had bin at Mum-chance my bones ratled so with jaunting? had it not bin for a friend in a corner. [Takes Aqua-vitae.] I had kickt up my heeles.
>
> DEKKER, West-ward Hoe, II, 2

Women in higher circles of society loved their bottle equally well. Dryden in Act III of *Marriage A-La-Mode* describes the visit of a citizen's wife to some country cousin "who treats her with furmity and custard, and opens her dear bottle of mirabilis beside, for a jill-glass of it at parting." Nor must one forget the famous proviso speech by Mirabel addressed to Millamant in

---

[29] Dr. Stephen's and similar waters were listed in early editions of the *Pharmacopoeia Londinensis* but were eventually expunged. "This water in our first pharmacopoeia stood under the name of *aqua hysterica*, or hysteric water, by which it is still commonly known; and the greatest part of women of condition, who have contracted the vice of dram drinking, have been betrayed into that abominable and pernicious habit by the use of this and the like waters under the notion of medicines: whereas, indeed, however spiritous liquors may give a momentary relief to the languors of hysteric and hypochondriacal persons, none suffer so soon the evil effects attending the constant use of such liquids" (*Dispensatory of the Royal College of Physicians*, London, p. 73).

Congreve's *Way of the World*, in which one of the items is the banishment of strong drink from her tea table.

Apparently the bucolic gentlefolk found in alcohol the true remedy for the monotony of country life. There is a familiar scene in which we see two young girls railing against the dullness of country breeding which forced them to learn:

EUGENIA. *To make clouted cream, and whipt sillabub?*
CLARA. *To make a caraway cake, and raise py-crust?*
EUGENIA. *And to learn the top of your skill in syrrup, sweat-meats,*
aqua-mirabilis, and snayl water.[30]

SHADWELL, Scowrers, II

It must have required no mean skill, by the way, to have prepared Aqua mirabilis, for Sir Kenelm Digby's recipe included a score of ingredients and a glass still with which to extract their essence.

While the number of lady tipplers on the stage was legion,[31] the other sex came in for its share of the dramatists' slaps. Again one example will be sufficient: [32]

SIR PATIENT FANCY. *But oh, I'm sick at heart. Maundy fetch me the*
bottle of mirabilis in the closet. . . .

APHRA BEHN, Sir Patient Fancy, IV, 3

Whereupon the old gentleman tipples his way into a frolicsome and lickerish state.

The caricature by Rowlandson of a midwife off on a professional visit with a bottle of brandy under a fat and frowsy arm finds a literary prototype in the seventeenth-century plays. Old

---

[30] G. Hartman, *True Preserver and Restorer of Health* (London, 1682), mentions "Dr. Harvey his excellent snail-water against consumptions and hecktick feavers."

[31] Other examples are the old widow Belliza who can hardly wait until her suitor arrives: "I shall never hold out without some aqua mirabilis, I grow so chill, and quake" (Shadwell, *Amorous Bigotte*, IV); and Lady Ninny, of whom it was said: "One may see by her nose, what pottage shee loves" (Field, *Woman is a Weathercocke*, I).

[32] A few others: "*Emilia*. Some rosa solis or aqua mirabilis ho! for our generall coward's in a swoune" (Day, *Law-trickes*, IV); also Ford, *'Tis Pitty Shee's a Whore*, III (Annabelle); Marston, *Dutch Courtezan*, II, 3 (Mulligrub); *Merry Devill of Edmonton*. Induction (Fabel); Shadwell, *Miser*, I (Goldingham).

Garrula, the midwife in Brome's *The Love-sick Court,* wishes for "volubility of tongue," though how she could talk more in five acts and still leave room for the other characters is incomprehensible to the reader of the play:

> But O
> *This tongue, that fails me now; for all the helps*
> *Of syrups, and sweet sippings, I still go*
> *Provided, as you see, to cherish it.*

The stage direction to this speech reads: "*She sips oft of a bottle at her girdle.*" And throughout the play Garrula is accompanied by her cherished bottle, which she samples at every opportunity.

Shakespeare had previously observed the same phenomenon:

> MARIA. *Nay, but say true, does it work upon him?*
> TOBY. *Like aqua-vitae with a midwife.*
> > *Twelfth Night,* II, 5

The doctors themselves had a quaint belief in the power of alcohol to cure all ills. James Atkinson recalls that Asclepiades of Prusa "prescribed wine for himself, and for his patients, something to excess." Pliny relates that he died from a fall.[33] Of him says the comical poet:

> *Wherefore to cure all his bruises and knocks,*
> *He was used to drink vinum orthodox;*
> *And one day did it so effectually,*
> *He dislocated his epistrophe.*[34]

Avicenna was another devotee of wine, like Jean Pecquet, the illustrious seventeenth-century discoverer of the thoracic duct.

---

[33] "But Asclepiades the Prusian . . . found out the way and means to make wine wholesome and medicinable for sicke folke: and recovered a man to his former state of health, who was caried forth upon his biere to be buried: and lastly he attained the greatest name; for laying a wager against fortune, and pawning his credit so farre as he should not be reputed a physitian, in case he ever were known to be sicke or any way diseased. And in truth the wager hee woon; for his hap was to live in health untill he was very aged, and then to fall downe from a paire of staires, and so to die suddenly" (*Natural Historie,* Bk. VII, Ch. 37). Pliny's account gives a far different impression than the "comical poet's" quatrain.

[34] *Medical Bibliography* (London, 1834), p. 14.

Dr. Pecquet prescribed brandy for his patients and himself, until his career tumbled down about his ears in ruin.

The therapeutic triumph of the century was not the popularization of brandy, however, but the introduction into Europe of Peruvian bark or cinchona. In the early days of the seventeenth century the Countess of Chinchon, wife of the viceroy of Peru, was cured of malaria by means of the bark of a certain tree. Brought back to Europe in 1632 by the Jesuits, this drug had to overcome the prejudice of a medical profession opposed to anything new. Gui Patin, of course, expressed his disapproval to a correspondent: "This powder of cinchona has not any credit here. Fools run after it because it is sold at a very high price, but having proved ineffective it is mocked at now." [35]

This was in 1653. Two years afterwards, cinchona was first sold and used in England. In 1658, when Cromwell died of his ague, *Mercurius Politicus* in four numbers advertised: "The excellent powder known by the name of 'Jesuites powder' may be obtained from several London chemists."

To Sydenham is usually assigned the credit for having introduced cinchona into medical practice in England and for having overcome the initial prejudice against its use. Certainly, we owe to him the classification of Peruvian bark as a *specific* remedy for intermittent fevers. It was a new and highly gratifying experience for the seventeenth-century physician to watch this drug cure an ague in hours, whereas under older and nonspecific treatments such fevers took weeks to disappear. There were elements of drama in such a contrast, nor did they escape the observant eye of the contemporary playwright.

CARLOS. *Oh, Madam! Marriage—*
THEODOSIA. *Is to love as the Jesuits powder to an ague; it stops the fit, and in a little time wears it quite off.*

The allusion comes from the ever-attentive Thomas Shadwell's pen in Act V of A *True Widow*, produced in 1678. It is indeed remarkable that the first widespread use of cinchona (in 1663) should be followed only fifteen years later by a beautifully

[35] Packard, *Gui Patin*, p. 155.

turned epigram spoken from the stage. Normally the lag between a medical discovery and its appearance in the popular literature was then nearer a century than a decade, but Shadwell's peculiar genius provides us with more than one exception to this rule. "Og's" writing may have lacked poetic finish, but it did not lack timeliness of appeal; and he was ever ahead of his scribbling colleagues in turning medicine's new tools into satire's new weapons.

A second reference to the bark comes from Congreve's *The Old Batchelour,* staged in 1693:

BLUFFE. *But? Look you here boy, here's your antidote; here's your Jesuit's powder for a shaking fit. . . .*

II

A more sober account of the standing of Peruvian bark is given by John Evelyn a year later:

> *I visited the Marquis of Normanby, and had much discourse concerning King Charles II. being poisoned.—Also concerning the quinquina which the physicians would not give to the King, at a time when, in a dangerous ague, it was the only thing that could cure him (out of envy because it had been brought into vogue by Mr. Tudor, an apothecary) till Dr. Short, to whom the King sent to know his opinion of it privately, . . . sent word to the King it was the only thing which could save his life, and then the King enjoined his physicians to give it to him, which they did, and he recovered. Being asked by this lord why they would not prescribe it, Dr. Lower said it would spoil their practice, or some such expression, and at last confessed it was a remedy fit only for kings.*
>
> Diary, II, 334

The "Mr. Tudor" mentioned above was Robert Talbor, a strong though quackish contender for the honor of having first successfully prescribed cinchona in England.[36] Gideon Harvey in

[36] For accounts of Talbor and the controversy (a dull one these many years after the event) over the introduction of cinchona, see Doctor Latham's introduction to Sydenham's *Works* (London: Sydenham Society, 1848), I, lxxiv ff.; also G. Dock, "Robert Talbor, Mme. de Sévigné and the Introduction of Cinchona," *Annals of Medical History,* IV (1922), 241.

one of his bombastic tirades called Talbor a "debauched apothecary's apprentice," but the fascinating Dr. Harvey was notorious in his day for his low opinion of his colleagues and his high
opinion of himself.[37] Probably Talbor's main fault in the eyes of
his professional brethren was his unprecedented success, which
brought him eventually to fortune and a knighthood. Poor
Gideon, by contrast, tried his unavailing best to get elected to
the Royal College of Physicians without stopping to take the
entrance examinations he considered beneath his dignity.

[37] James Atkinson's remark that "quackery is so pleasing, so natural and
recondite a passion, that we may sometimes excuse it," applies perfectly to
Gideon Harvey. Dr. Harvey is too entertaining a character to be dismissed thus
lightly, but fortunately there is H. A. Colwell's delightful "Gideon Harvey:
Sidelights on Medical Life from the Restoration to the End of the XVIIth
Century," Annals of Medical History, III (1921), 205.

4
Charms and Potions

Common experience confirms to our astonishment that Magicians can work such feats . . . and that the Devil without impediment can penetrate through all our bodies and cure such maladies by means to us unknown.
— ROBERT BURTON, Anatomy of Melancholy

THUS FAR WE HAVE DEALT WITH REMEDIES ANIMAL, VEGETABLE, and mineral, but the century had spiritual ones also. Charms were an essential part of the armamentarium of every patient, and sometimes of the physician as well. For example, the lady who felt a faintness coming on had the choice of a tot of brandy, a whiff of ammonia, or:

LEONORA. *I have within my closet a choyce relicke,*
   Preservative 'gainst swounding, and some earth,
   Brought from the Holy Land, right soveraigne
   To staunch blood.
                         WEBSTER, Devils Law-case, II, 3

Flowing blood could be controlled in many ways. Aside from Holy Earth

SCÆVINUS. . . . *There are about the house*
   Some stones that will staunch blood, see them set up.
                         Nero, III, 5

These were the blood-stones, like red jasper, which not only stopped bleeding at the nose and other fluxes of blood, but also the flux of the terms. Sapphires, too, when laid to the forehead stayed bleeding at the nose.

There were hemostatic virtues even in words, such as Pepys' magic rhyme:

> *Sanguis mane in te,*
> *Sicut Christus fuit in se;*
> *Sanguis mane in tua vena*
> *Sicut Christus in sua poena;*
> *Sanguis mane fixus,*
> *Sicut Christus quando fuit crucifixus.*
>
> [*Let the blood be in yourself*
> *As Christ was in Himself;*
> *Let the blood stay in your veins*
> *As Christ in his pains;*
> *Let your blood in place abide*
> *Just as Christ when crucified.*]

But rhymes, one would think, were useful only until the doctor came, or when more mundane remedies were not available. There were many homely ways to staunch blood, and some of them in rustic use even today.[1]

LADY BOUNTIFUL. Let me see your arm, sir. —I must have some powder-sugar to stop the blood—O me! an ugly gash upon my word, sir, you must go into bed . . . while I get the lint and the probe and the plaister ready.
                                    FARQUHAR, Beaux Stratagem, V

3 SERVANT. Go thou. I'll fetch some flax and whites of eggs
    To apply to his bleeding face. Now heaven help him!
                                    SHAKESPEARE, King Lear, III, 7

BOTTOM.   . . . I beseech your worship's name.
COBWEB. Cobweb.
BOTTOM. I shall desire you of more acquaintance, good Master Cobweb. If I cut my finger, I shall make bold with you.
                                    SHAKESPEARE, Midsummer Night's Dream, III, 1

---

[1] See notes 12 and 13 to ch. 2.

One would expect the credulous Pepys to be an authority on charms, and in point of fact he is. To round out his record of the year 1664 he gives five charms in verse: one for "stenching of blood" (transcribed above), two for a "thorne," one each for a cramp and a burning. At the same time he is experimenting with a hare's foot for the relief of a troublesome colic, and on the last day of the old year he writes:

> *I bless God I have never been in so good plight as to my health in so very cold weather as this is, nor indeed in any hot weather, these ten years, as I am this day, and have been these four or five months. But I am at a great loss to know whether it be my hare's foote, or taking every morning of a pill of turpentine, or my having left off the wearing of a gowne.*
> Diary, December 31, 1664

And a fortnight later (January 20, 1664/5):

> *So homeward, in my way buying a hare and taking it home, which arose upon my discourse today with Mr. Batten, in Westminster Hall, who showed me my mistake that my hare's foote hath not the joynt to it; and assures me he never had his colique since he carried it about him: and it is a strange thing how fancy works, but I no sooner almost handled his foote but my belly began to be loose and to break wind, and whereas I was in some pain yesterday and tother day and in fear of more today, I became very well and so continue.*

On the following day: "To my office till past 12, and then home to supper and to bed, being now mighty well, and truly I cannot but impute it to my fresh hare's foote."

On March 26 of the same year Pepys is still well and still undecided whether his health is due to his hare's foot, his turpentine pills, or his sleeping without a gown. Or to all together! The attempt to resolve similar questions has led many a more learned doctor a merry chase.

The stage provides many counterparts of Pepys' hare's foot:

DUCHESS. *Fye, fie, what's all this?*
   One of your eyes is blood-shot, use my ring to't,

They say 'tis very soveraigne. . . .
WEBSTER, Dutchesse of Malfy, I, 1

MISTRESSE OPENWORKE. *Because goshawke goe, in a shag-ruffe band, with a face sticking up in't, which showes like an agget set in a crampe ring, he thinkes I'me in love with him.*[2]
MIDDLETON, Roaring Girle, IV

LADY SQUEAMISH. *. . . And d'ye hear, bring me a mask with an amber-bead, for I fear I may have fits to night.*[3]
OTWAY, Friendship in Fashion, III

LADY ADDLEPLOT.   *. . . and truly*
I think pearls are good against the spleen.
D'URFEY, Love for Money, II, 1

Lady Addleplot's remark is a neat *double entendre*, for not only do strings of pearls assuage feminine wrath, but the jewels powdered were precious ingredients of many restorative and invigorating medicines.[4]

Rhymes to charm away diseases abounded:

PLAYFAIR.   *. . . get a rime*
To bless her when she sneezes.
T[HOMAS] B[ETTERTON], Love Will Find Out the Way, II

[2] "The kynges of Englande doth halowe every yere crampe rynges, the whyche rynges, worne on ones fynger, dothe helpe them the whyche hath the crampe" (Andrew Borde, *The fyrst boke of the Introduction of Knowledge*, ed. Furnivall, p. 121).

[3] "True it is that a collar of ambre beads worne about the neck of yong infants, is a singular preservative to them against secret poyson, & a countercharme for witchcraft and sorcerie. Callistratus saith, that such collars are very good for all ages, and namely to preserve as many as weare them against fantasticall illusions and frights that drive folke out of their wits" (Pliny *Natural Historie*, trans. Philemon Holland [London, 1634] Bk. XXXVII, Ch. 3).

[4] From Marston's *The Malcontent* comes this recipe for a posset which "purifieth the blood, smootheth the skinne, inlifeneth the eye, strengthneth the vaines, mundefieth the teeth, comforteth the stomacke, fortifieth the backe, and quickneth the wit, thats all": "Seaven and thirty yowlks of Barbarie hennes eggs, eighteene spoonfulles and a halfe of the joice of cocksparrowe bones, one ounce, three drams, foure scruples, and one quarter of the sirrop of Ethiopian dates, sweetned with three quarters of a pound of pure candid Indian eringos, strow'd over with the powder of pearle of America, amber of Cataia, and lambe stones of Muscovia." Commonly, of course, mother-of-pearl was the ingredient employed.

VOLPONE.   *I do feele the fever*
    Entring, in at mine eares; O, for a charme,
    To fright it hence.

                        JONSON, *Volpone*, III, 4

Samuel Butler's "Sidrophel, the Rosy-Crucian," had a full supply to

    Cure warts and corns, with application
    Of med'cines to th' imagination.
    Fright agues into dogs, and scare
    With rimes, the tooth-ach and catarrh.

                      Hudibras, Pt. II, Canto 3

Charms for the toothache were particularly popular. When Sorano is rummaging through his sister's cabinet to find out whom she loves, he comes across a suspicious-looking paper. But far from a love letter, what should it be but "A charm for the tooth-ach, here's nothing but saints and crosses" (Beaumont and Fletcher, *A Wife for a Month*, I).

Such a charm Elias Ashmole, the famous antiquary, gave John Aubrey, "writ with his own hand."

    Mars, hur, abursa, aburse.

    Jesu Christ for Mary's sake,
    Take away this tooth-ach.

    Write the words three times; and as you say the words, let the party burn one paper, then another, and then the last.

                      Miscellanies, p. 135

Evidently people were willing to go to even greater lengths to avoid the tender manipulations of the barber-surgeons. Deprived by the accident of too-early birth of the benefits of gold and silver amalgams, seventeenth-century men with rotten teeth stuffed the cavities with other substances:

DELIO. *He has worne gun-powder, in's hollow tooth,*
    For the tooth-ache.

            WEBSTER, *Dutchesse of Malfy*, III, 3 [5]

[5] Compare Webster's character of "A Roaring Boy": "Souldier he is none, for hee cannot distinguish 'tweene onion seede and gunpowder: if he have worne it in his hollow tooth for the tooth-ach, and so come to the knowledge of it, that's all" (*Complete Works*, ed. F. L. Lucas [Boston, 1928], IV, 32).

PETULUS. *O my teeth! Deare barber ease me,*
  Tongue, tell me why my teeth disease mee,
  O! what will rid me of this pain?
MOTTO. *Some pellitory fetcht from Spaine.*

LYLY, *Midas*, III, 2

"Pellitory of Spain" was an herb with a hot and fiery taste, like ginger and peppermint, which "easeth the paine of the teeth, especially if it be stamped with a little Staves-acre, and hid in a small bag, and put into the mouth, and there suffered to remaine a certain space," according to John Gerard's *The Herball* (London, 1597).

But, said a more perspicacious observer: "They invented as many enchauntments for love, as they did for the tooth-ach, but he that hath tryed both will say, that the best charme for a toothe, is to pull it out, and the best remedie for love to weare it out" (Lyly, *Euphues and His England*, II, 116).[6]

In the broader realm of "med'cines to th' imagination" were the seventeenth-century faith-healers. The reigns of Elizabeth and her immediate predecessors abounded in medical and surgical amateurs, and faith was compounded in their recipes equally with skill. Henry VIII composed plasters and waters which, on paper at least, have as professional an air as those concocted by his physicians, Drs. Augustyne, Butts, Cromer, and Chambre.[7] J. C. Jeaffreson mentions Sir Thomas Eliot, Sir Philip Parras, Sir William Gasgoyne, Lady Taylor, Lady Darrel, Sir Andrew Hav-

---

[6] Pliny's *Natural Historie*, Bk. XXX, Ch. 3, contains a multitude of charms for toothache, for example: The "tooth of a moule-warp taken out of her head whiles shee is alive" and hung around the neck or about the body; "ashes of a dogs head (dying of madnesse) . . . mixed with the oile Cyprinum" dropped into the ear of the painful side; "bones taken out of a lizards forhead at the ful of the moon" used to scarify the gums about the teeth; and "if the teeth that ake be hollow . . . put into the concavity thereof, the said ashes [of dog's teeth] incorporat in mice dung, or els the liver of a lizard dried."

[7] Appendix IX to Vicary's *The Anatomie of the Bodie of Man*, ed. Furnivall, E.E.T.S., e.s. 53 (London, 1888). I transcribe one of the royal prescriptions, "A blacke plastre devised by the kinges hieghnes": Take gummi armoniaci .℥. iiij. olei omphacini ℥,iij, fyne therebinthine .℥.vj. gummi Elennij .℥.i., Resun pini ℥.x. Boyle [them] to-guether strongly on a softe fyre of coolys in a faire lateñ basyñ, allwayes styrring it untill it be plaster-wyse; and so make it uppe in rolles, and kepe it to your use."

eningham, an Earl of Derby, the Earl of Herfurth, and James IV
of Scotland; and in sad recognition of his own century's decadence he remarks: "The only art which fashionable people now-
a-days care much to meddle with is literature." [8]

John Aubrey's *Lives* contains thumbnail portraits of a number
of iatric amateurs. William Penn's wife was "virtuous, generous,
wise, humble; generally beloved for those good qualities and one
more—the great cures she does, having great skill in physic and
surgery, which she freely bestows" (II, 34). The Reverend William Holder's wife: "Amongst many other gifts she has a strange
sagacity as to curing of wounds, which she does not doe so much
by presedents and receipt bookes, as by her owne excogitancy,
considering the causes, effects and circumstances" (I, 405). Sir
Walter Raleigh "made an excellent cordiall, good in feavers,
etc.; Mr. R. Boyle has the recipe, and makes it and does great
cures by it" (II, 192). Judge Walter Rumsey

> was much troubled with flegme, and being so one winter at the
> court at Ludlowe . . . sitting by the fire, spitting and spawling,
> he tooke a fine tender spring, and tied a ragge at the end, and
> conceited he might putt it downe his throate, and fetch-up the
> flegme, and he did so. Afterwards he made this instrument of
> whalebone. . . . It makes you vomit without any paine, and
> besides, the vomits of apothecaries have aliquid veneni in them.
> He wrote a little 8vo booke, of this way of medicine, called
> Organon Salutis: London . . . 1659. . . .
>
> II, 206

Sir Jonas Moore: "Sciatica he cured it, by boyling his buttock"
(II, 78).

To round out this medical portrait gallery, there was the wife
of Dr. Thomas Iles, one of the canons of Christ Church. She was
not only "a knowing woman in physic and surgery, and did many
cures," but it was to her that Thomas Willis owed the early
training which culminated in enduring fame:

> Tom Willis then wore a blew livery-cloak, and studied at the
> lower end of the hall, by the hall-dore; was pretty handy, and his

[8] *A Book about Doctors*, pp. 166 f.

mistresse would oftentimes have him to assist her in making of medicines. This did him no hurt, and allured him on.

II, 303

Robert Burton's mother was another who had "excellent skill in chirurgery, sore eyes, aches, &c." (*Anatomy of Melancholy,* II.v.1.5).

With so many living examples to draw from, it is no wonder that Madam Strangeloves and Lady Bountifuls appeared on the stage. "Lady Bountiful," before the Great Society took over, once signified an overpoweringly gracious lady irresistibly soothing the ills of the hapless poor; she was the creation of Farquhar. In Act I of *The Beaux Stratagem,* Bonniface the landlord is expatiating on her virtues for the benefit of two skeptical gentlemen from London:

> My Lady Bountiful is one of the best of women: her last husband Sir Charles Bountiful left her worth a thousand pound a year; and I believe she lays out one half on't in charitable uses for the good of her neighbours; she cures rheumatisms, ruptures, and broken shins in men, green sickness, obstructions, and fits of the mother in women;—The king's evil, chin-cough, and chilblains in children; in short, she has cured more people in and about Litchfield within ten years than the doctors have kill'd in twenty; and that's a bold word.

Later, in Act IV, Lady Bountiful herself confutes another skeptic:

> Well, Daughter Sullen, tho' you laugh, I have done miracles about the country here with my receipts.
> MRS. SULLEN. Miracles, indeed, if they have cur'd any body, but, I believe, madam, the patient's faith goes farther toward the miracle than your prescription.
> LADY BOUNTIFUL. Fancy helps in some cases. . . .

London citizens, indeed, had little liking and less respect for Lady Bountiful's "pretty, innocent huswifely-life in the country." Shadwell's Lucia, like Mrs. Sullen, scorned

> To have my closet stink, like a pothecaries shop, with drugs and medicines, to administer to my sick neighbours, and spoil the

next quack's practice with the receipt-book that belongs to the
family. . . . And then to have one approved green-salve, and
dress sore legs with it; and all this to deserve the name of as good
a neighbourly body as ever came into Sussex.

Epsom-Wells, II

Even in the presence of the almost 2,000 remedies of the
London pharmacopoeia, there were physicians who disdained
them all. Such a one was the doctor in Brome's *The Antipodes*,
of whom Blaze said:

> . . . *it will astonish you*
> *To heare the mervailes he hath done in cures*
> *Of such distracted ones, as is your sonne,*
> *And not so much by bodily physicke (no!*
> *He sends few recipes to th' apothecaries)*
> *As medicine of the minde. . . .*

I, 1

"Medicine of the minde" was what Sir William Ferfers
needed, whose inamorata disdained his love on the entirely ficti-
tious ground that he possessed "an ill-favoured great nose, that
hangs sagging so lothsomely to your lips, that I cannot find it in
my heart so much as to kisse you."

> *What, my nose (quoth he)? is my nose so great and I never
> knew it? certainly I thought my nose to be as comely as any
> mans: but this it is we are all apt to think well of our selves, and a
> great deale better than we ought: but let me see? my nose! by the
> masse, tis true, I do now feele it my selfe: Good Lord, how was I
> blinded before?*

> *Hereupon it is certaine, that the knight was driven into such a
> conceit, as none could perswade him but his nose was so great
> indeed. . . .*

> *Whereupon [his] lady having conferred with a phisitian that
> boare a great name in the countrey, hee undertooke to remove
> this fond conceit by his skill. . . .*

> *The phisitian being come, hee had filled a certaine bladder
> with sheepes blood, and conveyed it into his sleeve, where at the
> issue of the bladder he had put in a piece of swane quil, through
> the which the bloud should runne out of the bladder so close by*

his hand, that he holding the knight by the nose, it might not be perceived, but that it issued thence. All things being prepared, he told the knight, that by a foule corrupt bloud wherewith the veines of his nose were overcharged, his impediment did grow, therefore (quoth he) to have redresse for this disease, you must have a veine opened in your nose, whence this foul corruption must be taken; whereupon it will follow, that your nose will fall againe to his naturall proportion, and never shall you be troubled with this griefe any more, and thereupon will I gage my life.

I pray you Master Doctor (said the knight), is my nose so big as you make it?

With reverence I may speake it (said the phisitian) to tell the truth, and avoid flattery, I never saw a more misshapen nose so foule to sight. . . .

All this we wil quickly remedy, said the phisitian, have no doubt; and with that, he very orderly prickt him in the nose, but not in any veine whereby he might bleed; and presently having a tricke finely to unstop the quill, the blood ranne into a basen in great abundance; and when the bladder was empty, and the basen almost full, the phisitian seemed to close the veine, and asked him how he felt his nose, showing the great quantitie of filthy blood which from thence he had taken.

The knight beholding it with great wonder, said, he thought no man in the world had bin troubled with such abundance of currupt blood in his whole bodie, as lay in his mis-shapen nose, and therewithall he began to touch and handle his nose, saying that he felt it mightily asswaged. Immediately a glasse was brought wherein he might behold himselfe.

Yea mary (qd. he), now I praise God, I see my nose is come into some reasonable proportion, and I feele my selfe very well eased of the burthen thereof; but if it continue thus, thats all.

I will warrant your worship (said the phisitian) for ever being troubled with the like againe.

Whereupon the knight received great joy, and the doctor a high reward.

DELONEY, *Thomas of Reading*, Ch. 10

There were malingerers, too, and gullible husbands who, better versed in merchant's wiles than woman's ills, cured diseases with remedies not found in the pharmacopoeias. Such a one was

that thrifty weaver, Simon of Southampton, in another of Deloney's tales (*Thomas of Reading*, Ch. 6). Simon's wife han-
kered after the fineries of London town, and when he offered her
gray russet and good homespun cloth she scorned the offer and
straightway fell into a swoon; nor was to be recovered from
death's door until the weaver promised her a Cheapside gown.

And even in that robust age there were hypochondriacs to
keep the doctors busy—and wealthy: "He that for every qualme
wil take a receipt, and can-not make two meales, unless Galen be
his Gods good: shall be sure to make the phisitian rich, and
himselfe a begger: his bodye will never be with-out diseases, and
his pursse ever with-out money" (Lyly, *Euphues and His England*, II, 17). Tradition has it that such patients are the backlog of
a physician's practice, yet here we see a doctor making the in-
excusable error of telling a psychosomatic patient that he isn't
really sick:

> *A gentleman not richest in discretion,*
> *Was always sending for his own phisitian.*
> *And on a time he needs would of him know,*
> *What was the cause his pulse did go so slow?*
> *Why (quoth the doctor) thus it comes to passe.*
> *Must needs go slow, which goes upon an asse.*[9]

The classic example was Sir Patient Fancy, "an old rich Alderman, and one that fancies himself always sick." He enters the
stage in a nightgown, reading an apothecary's bill, and solilo-
quizing between items:

> *Hum,—twelve purges for this present January—as I take it,*
> *good Mr. Doctor, I took but ten in all December.—By this rule I*
> *am sicker this month than I was the last.—And good Master*
> *Apothecary, methinks your prizes are somewhat too high: at this*
> *rate no body would be sick. . . .*
>
> APHRA BEHN, *Sir Patient Fancy*, II

This scene is, of course, borrowed from Argan's speech opening
Le Malade Imaginaire. But even though Mrs. Behn plagiarized

---

[9] *England's Jests Refin'd and Improv'd* (London, 1693), quoted by J. Ashton,
Humour, Wit and Satire of the XVII Century (New York, 1884), p. 260.

from Molière, Englishmen were as subject as Frenchmen to delusions of disease.

Perhaps the most fantastic of the magical remedies of the time was the sympathetic powder of Sir Kenelm Digby. Its sponsor was no less remarkable than the medicine itself. Aubrey, who was Sir Kenelm's fervent admirer, held him to be "the most accomplished cavalier of his time." "He was such a goodly handsome person, gigantique and great voice, and had so graceful elocution and noble addresse, etc., that had he been drop't out of the clowdes in any part of the world, he would have made himselfe respected" (*Brief Lives*, I, 225).

Sir Anthony Van Dyck's portrait of Digby, surrounded by his family, bears eloquent testimony to the truth of Aubrey's description. Still, one must not forget that on November 7, 1651, John Evelyn had a conversation with Digby and afterwards impolitely recorded in his diary, "the truth is, Sir Kenelm was an errant mountebank." Another of his contemporaries called him "the very Pliny of the age for lying." He was a man to be greatly admired or cordially hated, and he was both.[10]

At some time before the middle of the century Sir Kenelm met a friar who was in possession of a marvelous secret, and happily did him a favor. In return for this, Digby received the recipe for the notorious powder of sympathy. This remarkable substance cured wounds when applied, not to the sword-thrust itself, but to a portion of the wearing apparel of the injured man or to the bandage with which the wound had been bound. Hence from the dramatists:

---

[10] Digby's epitaph by R. Ferrar was quoted by Aubrey (*Miscellanies*, p. 4) with approval:

> Under this stone the matchless Digby lies,
> Digby the great, the valiant and the wise:
> This age's wonder for his noble parts;
> Skill'd in six tongues, and learn'd in all the arts.
> Born on the day he died, th' eleventh of June,
> On which he bravely fought at Scanderoon.
> 'Tis rare that one and self-same day should be
> His day of birth, of death, of victory.

> Our medecine we apply,
> Like the weapon-salve, not to ourselves but him
> Who was the sword that made the wound.
>
> DAVENANT, *Unfortunate Lover*, II

MODISH. Have you receiv'd any hurt in your face, that you cover it with your handker cher?

FORECAST. A slight one only.

ESTRANGE. I have sympathy-powder about me, if you will give me your handkercher while the blood is warm, will cure it immediately.

SEDLEY, *Mulberry Garden*, III, 3

SCARAMOUCH. Why, madam, he is run—quite thro the heart,—but the man may live, if I please.

ELARIA. Thou please! torment me not with riddles.

SCARAMOUCH. Why, madam, there is a certain cordial balsam, call'd a fair lady; which outwardly applied to his bosom, will prove a better cure than all your weapon or sympathetic powder, meaning your ladyship.

ELARIA. Is Cinthio then not wounded?

SCARAMOUCH. No otherways than by your fair eyes, madam. . . .

APHRA BEHN, *Emperor of the Moon*, I

In *The Tempest, or the Enchanted Island*, the Davenant-Dryden alteration of Shakespeare's play, Hippolyto is wounded in a duel with Ferdinand, and Ariel is enjoined to see to his cure:

ARIEL. When I was chidden by my mighty lord, for my
    Neglect of young Hippolyto, I went to view
    His body, and soon found his soul was but retir'd,
    Not sally'd out: then I collected
    The best of simples underneath the moon,
    The best of balms, and to the wound apply'd
    The healing juice of vulnerary herbs. . . .
    Anoint the sword which pierc'd him with this
    Weapon-salve, and wrap it close from air till
    I have time to visit him again.

                    V

In the next scene Miranda enters with Hippolyto's sword wrapped up. As she unwraps the weapon, Hippolyto moans:

> *Alas! I feel the cold air come to me,*
> *My wound shoots worse than ever.*

Miranda then wipes and anoints the sword with Ariel's weapon-salve, and asks:

> *Does it still grieve you?*
> HIPPOLYTO. *Now methinks there's something laid just upon it.*
> MIRANDA. *Do you find no ease?*
> HIPPOLYTO. *Yes, yes, upon the sudden all the pain*
> *Is leaving me: Sweet Heaven, how I am eas'd.*

Miranda should, of course, have anointed Ferdinand's sword, which was the weapon that gave the wound. The mistake lay only in the stage directions, however, for Ariel's instructions were entirely correct.

Digby's secret, when it emerged, was found to be simply green vitriol recrystallized three times and dried in the midsummer sun. Samuel Butler took a satirical crack at the whole business in 1662:

> *Learned he was in med'c'nal lore,*
> *For by his side a pouch he wore*
> *Replete with strange hermetick powder,*
> *That wounds nine miles point-blank would solder,*
> *By skilfull chymist with great cost*
> *Extracted from a rotten post;*
> *But of a heav'nlier influence*
> *Than which mountebanks dispense;*
> *Though by Promethean fire made,*
> *As they do quack that drive that trade.*
> *For as when slovens doe amiss*
> *At others doors by stool or piss,*
> *The learned write, a red-hot spit,*
> *B'ing prudently apply'd to it,*
> *Will convey mischief from the dung*
> *Unto the breech that did the wrong:*
> *So this did healing, and as sure*
> *As that did mischief, this would cure.*
>
> Hudibras, Pt. I, Canto 2

By 1678, apparently, Butler's indignation had subsided, for his allusion in the third part of *Hudibras* (Canto 2) lacks the true Hudibrastic sting:

> *'Tis true, a scorpion's oyl is said*
> *To cure the wounds the vermine made;*
> *And weapons dress'd with salves restore*
> *And heal the hurts they gave before.*

We come across Sir Kenelm Digby again in connection with another of the interesting remedies of the time. This was viper-wine, a decoction in high repute with the superannuated Lotharios who in later days would have submitted to Voronoff's monkey-gland treatments, or the Steinach operation. The official *Vinum viperinum* was quite simply prepared: "Take of dried vipers two ounces, of white wine three pints. Infuse with a gentle heat for a week, and then strain the wine off." [11] From that point on let the wits take charge.

In Tom Brown's *Letters from the Dead to the Living,* "Madam Creswel of pious Memory" writes "to her Sister in Iniquity Moll Quarles of known Integrity": "I was never without viper-wine for a fumbler, to give a spur to old age and assist impotency." Both these ladies were noted bawds of the day, and kept bordellos famed in song and story.

Another procuress turned a neat compliment around the drink. Mrs. Cheatley says to old Goldingham the miser, "I never saw any creature so chang'd in all my life, sure you drink nothing but Viper Wine." And he simpers, flattered, "Nay you wheadle" (Shadwell, *Miser,* II).

There were aphrodisiacs even more potent than viper wine, for Sempronius says of a lady:

> . . . *your viper wine*
> *Soe much in practise with gray bearded gallants*
> *But vappa to the nectar of her lippe.*
>   MASSINGER, *Beleeve As Ye List,* IV

---

[11] "The committee proposed this medicine in their plan, with living vipers and intire. But this form is chosen by the college, as prepared in less time" (*Dispensatory of the Royal College of Physicians, London,* p. 262).

"Vappa" was a vapid or insipid wine.[12] What a seductive creature this lady must have been!

The virtue of viper wine lay partly in the fact that the viper
was an extremely prolific animal, and partly in the fancy that it
delighted in the act of generation.[13] This serpent was, on the
whole, medicinally very valuable. Besides viper wine, a broth of
vipers and also its meat, fresh and dried, were employed. Said
Pliny: "Some burn a viper with salt in an earthen pot; and they
are of opinion, that whosoever do lick the same salt, or let it melt
at the tongues end, it clarifieth the eies: and that they shall keep
the stomacke and all the body besides in good temper, yea, and
live long by that meanes." [14] From this came the metaphorical
recipe for remaining young, "to eat snakes":

HIPPOLITO. *Scarce can I read the stories on your brow,*
   Which age hath writ there; you looke youthfull still.
ORLANDO. *I eate snakes, my Lord, I eate snakes. My heart shall never*
   have a wrinkle in it, so long as I can cry hem with a cleare voice.
                              DEKKER, *Honest Whore*, Pt. II, I

And in Beaumont and Fletcher's *The Elder Brother*, "What,"
cries Andrew to old Brisac, who is about to cuckold him,

   you have eate a snake,
And are grown young, gamesom, and rampant.
                                                        IV, 4

[12] "In some countries, if new wine worke of it selfe a second time, it is thought
to be a fault and means to corrupt it: and indeed upon such a chance & unhappy
accident, it loseth the verdure and quick tast: whereupon it gets the name of
Vappa, and is clean turned to be dead or soure: in which regard also we give a
man that name by way of scorne and reproch, calling him Vappa, when he is
heartlesse, void of reason and understanding" (Pliny, *Natural Historie*, Bk.
XXIV, Ch. 20).

[13] "In the very act of generation the male viper thrusteth his head into the
mouth of the female; which she (for the pleasure and delectation that she hath)
gnaweth and biteth off. No land creature els but she lath egs within her belly, of
one colour and soft, like as fishes have. Now after three daies they be quicke, and
then come forth as they be hatched, but no more than one at once every day: and
20 commonly she hath. When she is delivered of the first, the rest (impatient of
so long delay) eat through their dams sides, and kil her" (*ibid.*, Bk. X, Ch. 62).

[14] *Ibid.*, Bk. XXIX, Ch. 6.

Digby's connection with viper-wine is retailed in unblushing detail by John Aubrey. His wife Venetia had been, before her marriage to the knight, the mistress of the Earl of Dorset, who "had one if not more children by her. He settled on her an annuity of 500 *li.* per annum" (*Brief Lives*, I, 230), "which after Sir K.D. maried was unpayd by the earle; and for which annuity Sir Kenelme sued the earle after mariage, and recovered it" (*Brief Lives*, I, 226). When Digby married his Venetia, much against the good will of his mother, "he would say that 'a wise man, and lusty, could make an honest woman out of a brothell-house.'" Lady Digby

> . . . dyed in her bed suddenly. Some suspected that she was poysoned. When her head was opened there was found but little braine, which her husband imputed to her drinking of viper-wine; but spiteful woemen would say 'twas a viper-husband who was jealous of her that she would steale a leape.
>
> Brief Lives, I, 231

But Aubrey had it on good authority that after her marriage Venetia redeemed her honor by her "strickt living." [15] Perhaps Sir Kenelm was the one who should have drunk the wine.

It seems fitting at this point to say a few words about a favorite anaphrodisiac of the day. This antidote to viper-wine was camphor.

> GOMEZ. But oh, this Jezabel of mine! I'll get a physician that shall prescribe her an ounce of camphire every morning for her breakfast, to abate incontinency. . . .
>
> DRYDEN, Spanish Fryar, I, 2

In Mrs. Behn's *The Amorous Prince* Lorenzo has gone a-whoring (as so many of her heroes regrettably do), and has tumbled into more than a lecher's share of trouble. "May I turn Franciscan," he exclaims, "if I could not find it in my heart to do penance in camphire posset, this month, for this" (IV, 4).

Then there is old Lady Wishfort, who, dissembling her ardent desire to be remarried, protests:

---

[15] The stories of the intimate relations between Lady Digby and Sir Anthony Van Dyck, the artist, lead one to question this. See *Stories of the Flemish and Dutch Artists*, ed. V. Reynolds (London, 1908), pp. 185–192.

> If you think the least scruple of carnality was an ingredient—
> WAITWELL. Dear madam, no. You are all camphire and frankincense,
> all chastity and odour.
>
> CONGREVE, Way of the World, IV

To Sir Thomas Browne, however, attributing this quality to camphor was one of the vulgar errors. He wrote:

> That camphire eunuchates, or begets in men an impotency unto
> venery, observation will hardly confirm; and we have found it to
> fail in cocks and hens, though given for many days; which was a
> more favourable trial then that of Scaliger, when he gave it unto
> a bitch that was proud.
>
> Pseudodoxia Epidemica, Bk. II, Ch. 7

From aphrodisiacs and their opposites it is but a step to the broader and inclusive subject of love. It was the perennial complaint of the poets, abroad as in England, that love was one disease which physic could not cure. The reader will recall Sappho's plaint in regard to mithridatium. Other remedies were as useless.

> O ye gods, have ye ordayned for everye maladye a medicine, for
> every sore a salve, for every payne a plaister, leving only love
> remedilesse?
>
> LYLY, Euphues, I, 226

> PHYSITIAN. No I have found you out, you are in love.
> JANE. I thinke I am, what your appliance now?
>   Can all your Paracelsian mixtures cure it?
>
> MIDDLETON, Faire Quarrell, II

> CHYRURGION. Courage, brave sir; do not mistrust my art.
> BRUCE. Tell me, didst thou e'er cure a wounded heart?
>   Thy skill, fond man, thou here imploy'st in vain;
>   The ease thou givest does but encrease my pain.
>
> ETHEREGE, Comical Revenge, V

> UNE BERGÈRE. Votre plus haut savoir n'est que pure chimère,
>   Vains et peu sages médecins;
>   Vous ne pouvez guérir, par vos grands mots latins,
>   La Douleur qui me désespère.

Votre plus haut savoir n'est que pure chimère.
                    Molière, *Le Malade Imaginaire*, Prologue [16]

Love is also a poison with only a single antidote. But there
were other poisons as well, fatal in a more literal sense. The old
plays abound in poisoning scenes, which as a rule run something
like this:

                                                    [Takes poison.]
[*Then follows a soliloquy.*]
                                                          [Dies.]

From the medical point of view such stage directions are not
very enlightening. An allusion as explicit as the following is very
rare:

FLAMINIUS.   . . . *see that they want not*
     Amonge their other delicates.
CHRYSALUS. *Marke that.*
FLAMINIUS. [Aside to Demetrius] *A sublimated pill of mercurie*
     For sugar to their wine.
DEMETRIUS. *I understande you.*
                              Massinger, *Beleeve As Ye List*, II

When poisoning was suspected, there was a toxicological
court of appeal. Thus, when an apothecary prescribes for the
politic senator Lupus, the latter thinks the potion is poison and
cries:

> . . . *take the potion from him there, I have an antidote more*
> *than you wote off, sir: throw it on the ground there: So. Now*
> *fetch in the dogge; And yet we cannot tarrie to trie experiments*
> *now: arrest him, you shall goe with me, sir; I'le tickle you,*
> *pothecarie; I'le give you a glister, i' faith.*
>   Jonson, *Poetaster*, IV, 4

---

[16] The prologue is not included in the English edition. Roughly translated, this
passage reads:

   A *Shepherdess.* Your lofty knowledge is nothing but illusion,
      Vain, unperceptive doctors;
      With all your big Latin words you cannot cure
      The sorrow that leaves me hopeless.
      Your lofty knowledge is nothing but illusion.

HUNT LIBRARY
CARNEGIE-MELLON UNIVERSITY

The poor dog! He ranks with Dr. Alvar Fanez's journeyman as a martyr to medicine.

The subtle and mysterious poisons of the sixteenth and seventeenth centuries owe their reputations more to legend than to fact. Many of the deaths attributed to secret poisoning were probably due to appendicitis, intestinal obstruction, extra-uterine pregnancy, or a number of other pathological processes with which the diagnostic ability of the old physicians could not cope. Of the actual poisons used, arsenic gained early the popularity it still keeps as a homicidal potion and, with bichloride of mercury, made up in potency what it lacked in subtlety. There is an interesting episode in Aphra Behn's novel *The Fair Jilt* which illustrates a crude bit of poisoning but a clever bit of detective work. The tale is too long to quote in full. Suffice it that "the doctors said, she [Alcidiana] had taken mercury. So that there was never so formidable a sight as this fair young creature; her head and body swoln, her eyes starting out, her face black, and all deformed. . . ." After questioning cook, butler, and footmen, the inquisitors arrived at the page: "He was examined, and show'd a thousand guilty looks: and the apothecary, then attending among the doctors, proved he had bought mercury of him three or four days before; which he could not deny; and making many excuses for his buying it, betray'd him the more; so ill he chanced to dissemble" (V, 255 ff.).

It was fortunate for Alcidiana (who finally recovered from the effects of the mercury) that the page was not as subtle as the doctor in *The White Divel*, who, Flamineo jeers, "will shoot pils into a mans guts, shall make them have more ventages then a cornet or a lamprey; hee will poyson a kisse, and was once minded, for his masterpiece, because *Ireland* breeds no poyson, to have prepared a deadly vapour in a *Spaniards* fart that should have poison'd all *Dublin*" (II, 1).

According to traditional theory poisons were of two sorts, hot and cold; and their antidotes were respectively cold and hot. Thus, says Colax:

> As when the skilfull and deep learn'd physitian
> Does take too different poysons, one thats cold,

> The other in the same degree of heate,
> And blends them both to make an antidote.
> > RANDOLPH, *Muses Looking-Glasse*, IV, 5

This process took place inadvertently, but fortunately for the well-being of one of Dryden's characters:

BENDUCAR [to Dorax]. *I'm sure I did my part to poyson thee,*
What saint soe'ere has sodder'd thee again.
A dose less hot had burst through ribs of iron.
MUFTI. *Not knowing that, I poyson'd him once more,*
And drench'd him with a draft so deadly cold
That, had'st not thou prevented, had congeal'd
The channels of his blood, and froze him dry. . . .
DORAX. *Thus, when Heaven pleases, double poysons cure.*
> > *Don Sebastian*, IV, 3

This belief has been carried down the centuries in the proverbial "hair of the dog" treatment for the morning after. Expressed in a more elegant fashion:

KING. *I'm stung, and won't the torture long endure;*
Serpents that wound, have blood those wounds to cure.
> > OTWAY, *Don Carlos*, II

And even more elegantly:

> As hee which is wounded of the Porcuntine, can never be healed unlesse his woundes be washt with the bloud of the same beast; as there is nothing better against the stinging of a snake, then to be rubbed with an adders slough, and as he which is hurt of the scorpion [must] seeke a salve from whom he received the sore, so love onelie is remedied by love, and fancie by mutuall affection. . . .[17]

The tradition of paired poisons, if traced to its source, would encounter there the ancient legend of the Ark; for the basis of the idea is not medical but mystical. Sir Thomas Browne states the orthodox case, but, in the end, his medical training asserts itself in a plaintive realization that medicine does not always follow mathematical laws.

[17] Greene, *Carde of Fancie*, in *Shorter Novels* (London [1929]), I, *Elizabethan and Jacobean*, 185.

> *And though also it be true, that God made all things double, and that if we look upon the works of the most High, there are two and two, one against another; that one contrary hath another, and poyson is not without a poyson unto it self; yet hath the curse so far prevailed, or else our industry defected that poysons are better known than their antidotes, and some thereof do scarce admit of any.*
>
> Pseudodoxia Epidemica, Bk. VII, Ch. 17

Although one poison may have had its special antidote in another, there was one antidote which was effective against them all. This was the unicorn's horn.

The legends of the unicorn do not need lengthy retelling here.[18] The animal was so swift of foot that neither horses nor dogs could overtake it. Curiosity, however, was the monster's fatal weakness. The sight of a virgin (so different from its bearded enemy, man) proved an irresistible attraction, and hunters took advantage of the unicorn's failing by disguising a beardless youth in woman's clothes. Then, when the animal timidly approached, the supposed virgin reached out a brawny arm and twisted off the precious horn. According to other authorities it was the virginal scent rather than sight which attracted the beast. The feminine effluvium acted as a soporific: the unicorn trotted up to the maid, lay down with its head in her lap, and fell asleep. Here, too, sweetly scented boys took the place of the virgins, who after all were much too rare and valuable to be risked in such dangerous games.

In the Golden Age the unicorn lived at peace, for there was then no poison in the world. "The Unicorne did not put his horne into the streame to chase awaye venome before hee dranke, for then there was no suche thing extant in the water or on the earth" (Nashe, *Unfortunate Traveller*, p. 80).[19] Later

---

[18] See O. Shepard, *The Lore of the Unicorn* (London, 1930). Also W. G. A. Robertson, "The Use of the Unicorn's Horn, Coral and Stones in Medicine," *Annals of Medical History*, VIII (1926), 240.

[19] "And even in our times, it is said, venemous animals poison that water after the setting of the sun, so that the good animals cannot drink of it; but in the morning, after the sunrise, comes the unicorn and dips his horn into the stream, driving the poison from it so that the good animals can drink there during the day" (*Itinerarium Joannis de Hese presbyteri ad Hierusalem* [Daventria, 1499]).

there was poison enough, and not enough unicorn's horn to go around.

Belief in the efficacy of the horn received a mortal affront, if not quite a mortal blow, when the surgeon Ambroise Paré bravely published in 1582 his *Discourse, a scavoir, de la mumie, des venins, de la licorne et de la peste.* In this book he categorically denied the medicinal virtue of what was later called

> That most unvalued horn the unicorn
> Bears to oppose the huntsman. . . .
>   BEAUMONT AND FLETCHER, *Valentinian,* I, 2

Paré's scandalized contemporaries replied in the only way possible: A material so costly must be potent. Otherwise would a Russian have paid half a million rubles for three small pieces of horn? Moreover, only a few years before the surgeon's impertinent discourse, the great Jerome Cardan, on his way from Italy to an important consultation in Edinburgh, stopped at Paris and was impressed by three things: the filthiness of the streets, the density of the population, and (most of all) with the unicorn's horn the royal physician showed him in the Church of St Dionysius.[20] And Cardan, the most celebrated astrologer and physician in all Europe, was properly hard to impress.

It is no wonder, then, that naïve Tom Coryat, who saw the same sights on May 24, 1608, recorded his amazement at "an unicornes horne valued at one hundred thousand crownes, being about three yardes high, even so high that I could hardly reach to the top of it . . ." (*Crudities,* I, 184).

In 1646 the author of *Pseudodoxia Epidemica* treated the subject with characteristically credulous skepticism (Ch. XXIII). It was not so much the efficacy of the horn that Browne doubted, as its genuineness. He was willing to believe that the horn of a real unicorn would possess many of the traditional virtues, but with the horns of at least five different animals masquerading under the name of unicorn, he was not quite

---

[20] C. L. Dana, "The Story of a Great Consultation: Jerome Cardan Goes to Edinburgh," *Annals of Medical History,* III (1921), 122.

convinced of the actual existence of the substance in apothecaries' shops.

There was, fortunately, a test for the genuineness of the horn:

> As men to try the precious unicornes horne
> Make of the powder a preservative circle
> And in it put a spider. . . .
>
> WEBSTER, White Divel, II, 1

If the horn were authentic, the spider found itself unable to pass
the barrier.[21] An inquisitive budding poet put the question to
experimental test. Will Davenant "was preferred to the first
Duchess of Richmond to wait on her as a page. I remember he
told me, she sent him to a famous apothecary for some unicorn's-horn, which he was resolved to try with a spider which he
encircled in it, but without the expected success; the spider
would go over, and through and through, unconcerned"
(Aubrey, Brief Lives, I, 205).

In seventeenth-century England the unicorn's horn no longer
maintained its once-proud position in the esteem of physician or
layman. Most of the dramatic allusions to the antidote carry a
mocking note. Thus, in Jonson's Every Man out of His Humour,
Sir Puntarvolo's dog has been poisoned, and Carlo exclaims:
" 'Fore god, sir Puntarvolo, I am sorry for your heaviness: body a
men, a shrewd mischance! why, had you no unicornes horne, nor
bezoars stone about you? ha?" (V, 5).

Medico de Campo, an arrant mountebank, touts his remedies
in the following terms: "Poxe of your old wives medicines; the
worst of mine ingredients is an unicornes horne, and bezars
stone; raw beefe, and inkehornes!" (Randolph, Aristippus, p.
25). And a discontented patient makes a resolve:

> PHILARGUS.   . . . His pills, his cordials, his electuaries,
>   His sirrups, julips, bezerstone, nor his
>   Imagin'd unicornes horne comes in my bellie,
>   My mouth shall be a draught first, 'Tis resolv'd.
>
> MASSINGER, Roman Actor, II

[21] Another test, apparently unknown to the dramatists, was to "put silke upon
a burning cole, and upon the silke the aforesaid horne, and if so be that it be true
the silke will not be a whit consumed" (E. Topsell, The Historie of Foure-Footed
Beastes [London, 1607], p. 720).

Two scoundrelly surgeons talk over a case:

1 SURGEON. *But let's take heed he doe not poyson us.*
2 SURGEON. *Oh, I will never eate nor drinke with him,*
  Without unicornes horne in a hollow tooth.
                        WEBSTER, *Devils Law-case*, III, 2

What Browne called "the brother antidote bezoar" was commonly linked in the allusions with unicorn's horn. Such stones
were of two varieties, the *orientale*, formed in the fourth stomach of the gazelle of India, and the *occidentale*, found in the
fourth stomach of the wild goat or chamois of Peru. Just as
rhinoceros and narwhal horns, fossil wood, bones, and teeth
passed for unicorn's horn, so other animal concretions, crabs'
eyes and claws, bruised and mixed with musk and ambergris,
were sold for true bezoars. In medieval days bezoar stones had a
reputation as an antidote second only to the rarer horn, but in
the seventeenth century they had fallen into corresponding disrepute.

In spite of the comedies on the stage, the century's temper
was a melancholy one, preoccupied with thoughts of mortality.
Quack medicines, simples, alchemical remedies; live animals and
dead organs; magic, charms, and sympathetic powders; mithridatium and unicorn's horn—all might fail to cure, but one recourse always remained:

MELEANDER. *The hangman is a rare phisician.* . . .[22]
  All the buzz of drugs, and myneralls and simples,
  Bloud-lettings, vomits, purges, or what else
  Is conjured up by men of art, to gull
  Liege-people, and reare golden piles, are trash
  To a well-strong-wrought halter; there the goute,
  The stone, yes and the melancholy devill,
  Are cur'd in lesse time then a paire of minutes.
  Build me a gallows in this very plot,
  And Ile dispatch your businesse.
                        FORD, *Lovers Melancholy*, IV

[22] Sir Walter Raleigh said, as he kissed the axe on the scaffold, " 'Tis a sharp
medicine, but a sure cure for all diseases."

5

Great Men and Quacks

Since Hippocrates says it, it must be done.
                    —Molière, *The Forced Physician*
                              [*Le Médecin Malgré Lui*]

As late as the seventeenth century, the teachings of the Greco-Arabic authorities were still an infallible dogma. The doctrines of medical science were a finished book, just as the authorities of the church were final. They might be commented upon, expounded, and interpreted but not contradicted nor even seriously questioned. The three rocks upon which these medical doctrines were so firmly founded were Hippocrates, the Father of Medicine, the Divine Old Man; Galen; and Avicenna.

To the old physicians this trinity was hardly less revered than God the Father, the Son, and the Holy Ghost. Nor did worship of these iatric idols stop with medical men. Laymen also invoked their names as representing the apogee of the healing art.

d'amville. *Doctor! Behold two patients, in whose cure*
    Thy skill may purchase an eternall fame.
    If thou hast any reading in Hipocrates,
    Galen, or Avicen; if hearbes, or drugges,
    Or mineralles have any power to save;
    Now let thy practise and their soveraigne use,
    Raise thee to wealth and honour.
                    Tourneur, *Atheist's Tragedie*, V, 1

They were, as Ben Jonson said, names to conjure with:

COMPASSE. *The doctor is an asse then, if hee say so,*
  And cannot with his conjuring names, Hippocrates,
  Galen, or Rasis, Avicen, Averroes,
  Cure a poore wenches falling in a swoune:
  Which a poore farthing chang'd in rosa solis,
  Or cynnamon water would.

                                        Magnetick Lady, III, 2

Here the most learned of poets has listed in true chronological order the most famous names of ancient and medieval medicine. A eulogy of Hippocrates would be a presumption here. His sobriquets are sufficient unto themselves; and, when he died in 377 B.C., the apotheosis of medicine had reached its peak.

To Galen (130–200 A.D.), Hippocrates and his contemporaries were "the ancients"; and this Greek-speaking Roman born in Asia Minor, with his "imperious temper and tendency to self-glorification," became in turn the touchstone to which all medical theory was applied. The Greek mist does not cling to Galen. In him one can recognize a later type of doctor in whom genius, enthusiasm, and ability are tempered with more worldly qualities. Hippocrates has become a myth; but let Galen change his terminology and toga for polysyllabic English and a white jacket, and he might have been the most famous and fashionable physician of modern London or New York as he was in the Rome of Marcus Aurelius' day.

The names of no physicians are more prevalent in the old plays than those of Galen and Hippocrates.[1] The dramatists

---

[1] The fame of Hippocrates and Galen recognized no geographical frontier; Molière called on the same medical authorities as his contemporaries in England.

  Sganarelle. Hippocrates says, and Galen by lively reasons, argues, that a
    person does not feel well when he is sick.
      (*The Flying Physician* [*Le Médecin Volant*], I, 4)

  Sganarelle [*in a physician's gown and a high crown'd hat*]. Hippocrates says
    —let's be cover'd.
  Geronte. Does Hippocrates say that?
  Sganarelle. Yes.
  Geronte. In what chapter pray?
  Sganarelle. In his chapter—of hats.

slipped them into their dialogue, not out of a desire to display their erudition, but simply as a matter of course; and it is apparent that even the groundlings understood the allusions.

PURSUIVANT.   Good Mr. Doctor,
   Teach your Apoethecary: Galen nor
   Hippocrates can perswade me from my duty.
                    BETTERTON, Love Will Find Out the Way, II

FERDINAND.   You are a brace of quacks,
   That tie your knowledge unto dayes and houres
   Mark'd out for good or ill i' th' almanack.
   Your best receipts are candy for a cold;
   And carduus benedictus for an ague,
   Could you give life as Æsculapius
   Did to unjustly slaine Hippolitus,
   You could prescribe no remedy for me.
   Goe study Gallen, and Hippocrates,
   And when your rare simplicities have found
   Simples to cure the lunacy of love,
   Compose a potion, and administer't
   Unto the family at Amsterdam.
                    BROME, The Court Beggar, III, 1

The medieval Arabs translated the works of the Greeks into their own language and added to Hellenic theory a mass of practical knowledge. Their great compendiums were then recast into Latin by twelfth- and thirteenth-century translators, and these conquered Europe completely, as the arms of the Crescent tried in vain to do.

Rhazes (ca. 850–923 or 932 A.D.), the "Rasis" of the poets, is the apocryphal author of an aphorism which strikes the keynote

---

Geronte. Since Hippocrates says it, it must be done.
                (The Forced Physician [Le Médecin Malgré Lui], II, 2)

One of the few instances in which an adaptation of Molière surpassed the original is Lacy's rendition of this passage in Act II of The Dumb Lady:

Doctor. Hippocrates says, I pray you be cover'd.
Geronte. Pray you, in what chapter of Hippocrates does he bid you be cover'd?
Doctor. In the first chapter of keeping your head warm.

of medieval medicine: "The study of a thousand books is more important for the physician than seeing a thousand patients." Rhazes himself, however, far from followed this advice, for in erudition he was surpassed by both Avicenna and Averroes, while as a clinician with diagnostic and therapeutic skill he stands unequalled among medieval physicians.

He lived, according to a report taken and transmitted *cum grano salis* by James Atkinson, "one hundred and twenty years; began his medical tricks at thirty, turned quack or empiricus for forty years, and a rational being or physician, for forty more, so that he was eighty years practising physic, before he came to his senses, his medical senses." [2] This does not sound like Rhazes, who after a brilliant manhood died embittered, blind, and impoverished. It would lead to a dismal conclusion to superimpose Dr. Atkinson's chronology on the facts of Rhazes's life.

The Persian "Prince of Physicians" was Avicenna (980–1038). He was the author of the renowned *Qānūn* (*Canon*), in which he expressed the quintessence of Greco-Arabic medicine in a comprehensive system and thereby established medical thought upon foundations apparently immutable. This book remained the medical bible of Christendom until recent times, and of Islam until yesterday or even today. [3] But Avicenna tinctured his scientific life with an immorality which today would have caused a sad clucking of academic tongues. During the day he practiced and wrote, but each evening found him sampling Bacchus and investigating Venus. Eventually wine and women proved too much for him, and he died at the age of fifty-eight. Apparently he had not heard "wise clearkes say, that *Galen* being asked what dyet he used that he lyved so long, aunswered: I have drunk no wine, I have touched no woman, I have kept my selfe warme" (Lyly, *Euphues and his England*, II, 55). But in answer Avicenna could have coined la Rochefoucauld's epigram six hundred years in advance: "Preserving the health by too strict a regimen is a wearisome malady."

Averroes (1126–1198) matched his predecessor in knowledge

[2] *Medical Bibliography* (London, 1834), p. 85.
[3] G. Sarton, *Introduction to the History of Science* (Baltimore, 1931), II, 72.

(his complete system of medicine, the *Kullīyāt* [*Colliget*], had
almost as much authority as the *Canon*), but hardly in dissipa-
tion. For Averroes was a prodigious worker and spent only two
nights of his long life away from his books and quill. One was
the night of his father's death, the other that of his own wedding
day.[4]

The dramatists added other names to the trinity, but more or
less unsystematically, according to quaint leanings of their own.
Richard Brome had a fancy for Dioscorides (40–90 A.D.), known
as the Father of Pharmacy.

DOCTOR.   . . . *I will warrant*
   His speedy cure without the helpe of Gallen, Hippocrates, Avi-
   cen, or Dioscorides.

                                        Antipodes, I, 6

STRANGELOVE. *Now Mr. Doctor! you come to aske my counsell I*
   know for your impatient patient. But let me tell you first, the
   most learned authors, that I can turne over; as Dioscorides,
   Avicen, Galen, and Hyppocrates are much discrepant in their
   opinions concerning the remedies for his disease.

                                        Court Beggar, III, 1

Ben Jonson in another play turns again to Rhazes in an illus-
tration of how deeply the legend of the famous Arabs sank into
even the inarticulate life of the times:

CLENCH. *As I am a varrier, and a visicarie:*
   Horse-smith of Hamsted, and the whole towne leach—.
MEDLAY. *Yes, you ha' done woundy cures, Gossip Clench.*
CLENCH. *An' I can see the stale once, through a urine-hole,*
   Ile give a shrew'd ghesse, be it man, or beast.
   I cur'd an ale-wife once, that had the staggers
   Worse then five horses, without rowelling.
   My God-phere was a Rabian, or a Jew.
   (You can tell D'oge!) They call'd him Doctor Rasi.

[4] An excellent account of Arabic medicine and medical men, from which the
above is largely taken, may be found in M. Neuberger's *History of Medicine*,
trans. E. Playfair (Oxford, 1910), I. For accounts of the Greek physicians, see A.
J. Brock's *Greek Medicine* (London, 1929).

SCRIBEN. *One Rasis was a great Arabick doctor.*
CLENCH. *Hee was King Harry's doctor, and my God-phere.*

Tale of a Tub, IV, 1

The tradition of the Greek fathers was as deeply ingrained in the popular mind:

GERNETTE. *And is he so famous a physician, say you?*
JARVIS. *Why, sir, Æsculapius, as you call him, is a meer mountebank to him.*
SOFTHEAD. *I, and that fellow Galen Hippocrates, as you call him, not worthy to be his apothecary.*

LACY, Dumb Lady, II

One wonders how comprehensible analogous allusions would be to a modern audience, even to the medical men scattered throughout it.

But it was "the huge, overshadowing figure of Galen" which eclipsed every other medical luminary in the playwrights' minds, even that of Hippocrates himself. Galen's genius is not to be denied, but forces even greater than this operated to place the halo on his brow. His piety, monotheism, and all-embracing teleology appealed to the medieval church, and his voluminous works were copied by the monks and disseminated, not only widely, but with the apostolic blessing. Then, too, Galen was not only omniscient, medically speaking, but dogmatic about it. To a world imbued with respect for authority, he offered the ultimate word. His name sanctioned any medical custom and sanctified any medical act, no matter how trivial, as in Davenant's song:

> *Arise, arise! Your breakfast stays—*
> *Good water-gruel warm,*
> *Or sugar-sops, which Galen says*
> *With mace will do no harm.*

And Galen became synonomous with Gospel:

MASTER GOURSEY. *. . . I like this motion,*
And it hath my consent, because my wife, is sore infected and hart sick with hate: & I have sought the Galē of advice, which

onely tells me this same potion, to be most soveraigne for her
sicknes cure.

PORTER, *Two Angry Women,* II

It appears that at least one of the poets had a nodding acquaintance with the works of Galen. In James Shirley's *The*
Wittie Faire One one of the characters is sick, and Manly,
disguised as a physician, is attending him. The pretended doctor
is descanting upon his patient's illness: "For I observed so soone
as his searching eye had fastned on her, his labouring pulse that
through his feavor did, before sticke hard and frequent now
exceeds in both these differences and this *Gallen* himselfe found
true upon a woman, that had doted uppon a fencer" (III).

This scene represents the ancient literary device of a lover
feigning illness while a confederate plays the doctor. The coy or
unwilling inamorata never penetrates the stratagem or the disguise, or perhaps she merely pretends not to. The physician has
thus played the pander in many a seventeenth-century romance.

Galen's case, to which the pretended doctor refers, illustrates
the ingenuity and penetration of the first-rate physician. Galen,
as he tells us in his book *On Prognosis,* had been called in "to see
a woman who was stated to be sleepless at night and to lie
tossing about from one position into another. . . ."

> After I had diagnosed that there was no bodily trouble, and that
> the woman was suffering from some mental uneasiness, it hap-
> pened that, at the very time I was examining her, this was
> confirmed. Somebody came from the theater and said he had
> seen Pylades dancing. Then both her expression and the colour
> of her face changed. Seeing this, I applied my hand to her wrist,
> and noticed that her pulse had suddenly become extremely irreg-
> ular. This kind of pulse indicates that the mind is disturbed; thus
> it occurs also in people who are disputing over any subject. So on
> the next day I said to one of my followers, that, when I paid my
> visit to the woman, he was to come a little later and announce to
> me, "Morphus is dancing today." When he said this, I found the
> pulse was unaffected. Similarly on the next day, when I had an
> announcement made about the third member of the troupe, the
> pulse remained unchanged as before. On the fourth evening I

kept very careful watch when it was announced that Pylades was dancing, and I noticed that the pulse was very much disturbed. Thus I found out that the woman was in love with Pylades, and by careful watch on the succeeding days my discovery was confirmed.[5]

Modern physicians will approve of Galen's "control observations." And psychiatrists can claim the now helpless master as one of the first luminaries of their art.

Until the Renaissance Galen remained the dictator of medicine, and no physician dared oppose even the memory of this autocrat of the healing art. As late as 1559 in England a certain Dr. Gaynes was haled before the College of Physicians for impugning the infallibility of Galen, and only upon acknowledgment of error and humble recantation was he readmitted to standing.[6] Nevertheless, thirty years before Dr. Gaynes's heterodoxy, a Swiss megalomaniac was vociferously and pugnaciously engaged in sawing planks for Galen's coffin and forging nails with which his followers were to fasten them together. His name was Theophrastus Bombastus von Hohenheim, called Paracelsus by history, quacksalver by his enemies, and messiah by his disciples and friends.

Modern commentators have succeeded in deciphering enough of Paracelsus' polyphonic German to secure him a high place in the annals of medicine and chemistry. We are not here, however, particularly concerned with his position in science, but rather with his standing among the seventeenth-century dramatists. To them Paracelsus was the arch opponent of Galen, and "Paracelsian" the antonym of "Galenical." Again Ben Jonson speaks for the century's attitude:

MAMMON. No, h'is a rare physitian, doe him right.
    An excellent Paracelsian! and has done
    Strange cures with minerall physicke. He deales all
    With spirits, he. He will not heare a word
    Of Galen, or his tedious recipe's.

                                   Alchemist, II, 3

[5] Brock, *Greek Medicine*, p. 213.
[6] J. M. Stillman, *Paracelsus* (Chicago, 1920), p. 66.

It followed that the disciples of the two men formed sharply antagonistic schools, until the eighteenth-century theorists and system-makers substituted their own ephemeral brain-children for those of the infinitely greater Pergamene and Swiss. In a neat couplet:

> The Gallenist and Paracelsian,
> Condemn the way, each other deals in.
>
> BUTLER, *Hudibras*, Pt. III, Canto 3

This is nowhere more clearly evident than in the conversation of three learned doctors who are wondering whether to permit a disciple of Paracelsus to consult with them:

1 DOCTOR. *Why I, for if he be a chymist, his opinion and ours must needs differ, and consequently not agree in consultation.*

2 DOCTOR. *I am, sir, of your opinion, for I think it* infra dignitatem *to hold consultation with mountebanks.*

3 DOCTOR. *We know not yet, sir, what the man is.*

1 DOCTOR. *If he be a chymist, sir, he is* eo nomine, *a declared enemy to the Galenical way, to all truth and learning, and a denyer of principles; and therefore not to be consulted with.*

2 DOCTOR. *Right, sir;* contra principia negantem non est disputandum; *he that replies but with submission to* sic dixit Galenus, *is not to be lookt on as a physician.*

3 DOCTOR. *Pardon me gentlemen, I have known some chymical physicians learned and rational men; and although not strict adherers to the Galenical method, proceed with great reason, and good success, which, I take it, answers all we can say or do.*

2 DOCTOR. *I profess I think it as bad as murder to cure out of the methodical way. Oh what satisfaction 'tis to have a patient dye according to all the rules of art!*

> LACY, *Dumb Lady*, V

Nevertheless, in spite of the opposition of the traditional physicians, the public held the abilities of each in equally high esteem:

SENILIS. Nor Galenist, nor Paracelsian
> *Shall ere read Physick lecture out of me:*
> *I'le be no subject for Anatomie.*

PHARMACOPOLIS. *They are two good artists, sir.*
SENILIS. *All that I know:*
　What the Creator did, they in part do:
　A true Physitian's a man-maker too.
　　　　　　　DAY, *Parliament of Bees,* Character ix [7]

Though Paracelsus was not the originator of all chemical remedies (minerall physicke), he invented many and popularized still more. He introduced into the pharmacopoeia mercury, lead, sulphur, iron, arsenic, copper sulphate, and potassium sulphate and did his best to expunge from that list empirical mixtures containing two score animal and vegetable ingredients. He was not, however, altogether consistent in his purging. He was responsible for "Zebethum occidentale," a concoction of dung, and for a weapon ointment consisting of moss from a human skull, human fat and blood, mummy, oil of roses, bole armeniac, and linseed oil, which was the precursor of Digby's Powder of Sympathy.[8] But, in spite of these occasional defections, Paracelsus bent his indomitable will, courage, and vocabulary to the task of reforming therapeutics. Such reform, however, is not achieved simply by admitting one class of remedies and expunging another. A remedy is any substance which will maintain or restore health, whether animal, vegetable, or mineral in nature. It is fortunate, therefore, that not all Galenicals were swept away by Paracelsus' impatient hand, to be enthusiastically replaced by

---

[7] Compare Day's later contribution to Dekker's *The Wonder of a Kingdome:*
　Jacomo Gentili. . . .
　　Nor Galenist nor Paracelsian,
　　Shall ere reade phisicall lecture upon me.
　Apothecary. Two excellent fellowes my lord.
　Gentleman. I honour their profession,
　　What the Creator does, they in part doe,
　　For a phisician's a man-maker too. . . .
　　　　　　　　　　　　　　　　　　(IV)

[8] It was to this salve that the great Bacon gave his seal of approval: "It is constantly received, and avouched, that the *anointing* of the *weapon,* that maketh the *wound,* wil heale the *wound* it selfe. . . . And thus much hath been tried, that the *ointment* (for *experiments* sake) hath been wiped off the *weapon,* without the knowledge of the *party hurt,* and presently the *party hurt,* hath been in great *rage of paine,* till the *weapon* was *reanointed*" (*Sylva Sylvarum* [6th ed.; London, 1651], p. 217).

mineral spirits of perhaps as doubtful therapeutic value. Paracelsus' greatest contribution lay in affirming that several hundred years of traditional use were in themselves powerless to lend efficacy to a worthless drug, and that the patient, not the pharmacopoeia, was the only valid court of appeal.

A recent medical dictionary defines "Galenicals" as: "medicines prepared according to the formulas of Galen. The term is now used to denote standard preparations containing one or several organic ingredients, as contrasted with pure chemical substances." In justice to Paracelsus, these pure chemical substances should be called "Paracelsicals," for it was he who first turned chemistry uncompromisingly to the service of medicine —a detour very distasteful to those seventeenth-century alchemical adepts who, like Aubrey's friend Mr. Lloyd, considered the search for the philosopher's stone a higher and holier purpose: "Meredith Lloyd tells me that, three or 400 yeares ago chymistry was in a greater perfection, much, then now; their process was then more seraphique and universall: now they looke only after medicines" (*Brief Lives*, I, 243).

Paracelsus felt differently. He wrote in his *Fragmenta medica*: "Many have said of alchemy that it is for making gold and silver. But here such is not the aim, but to consider only what virtue and power may lie in medicines. . . ." [9] And again in the *Paragranum*: "The purpose is to make arcana and direct them against diseases." By "arcana" Paracelsus meant the vital essence of a medicine, its curative power. When Ben Jonson wrote, "He deales all/With spirits," he was thinking of the arcana.

Thus, at one stroke, Paracelsus antagonized both the alchemists and the doctors. He alienated the alchemists, whose sole aim was the production of the philosopher's stone with which transmutation might be effected and immortality achieved. At the same time the traditional physicians (of whom Dr. Sangrado was one) regarded Paracelsus and his disciples as "medical baboons . . . dipping their paws into chemistry." The Hippocrates of Vallodalid was no more bitter against the iatrochemists than were his flesh-and-blood colleagues. Wailed old Sangrado:

[9] Stillman, *Paracelsus*, p. 102.

Why, sir, there are fellows in this town, calling themselves physicians, who drag their degraded persons at the *currus triumphalis antimonii*, or as it should properly be translated, the cart's tail of antimony. Apostates from the faith of Paracelsus, idolaters of filthy kermes, healers at haphazard, who make all the science of medicine to consist in the preparation and prescription of drugs.

Le Sage, Gil Blas, Bk. X, Ch. 1

Nowadays we are plagued with another sort of animal, with "chemical baboons dipping their paws into medicine." And Dr. Sangrado's eloquence is not too splenetic to describe these scientists to whom the body is merely a glorified test-tube into which they incontinently inject a dose of every new miracle drug; these apostates from the faith of Hippocrates forget that the body is neither a living anatomy, a physiological model, nor a chemical laboratory, but a sick and suffering patient. They too are healers at haphazard, inverting their patients into laboratory animals and exalting a novel experiment above a cure.

Not content with purging the pharmacopoeia, Paracelsus attacked the Faculty on a wider medical front. He insisted on the study of patients rather than books, lectured in German instead of the traditional Latin, and contemptuously threw the revered *Canon* of Avicenna (that epitome of Galenism) into a students' bonfire. The respectable physicians of Basel, in which university Paracelsus was professor of medicine, were appalled and barely restrained themselves from hiring an assassin to rid the world of this Luther of physicians. But they contented themselves with tacking scurrilous Latin verses to the university doors, and waited for the celebrated case of Canon Lichtenfels to free the city of its shame.

Canon Lichtenfels was a prominent and wealthy citizen of Basel who was obstinately ill. He offered a hundred gulden for his cure, and Paracelsus succeeded where his enemies the Galenists failed. He demanded his fee, but once relieved of his pain, the canon came quickly to his thrifty senses and offered Paracelsus six gulden and a written testimonial. The physician refused, then sued for the full amount, lost his case in the courts, and expressed his opinion of the judges in such terms that he was forced to flee from the outraged law.

Had Paracelsus paid more attention to his books and less to his patients, he might have remembered the advice of sage old Isaac Judaeus in his *Guide to Physicians:* "Demand thy fee of the patient when his illness is increasing or at its height; when he is healed he forgets what thou hast done for him."[10] Not that it was necessary to go all the way back to the tenth century to find wisdom: Paracelsus' own contemporary, Euricius Cordus, had this to say:

> *Three faces wears the doctor: when first sought,*
> *An angel's—and a God's, the cure half-wrought;*
> *But, when that cure complete, he seeks his fee,*
> *The Devil looks then less terrible than he.*

The trial took place in 1528. Paracelsus then roamed over Europe until the day of his death (said to have occurred, like Marlowe's, in a tavern brawl), squabbling, writing, curing, and drinking with Protestant fervor and megalomaniac zeal.

> *I am Theophrastus and greater than those to whom you liken me. I am Theophrastus, and am moreover Monarch of Physicians. . . .*
> *The stars did not make me a physician—God made me; it is not for the stars to make physicians, that is a work of God, not of the stars. I may well rejoice that rascals are my enemies—for the truth has no enemies but liars. . . . Could I protect my bald head from the flies as easily as I can my monarchy, and were Milan as safe from its enemies as I from you, neither Swiss nor foot-soldiers could gain entrance.*
>
> Paragranum, Preface [11]

By 1600 Paracelsus was a legend.[12] The events of his turbulent

---

[10] Neuberger, *History of Medicine,* I, 366.

[11] Stillman, *Paracelsus,* p. 74.

[12] The legend of Paracelsus is still current among the mystics and alchemists of the present day. F. Hartmann, M.D., writes: "An old tradition says—and those who are supposed to know confirm the tale—that his [Paracelsus'] astral body having already during physical existence become self-conscious and independent of the physical form, he is now a living adept, residing with other adepts of the same

life needed no embroidery to lend them popular appeal. His reputation as a healer, measured by the number of people he actually cured, was immense; it was natural for the dramatists to bracket the greatest physician of antiquity with the greatest physician of the Renaissance.

In *The Tragicall Historye of Doctor Faustus*, first produced in 1588, Paracelsus may even have appeared on the stage. Faustus welcomes "Germaine Valdes and Cornelius [Agrippa]." Literary authorities have advanced the suggestion that by "Valdes" Paracelsus was meant, and a medical historian has suggested that Faustus himself is in part a depiction of Paracelsus. There is no confusion, however, in later plays, for although Paracelsus never again actually treads the boards, he furnished the writers with a contrapuntal theme. Here is the sort of melody they composed:

CRASY [like a physitian]. *My name is Pulse-feel: A poor doctor of physick, that weares three-pile velvet in his cap; has paid a quarters rent of his house afore-hand; and as meanly as he stands here was made doctor beyond the seas. I vow (as I am right worshipfull) the taking of my degree cost me twelve French crowns, and five and thirty pounds of salt butter in upper Germany. I can make your beauty, and preserve it; rectifie your body, and maintain it; perfume your skin; tinct your haire; enliven your eye; heighten your appetite: as for gellies, dentrifices, diets, minerall fucusses, pomatums, fumes, Italian masks to sleep in, either to moysten, or dry the superficies of your face; paugh, Gallen was a goose, and Paracelsus a patch to Doctor Pulse-feel.*
                                               BROME, *City Wit*, II, 2

But it was when the plague raged that the poets called most loudly for Galen and Paracelsus, only to reproach them in the next breath for their inability to stem the pestilence:

Galen mught goe shooe the gander for any good he could doe, his secretaries had so long called him divine, that now he had lost al his vertue upon earth. Hippocrates might well helpe alma-

order in a certain place in Asia, from whence he still—invisibly, but nevertheless effectually—influences the minds of his followers, appearing to them occasionally even in visible and tangible shape" (*The Life of . . . Paracelsus* [2nd ed.; London, 1887], pp. 9–10).

*nacke-makers, but here he had not a word to say: a man might
sooner catch the sweate with plodding over him to no end, than
cure the sweate with anie of his impotent principles. Paracelsus
with his spirite of the butterie and his spirites of mineralls, could
not so much as saye, God amend him to the matter.*

NASHE, Unfortunate Traveller, p. 27

*Never let any man aske me what became of our phisitians in
this massacre, they hid their synodicall heads as well as the
proudest; and I cannot blame them, for their phlebotomies,
losenges, and electuraries, with their diacatholicons, diacodions,
amulets, and antidotes, had not so much strength to hold life and
soule together, as a pot of Pinders ale and a nutmeg: their drugs
turned to durt, their simples were simple things: Galen could do
no more good than Sir Giles Goosecap: Hipocrates, Avicen,
Paracelsus, Rasis, Fernelius, with all their succeeding rabble of
doctors and water-casters, were at their wits end, or I thinke
rather at the worlds end, for not one of them durst peepe abroad;
or if any one did take upon him to play the ventrous knight, the
plague put him to his nonplus: in such strange, and such change-
able shapes did this camelion-like sicknes appeare, that they
could not (with all the cunning in their budgets) make pursenets
to take him napping.*

DEKKER, Plague Pamphlets, pp. 36–37

It was popularly believed that Paracelsus' skill owed something to supernatural aid, and this not by the powers of good.
The Galenists even went so far as to intimate that Paracelsus
was a devil himself. They would have agreed with the exorcist
who, demanding the name of the devil in possession of a lady, is
answered by the fiend:

*Monsieur Devile: Don, or Signior Diavolo:
Mine Here Tifle: Herenagh mac Deul; or Sir
Duncan, in the Devil's name.*

To which the caster-out of devils cries:

*What's here? Philippus, Aureolus, Theophrastus,
Paracelsus, Bombastus of Hoenhayim?*

WILSON, Belphegor, V, 2

as if a legion of devils were in Paracelsus' very name.

But most people would not have gone that far; tradition said only that

> Bumbastus, *kept a devil's bird*
> *Shut in the pummel of his sword,*
> *That taught him all the cunning pranks,*
> *Of past, and future mountebanks.*[13]
>
> Butler, Hudibras, Pt. II, Canto 3

This weapon of Paracelsus was famous for a hundred years after his death. The zany, Nano, who supports Volpone's masquerade as a quack, sings:

[13] Dr. Mopus in Wilson's *The Cheats* (1664) was a disciple of Paracelsus after the popular tradition. His bill in Act II, scene 2, contains all the tricks of "past, and future mountebanks:"

> In the Name of God, through the light of the Son, by the revelation of the Spirit, I cure these diseases, perfectly, and speedily, without any annoyance to the body, which commonly happens through colledge bills, and apothecaries medicines, with which, the Devil has deceiv'd the world, these many hundreds of years.
>
> The new disease (otherwise called the Great Pox) with all its appendices, in few dayes, with herbs which I gather in the woods, and gums of trees.— Agues of all sorts, in three fits:—gout, whither-knotted, or running, in four or five dressings:—dropsie—timpany—rickets—spleen—convulsion—yellow, and black jaundies—stone—strangury—and chollick, in six hours:—all kinds of fluxes;—most distempers of the head—shortness of breath, and ptisick, at first sight:—And have ever by me a most approv'd remedy, against greensickness—barrenness—and fits of the mother. . . .
>
> As also (to let the world see, how wide of their mark, they are like to run, that as boldly as ignorantly, dare adventure on physick, without the knowledge of astrology) I resolve, these ensuing astrological questions.
>
> The sick, whither they shall recover, or not:—the party absent, whither living, or dead—how many husbands, or children, a woman shall have:— whither one shall marry the party desir'd, or whom else:—whither a woman has her maiden-head or not—or shall be honest after marriage—or her portion well paid:—if a man be wise, or a fool;—whither it be good to put on new cloaths:—if dreams, be for good, or evil;—whither a child be the reputed fathers; or shall be fortunate, or not:—ships at sea, whither safe, or not:—of law-suits, which side shall have the better:—and generally all astrological questions whatever.
>
> Iátros Iátrophilus Mopus,
A Servant of God, and Secretary of Nature

Had old Hippocrates, or Galen,
(That to their bookes put med'cines all in)
But knowne this secret, they had never
(Of which they will be guiltie ever)
Beene murderers of so muche paper,
Or wasted many a hurtlesse taper;
No Indian drug had ere beene famed
Tobacco, sassafras not named;
Ne yet, of guacum one small stick, sir,
Nor Raymund Lullies great elixer.
Ne, had been knowne the Danish Gonswart.
Or Paracelsus, with his long-sword.

JONSON, Volpone, II, 2

And Beaumont and Fletcher in *The Faire Maide of the Inne* speak of a "rare physitian" in this manner:

HOST. Why Ile tell you, were Paracelsus the German now living, hee'd take up his single rapier against his terrible long sword—he makes it a matter of nothing to cure the goute, sore eyes he takes out as familiarly, washes them, and puts them in againe, as you'd blanch almonds.

IV, 2

It is a singularly interesting coincidence that both the doctor and the alchemist in *The Faire Maide of the Inne* were, in the words of their creators, "rare physitians" and Paracelsians. Ben Jonson's alchemist was

MAMMON.   . . . A man, the Emp'rour
Has courted, above Kelley: sent his medalls,
And chaines, t'invite him.

IV, 1

And of the doctor in *The Faire Maide of the Inne*:

TAYLOR. They say he can make gold.
HOST. I, I, he learnt it of Kelly in Germany. There's not a chimist in christendome can goe beyond him for multiplying.

IV, 1

With Edward Kelley we come to a figure very nearly contemporary with the Elizabethan dramatists, for the notorious alchemist did not die until 1595, when Webster and Jonson were both young men. It was only a year after his death, in fact, that Thomas Nashe in *Have with you to Saffron-Walden* compared Kelley with Raymund Lully and Paracelsus, to the detriment of the greater men:

CARNEAD. *Let him call uppon Kelly, who is better than them both; and for the spirites and soules of the ancient alchemists, he hath them so close emprisoned in the firie purgatorie of his furnace, that for the welth of the King of Spaines Indies, it is not possible to release or get the third part of a nit of anie one of them, to helpe anie but himselfe.*

IMPORT. *Whether you call his fire Purgatory or no, the fire of alchumie hath wrought such a purgation or purgatory in a great number of mens purses in England that it hath clean fired them out of al they have.*[14]

Thus Kelley was not to the poets a mere legendary character, as were Galen and even Paracelsus, but an actual personage whose checkered career an Englishman could follow with attentive interest. Kelley was known variously and functioned vicariously as an apothecary, notary, forger, and counterfeiter (for which he had his ears cropped), necromancer, quack, charlatan, crystal-gazer, medium, and transmuter of base metal into gold. In 1583 he left England and was soon established at the court of Rudolph II of Bohemia (the "Emp'rour" of the dramatists), a hotbed, under the aegis of the king, of sixteenth-century alchemy. There is reliable contemporary evidence that Kelley reached the alchemist's goal and achieved projection, for he transmuted part of an iron skillet into silver by means of his elixir and sent the result to Queen Elizabeth.[15] This annoyed

---

[14] In Nashe, *Works*, ed. R. B. McKerrow (London, 1905), III, 52.

[15] T. J. Pettigrew, *Superstitions Connected with the History and Practise of Medicine and Surgery* (Philadelphia, 1844), p. 30.

 Edward Kelley:

  . . . committing certain foul matters, lost both his ears at Lancaster. . . .

  At Trebona, Kelley made projection 9 Dec. 1586, with one small grain of the elixir (in proportion no bigger than the least grain of sand) upon one ounce and a quarter of common mercury, and it produced almost an ounce

Rudolph considerably, and the next time Kelley ventured into Bohemia he was imprisoned, the price of his freedom being the Great Secret. Needless to say, neither protagonist consummated his desire: the Emperor's kitchen utensils remained iron and copper, and Kelley was slain trying to escape.

An alchemist has taken us to the shadowy borders of the medical art, but there is no virtue in listing here the allusions to famous ancients even more tenuously connected with medicine. Plato, Aristotle, Pliny, Ptolemy, Albertus Magnus, Copernicus, Galileo, and other notable names appear here and there in the plays, but none of them has an immediate interest for the commentator, and probably had little more to the average seventeenth-century playgoer.[16]

It will be of interest, however, to mention at this point the *Problems* of Aristotle, a book of medical questions and answers extremely popular with the curious of the day. This little volume is properly catalogued under Pseudo-Aristotle, for the great Peri-

---

of pure gold. [Elias Ashmole in his *Theatrum Chymicum Britannicum* Lond. 1652, qu. p. 481.] At another time he made projection upon a piece of metal cut out of a warming-pan, and without his touching or handling it, or melting the metal (only warming it in the fire,) the elixir being out thereon, it was transmuted to pure gold [silver, first edition]. The same warming-pan and piece were sent to Q. Elizabeth by her ambassador "the lord Willoughby" then residing at Prague, that by fitting the piece, with the place whence it was cut out, it might exactly appear to be a part of the said warming-pan.

"Nov. 25, an. 1595, news that sir E. K. was slain."—Dee's diary.
(Anthony à Wood, *Athenae Oxoniensis*. . . , ed.
P. Bliss [London, 1813], I, cols. 639–643)

[16] Butler's *Hudibras*, for example, is a storehouse of allusions to physicians and astrologers: Agrippa, Part I, Canto 1, line 539; II, 3, 635, 642; Albertus Magnus, II, 1, 438; Averroes, II, 3, 679; Friar Bacon, I, 2, 344; II, 1, 530; II, 3, 224; Jacob Behmen, I, 1, 542; II, 3, 643; Booker (the astrologer), II, 3, 1093; Friar Bongey, III, 3, 742; Tycho Brahe, I, 1, 120; Cardan, II, 3, 895; Copernicus, II, 3, 882; John Dee, II, 3, 235; Erra Pater (a legendary astrologer), I, 1, 120; Fisk (the astrologer), II, 3, 404; Robert Floud, I, 1, 541; Robert Grosseteste, II, 3, 224; Helmont, II, 2, 15; Sarah Jimmers (the astrologer), II, 3, 1093; Kelley, II, 3, 163, 237, 631; Athanasius Kircher, III, 2, 1585; Lilly, II, 3, 1093; Raimund Lully, II, 2, 15; Paracelsus, II, 3, 299, 627, 643; Alexander Ross, I, 2, 2; II, 2, 670; Rudolph II (the emperor), II, 3, 238, 646; Scaliger, II, 3, 881; and Taliacotius, I, 1, 281.

patetic had nothing to do with its composition. The first English edition appeared in 1595 as *The Problemes of Aristotle, with other Philosophers and Phisitions . . . touching the estate of man's body,* and by 1710 "The Twenty Fifth Edition" was published in London.

The questions, of which I shall transcribe a few in a footnote,[17] are largely anatomical and obstetrical, not pornographic. Nevertheless, some of the information, though it could easily be cast in a more titillating form, was not considered fit for virgin eyes. Yet as early as 1602, the *Problems* were furnishing information to the women. Old Nutriche, doing her best to cheer an unwilling bride, chatters:

> *I have had foure husbands my selfe. The first I called, Sweete Duck; the second, Deare Heart; the third, Prettie Pugge: but the fourth, most sweete, deare, prettie, all in all: he was the very cockcall of a husband. What, ladie? your skinne is smooth, your bloode warme, your cheeke fresh, your eye quick: change of pasture makes fat calves: choice of linnen, cleane bodies; and (no question) variety of husbands perfect wives. I would you should knowe it, as fewe teeth as I have in my heade, I have red Aristotle's Problemes, which saith: that women receiveth perfection by the man.*
>
> MARSTON, *Antonios Revenge,* Pt. II, III, 4

A few years later Viola complains: "I protest to thee *Fustigo,* I love him most affectionately; but I know not—I ha such a

---

[17]"Why have some women greater grief than others in child-birth?" "For three reasons; first, for the largeness of the child; secondly, the midwife being unskillful; and, thirdly, because the child is dead, and cannot be bowed. For the contrary causes some have less pain."

"Why is immoderate carnal copulation hurtful?" "Because it destroys the sight, drys the body, and impairs the brain; often causes fevers, as Avicen and experience show; it shortens life too, as is evident in the sparrow, which, by reason of its often coupling, lives but three years."

"How comes the imagination of the mother to bring forth a blackamoor, as Albertus Magnus reports of a queen, who, in the act of carnal copulation, imagined a black being printed, and in her sight?" "Avicen says the imagination of a fall makes a man fall, and the imagination of a leprosy makes a man a leper. So in this the imagination is above the forming power, and therefore the child born followeth the imagination, and not the power of forming and shaping, because it is weakest."

tickling within mee—such a strange longing; nay, verily I doe long." To which Fustigo answers: "Then y'are with childe sister, by all signes and tokens; nay, I am partly a physitian, and partly something else. I ha read *Albertus Magnus*,[18] and *Aristotles Emblemes*" (Dekker, *Honest Whore*, Pt. I, I).

There was no objection to hardened old nurses' or experienced young men's reading Aristotle, but the dramatists objected to unmarried girls' dipping too early into unseasonable knowledge. Alderman Wiseacres thus deplored the state of the times in 1682: "Girls now at sixteen are as knowing as matrons were formerly at sixty. I tell you in these days they understand *Aristotle's* Problems at twelve years of age." Old Doodle nods a resigned amen: " 'Tis true indeed; nothing in the nature of man or woman is a secret to them." (Ravenscroft, *London Cuckolds*, I).

It seems, indeed, that the dramatists objected as much to feminine dipping into Aristotle as into the aqua-vitae bottle. Sir Geoffrey Jolt cries: "What's here, a study? *Aristotles Problems*, excellent; and here's *Leschole de Filles*,[19] a pretty French book; and here *Annotations upon Aretines Postures*, three excellent books for a ladies chamber" (Leanerd, *Rambling Justice*, IV, 6).

And for a man's chamber, too. Lady Dunce in Otway's *The*

[18] *De secretis mulierum* [*The Secrets of Women*] was an extremely popular book attributed to Albertus Magnus. Many editions appeared before 1500 (the earliest English imprint was by William de Machlinia: London, 1485?), and the book was placed on the *Index Expurgatorius*, either because it was too popular or because its title was too suggestive. It treats of astrological influences, cosmetics, generation, fetuses, birth, miscarriage, etc., leaving little to the imagination of the reader. The earliest edition in English (British Museum Catalogue) is *De Secretis Mulierum: or, the Mysteries of Human Generation fully revealed . . .* Faithfully rendered into English [*sic*] with explanatory notes . . . by . . . John Quincy. E. Curll: London, 1725.

[19] Pepys records in his *Diary* for Jan. 13, 1667/68, having "stopped at Martin's, my bookseller, where I saw the French book which I did think to have had for my wife to translate, called 'Lescholle des filles' [by Helot, which was burnt at the foot of the gallows in 1672, and the author himself burnt in effigy], but when I came to look in it, it is the most bawdy, lewd book that ever I saw, rather worse than 'Putana errante' [by Aretine], so that I was ashamed of reading in it, and so away home. . . ."

Souldiers Fortune says to Sir Jolly Jumble, "Really, Sir Jolly, you are more a philosopher than I thought you were." "Philosopher, madam!" returns the knightly old procurer, "Yes, madam, I have read books in my time: odd, Aristotle, in some things, had very pretty notions; he was an understanding fellow" (V).

Now comes one of those minor confusions the elucidation of which is so dear to a commentator's heart (and which takes up more space than the whole business is worth). A bookseller's boy in Act III of *The Plain Dealer* asks the Widow Blackacre: "Will you see *Culpepper*, Mistress? *Aristotle's Problems? The Compleat Midwife?*" According to Wycherley's own statement made in his old age, this play was written when he was twenty-five years old, that is, in 1665/66. It was not staged, however, before 1672, nor printed until 1677. Now, a book entitled *The Compleat Midwife's Companion* by one "Jane Sharp" was published in London in 1671. One is therefore driven to conclude that Wycherley's senile memory had been playing him tricks, and that *The Plain Dealer* containing the above allusion could not have been written before 1671, when the author had reached the advanced age of thirty-one. This conclusion has already been reached by other critics from a consideration of similar anachronisms in the text, but I am glad of this corroborative opportunity to demonstrate that medical historians sometimes perform useful tasks.

This "Culpepper" Wycherley mentions was old Nicholas Culpeper (1616–1654), another engaging if not altogether respectable character. Like all men who arouse extraordinary interest or antagonism, Nicholas was something of a quack. He fell into disrepute in 1649 by translating (very filthily, it was said) the *Pharmacopoeia Londinensis* into English with inappropriately scurrilous comments regarding the medical profession. This scandalous act led to his characterization as a "frowzy-headed coxcomb" who

> by two years drunken labour hath gallimawfred the apothecaries'
> book into nonsense mixing every receipt therein with some sam-
> ples, at least, of rebellion or atheisme, besides the danger of
> poysoning men's bodies. And (to supply his drunkenness and

leachery with a thirty-shillings reward), endeavoured to bring into obloquy the famous societies of apothecaries and chyrurgions.[20]

He also wrote *The English Physician* in 1653 (very likely the *Culpepper* the bookseller's boy had in mind), a very popular book which took several slices of bread from the mouths of the licensed practitioners, although the author himself probably realized only another guinea or two. It was the publisher, of course, who made the money, for *The English Physician* entered many a home which poverty or prejudice barred to the English physicians. The esteem in which such books of household medicine were held must have been an added insult to the dignity of the profession.

> *Now comes the sage matron Experience, saying that she hath learnt a secret from a prudent doctor that's worth its weight in gold, nor can the vertue thereof be too much commended. And she hath already communicated it unto several persons; but there are none that tried it that do not praise it to be incomparable: therefore she hath been very vigilant to note it down in S. John Pain, and Nic-Culpeppers works; to the end that her posterity may not only make use of it, but participate it to others: This is, lapis calaminaris prepared, mingled with a small quantity of May-butter, and then temper them together with the point of a knife upon an earthen plate, just as the picture drawers do their colours upon their pallet, which will bring it to be a delicate salve: and it is also very soft and supple for the chops of the tipples; nay, though the child should suck it in, yet it doth no harm; and it doth not alone cure them, but prevents the coming of any more.*
>
> APHRA BEHN, *Ten Pleasures of Marriage*, p. 91

The reader has undoubtedly remarked by this time that all the great men of science immortalized in the plays had been dead for varying lengths of time before their appearance on the stage. Even Culpeper the quack had succumbed before his fame bridged the gap between the bookseller and the boards. In only very few cases of which I am aware were contemporary practi-

---

[20] B. Chance, "Nicholas Culpeper, Gent: Student in Physick and Astrologie," *Annals of Medical History*, n.s. III (1931), 394.

tioners of the medical art alive to hear their names spoken in a play, and the remarkable fact is that two of them were members of the famous Chamberlen family.

The Doctors Chamberlen were descendants of a Huguenot refugee, and practiced surgery and midwifery in England from 1569 to 1728. Peter the elder (died 1631), a son of the founder of the English branch, was believed to have been the inventor of the obstetrical forceps. He was the first of the family to serve at court; in 1614 he was awarded forty pounds for his services to the Queen, and in 1628:

> The Queen, Henrietta Maria, miscarried her first child. She had neither midwife nor surgeon about her, only the poor town midwife of Greenwich was sent for who swooned with fear as soon as she was brought into the Queen's chamber so as she was forced presently to be carried out; and Chamberlayne the surgeon was he alone that did the part of a midwife.[21]

Dr. Peter Chamberlen (1601–1683), nephew of Peter the elder and the first of the family to have academic degrees (from Padua, Oxford, and Cambridge), was appointed to attend the ladies of the court in 1647, "that with greater secrecy and ease their ladyships may be help and with their most troublesome and pressing affairs." [22] But apparently there was little secrecy involved, for Dr. Peter's duties were a byword about the town. In attestation, we find John Tatham writing in *The Rump; or, The Mirrour of the Late Times*, produced in June, 1660:

BERTLAM. . . . *the city's big with riches, and neer her time I hope to be delivered.*
HUSON. *Ile be the midwife, or what you will call me. Ile undertake to do my office as well as Dr. Chamberlen can do his.*

III

Forty-three years after Huson's obstetrical metaphor a character in Farquhar's *The Twin-Rivals* refers to Clelia, who discovers herself with child, in these significant words:

[21] *Quoted by E. M. Jameson, Gynecology and Obstetrics* (New York, 1936), p. 70.
[22] Quoted in *ibid.*, p. 73.

RICHMORE. . . . *Do's the silly creature imagine that any man would*
come near her in those circumstances, unless it were Doctor
Chamberlain—

I

Now, at the time Clelia found herself in this delicate condition, Dr. Hugh (1664–1728) was the reigning Chamberlen. By
1703, when Farquhar's play was produced, he had long been
engaged in helping London babies into the world with the aid of
the family "instrument of iron." Indeed, on April 17, 1692: "Dr.
Chamberlain had the honor to lay the princesse [Anne of Den-
mark, afterwards Queen Anne] of a son who immediately dyed.
He had a hundred guineas for his pains." [23] Dr. Chamberlen
cannot be blamed for the unfortunate outcome of his labor.
Anne had given birth to a daughter in October, 1690, and this
child too died soon after it was born. The Princess followed this
up with miscarriages in February, 1696; December, 1697; September, 1698; and January, 1700. The politicians blamed the
physicians and smelled out a plot to subject the Princess, will-
fully and treacherously, to a wrong course of treatment in order
that she might not be delivered of a living heir, thus giving
additional strength to the claims of the Pretender.[24]

The physician who attends royalty receives a measure of fame
whether his patient lives or dies (and sometimes more of it in
the latter case). There is no doubt that Farquhar's allusion was
immediately understood and heartily appreciated by the wits
and blushing ladies in the audience. One wonders what poor
Queen Anne, had she deigned to honor the production with her
presence, would have thought.

In the seventeenth century the midwives had almost a monopoly of the parturient trade. Male midwives or obstetricians were
rare exceptions, faintly comic and rather immoral.[25] A contempo-

---

[23] Quoted in *ibid.*, p. 80.
[24] J. R. Clemens, "Notes on English Medicine (Henry VIII–George IV),"
Annals of Medical History, n.s. III (1931), 312.
[25] Nevertheless, as shown by Peter Chamberlen's experience with Queen Hen-
rietta Maria, and Master Peepin's with the poor woman who had been misman-
aged by a midwife, the man midwife was the ultimate court of obstetrical appeal.
"Doe not you know mistresse, what serjeants are?" asks Dekker in *The Whore of*

rary opinion of such a doctor is found in *The Ten Pleasures of Marriage:*

> *In our parish there is a married woman brought to bed, but she was so miserably handled by the midwife, that no tongue can express it. Insomuch that Master Peepin the man midwife, was fain to be fetcht, to assist with his instrument; it was a very great wonder that the woman ever escaped it; and too sad indeed to be placed by me among the pleasures of marriage.*
>
> p. 102

It is an obvious assumption to identify Master Peepin and his instrument with Dr. Hugh Chamberlen and his obstetrical forceps.

In all this there is an interesting sidelight on comparative immorality. Until rather recently, we considered the seventeenth-century playwrights among the most amoral and immoral creatures who ever wielded pens, and it was usually the custom for the timid nineteenth-century scholar to introduce a volume of Restoration plays with some sentence such as this: "Yet I venture to assert that, in spite of their licentiousness, these comedies possess claims to recognition not lightly to be ignored." The plays were Wycherley's, but the author of the critical line might have been any one of a dozen thin-shanked pedants, and I forebear to particularize here. Turning the leaves of this volume at random, one comes across this choice bit of smut from Lady Fidget's lascivious lips: "I thought his very name obscenity; and I would as soon have lain with him as have named him." I do not have to point out wherein Wycherley's "immorality" lies. But Wycherley and Lady Fidget would have been fully as shocked to learn that a male midwife, and whole classes of medical students as well, routinely grope the pudenda of the twentieth-century fair sex.

A living quack was mentioned in Shadwell's *The Sullen Lovers*, produced in 1668. Emilia scornfully tells a fatuous drama-

---

Babylon, ". . . why they are certaine men-midwives, that never bring people to bed, but "when they are sore in labour, that nobody els can deliver them" (*Dramatic Works* [London, 1873], II, 213).

tist: "And your playes are below the dignity of a mountebanks
stage. Salvator Winter would have refus'd them" (III). Salvator Winter was a Neapolitan quack who operated near Covent
Garden and sold a remarkable compound called Elixir Vitae,
good for anything from catarrh to consumption and the French
pox.[26] It contained sixty-two ingredients, one correcting the
other. Apparently Salvator purveyed other remedies also, for in a
discussion about sore nipples Mistress Know-all says "that she
hath tried above an hundred other things, that were approved to
be good; yet of all things never found nothing under the sun that
were more noble than Salvator Winter's salve, for that cures
immediately: And you can have nothing better" (Aphra Behn,
Ten Pleasures of Marriage, p. 91).

A famous astrologer of the time was William Lilly (1602–
1681), probably satirized as "Sidrophel" in Butler's *Hudibras*,
Part II, Canto 3, and again in *An Heroical Epistle of Hudibras
to Sidrophel*.[27] A reading of these lines is heartily recommended
to those individuals who desire to be entertained by the lam-
pooning of folly and vice. For a more favorable estimate of Lilly
(and, despite Butler's prejudice, a less accurate one), we may
turn to Pepys: "Mr. Booker . . . did tell me a great many
fooleries, which may be done by nativities, and blaming Mr.
Lilly for writing to please his friends and to keep in with the
times (as he formerly did to his own dishonor), and not according to the rules of art, by which he could not well err, as he had
done" (*Diary*, October 23, 1660).

As Pepys implies, during the Protectorate Lilly backed the
wrong horses on several occasions (although he did predict the
defeat of Charles I at Naseby), and after the Restoration he was

---

[26] C. J. S. Thompson, *The Quacks of Old London* (Philadelphia, 1929), p. 94.
[27] Under "Unknown Authors" Langbaine lists a play called *"Levellers levelled,
or The Independents Conspiracy to root out Monarchy;* an Interlude written by
Mercurius Pragmaticus; printed quarto 1647. Who this author is, under this
disguise, I know not: but 'tis easy to discover him a Royalist, by his Dedication to
King Charles the Second; and an enemy to Lilly, the almanack-maker, whom he
lashes under the name of Orlotto" (*An Account of the English Dramatick Poets*
[Oxford, 1691], p. 538).

forced to swallow his prognostications. With that his reputation dwindled, and as far as the dramatists—Royalists almost all—were concerned, vanished completely. No sooner had General Monk overthrown the Rump Parliament than John Tatham dragged Lilly on the stage in person and confronted him with a mass of exploded prophecies. In the fourth act of *The Rump*, produced in June, 1660, a servant ushers Master Lilly onto the stage:

SERVANT. *Here's Master Lilly, an't please your Highness.*

LADY BERTLAM [i.e., Lambert]. *How now, Lilly, hast thou don what I commanded thee?*

LILLY. *I have examined the zodiac, searcht the 12 houses, and by my powerful art, put the whole regiment of gods and goddesses out of order, Saturn and Jupiter are by the ears, and Venus will be rampant, assisted by Mars, the god of battailes. . . .*

LADY BERTLAM. *How stands my husbands fortune?*

LILLY. *In the alnathy of Aries, or as some others have it salhaym being the head of Aries.*

LADY BERTLAM. *Aries, what is that Aries?*

LILLY. *'Tis a signe, and signifies a ram.*

LADY BERTLAM. *You rascal, do you put the horns upon my princely husband. . . .*

LILLY. *He's subtle, politick, and crafty.*

LADY BERTLAM. *Thou hitst pretty well there.*

LILLY. *Then in the allothanie, or as some have it, alhurto, being the tail of Aries, I find him eloquent, prodigal in neccesity proud, inconstant, and deceitful.*

LADY BERTLAM. *Dost thou abuse me, rascal?*

LILLY. *No such matter. . . . He's there denoted to be fortunate in warfare.*

LADY BERTLAM. *Go on, fellow.*

LILLY. *In adoldaya, being the head of Taurus.*

LADY BERTLAM. *Taurus, What's that?*

LILLY. *A bull.*

LADY BERTLAM. *Darst thou horn him again?*

LILLY. *'Tis a signe. . . . Had your lord a mark or mold upon his members? If he had, he vanquishes his enemies.*

LADY BERTLAM. *He has that, Pris, I'm sure on't.*

PRISSILA. *You are best acquainted with his secrets.*
LILLY. *For Mars being with the moon in the Sextile Aspect, incour-*
     ages men of war, and in the Trine promises success.
LADY BERTLAM. *Ile love that Trine while I live for't.*
PRISSILA. *I wonder where the fellow got all these hard words.*
LILLY. *Lose not an inch of your state, lest you diminish the lustre of*
     that planet predominates.

                                             [She struts it.]

LADY BERTLAM. *Why sirrah, you grow saucy. Pris, let the foot-boy pay*
     the fellow for his pains.
LILLY. *I hope she does not mean to pay me with kicks. Is she angry?*
PRISSILA. *No no, you have only put her in mind of her majesty, she*
     loves you ne're the worse for't; you must flatter her.
LILLY. *I have been bred to't. I take my leave of your Highness. . . .*
LADY BERTLAM. *Well, go thy ways, and if thy judgment falter,*
     To second thy gold chain expect a halter.

                                             [Exit LILLY.]

There is a Parthian shot in the last act, when Bertlam's [Lam-
bert's] downfall abruptly dissipates his wife's dreams of grandeur. The overjoyed populace is milling around in the streets,
and a prentice calls out, "Where is Lilly now?" "In one of the
twelve houses," jeers another.

A few years later Dryden, in spite of his own predilection for
astrology, took up the delightful task of what Jonson in the third
act of *The Staple of Newes* had called "drawing farts out of dead
bodies." In the Epilogue to *Sir Martin Mar-all* (1668) Dryden
wrote:

> *Thus, gallants, we like Lilly can foresee,*
> *But if you ask us what our doom will be,*
> *We by to morrow will our fortune cast,*
> *As he tells all things when the year is past.*

He continued his animadversions in his next play, *An Evening's
Love, or The Mock-Astrologer* (1664 to 1671), in which Bellamy's masquerade as a stargazer gave him a further opportunity
to ridicule Lilly's methods. Wildblood is coaching Bellamy how
to act: "And if at any time thou ventur'st at particulars, have an
evasion ready like Lilly: as thus, it will infallibly happen if our

sins hinder not. I would undertake, with one of his almanacks to give very good content to all Christendom, and what good luck fell not out in one kingdom, should in another" (II).

When Dryden left off there was Duffett to begin afresh. His *Psyche Debauch'd* (1674 to 1678), a clever and amusing burlesque of Shadwell's *Psyche*, contains an elaborate parody of the oracle scene in Shadwell's play. After a dance, the Invocation runs:

2 PRIEST. Hocus-pocus, Don Quixot, Jack Adams, Mary Ambry, Frier Bungey, William Lilly.
ANSWER. *Help our Opera, because 'tis very silly.*

Poor Lilly died in 1681 and so escaped his tormentors, in body at least. But around December of the same year, Aphra Behn laid a pair of ill-smelling bouquets on his grave. She resurrected *The Rump* under the title of *The Round-heads, or the Good Old Cause*, and in Act V pricked the astrologer's ghost with an unforgiving pen:

GILLIFLOWER. *Call up your courage, madam, do not let these things scoff you—you may be yet a queen: Remember what Lilly told you, madam.*
LADY LAMBERT. *Damn Lilly, who with lying prophecies has rais'd me to the hopes of majesty: a legion of his devils take him for't.*

And when the mob gathers:

CORPORAL RIGHT. *What say you now, lads, is not my prophecy truer than Lilly's? I told you the Rump would fall to our handling and drinking for: the King's proclaimed, rogues.*
CAPTAIN. *Ay, ay, Lilly, a plague on him, he prophesied Lambert should be uppermost.*
CORPORAL. *Yes, he meant perhaps on Westminster Pinacke; where's Lilly now, with all his prophecies against the royal family?*
CAPTAIN. *In one of his Twelve Houses.*

In another of Mrs. Behn's plays, produced in 1682, Wilding mocks the astrologer and one of his own satellites in one breath: "thou art out at elbows; and when I thrive, you show it i' th' pit, behind the scenes, and at coffee-houses. Thy breeches give a better account of my fortune, than Lilly with all his schemes and stars" (*City Heiress*, II, 2).

By 1695, when Congreve wrote his *Love for Love*, Lilly was a legend, and took his place with the famous astrologers of the past:

SCANDAL. *Something has appear'd to your son Valentine—he's gone to bed upon't, and very ill—he speaks little, yet says he has a world to say. Asks for his father and the wise foresight; talks of Raymond Lully, and the ghost of Lilly.* . . .

III

But the apotheosis of the astrologer had taken place even within Lilly's lifetime. "This rogue will invent more stories of me, than e'er were father'd upon Lilly," complained Bellamy in Dryden's *An Evening's Love.*

And so we take leave of Lilly, with the reflection (to paraphrase a pertinent bit of medical satire) that astrology "is the best trade of all; because, whether one prophesies well or prophesies badly, one is always paid the same."

In spite of the numerous allusions to men of science and pseudo-science in the old plays, remarkably few of them referred to persons who were actually living at the time the dramas were produced. Only the doctors Chamberlen, and Salvator Winter and William Lilly, of all the men in this chapter, might have heard their names spoken from the stage.[28] Winter was a simple

---

[28] There was one more: Sir Richard Blackmore, the physician-poet, who, in an inept attempt to raise the moral tone of the literature of the day by publishing incredibly dull epic poems, incurred the contempt of all true wits. Dryden, in his Prologue to Vanbrugh's *The Pilgrim* (1700), scornfully wrote of Blackmore:

Quack Maurus [i.e., Blackmore], tho' he never took degrees
In either of our universities; . . .
At leisure hours, in epique song he deals,
Writes to the rumbling of his coaches wheels,
Prescribes in hast, and seldom kills by rule,
But rides triumphant between stool and stool.
    Well, let him go; 'tis too early day,
To get himself a place in farce or play.
We know not by what means we should arraign him,
For no one category can contain him;

mountebank; Lilly a much more pretentious quack; and the Chamberlens with their secret instruments of iron certainly laid themselves open to the charge of unprofessional conduct verging on downright charlatanism. For the more respectable of the worthies mentioned by the dramatists, a long gap exists between the date of their death and the time of their rebirth in a dramatic allusion.

This lag is one of the most significant features of seventeenth-century references to scientists. Quacks, one concludes, insinuate themselves into popular literature infinitely more rapidly than their more sober and scientific fellows; the reason is not far to seek. A charlatan must have an arresting, and often an engaging, personality to make up for his deficiency of knowledge; while most of our learned scientists, both ancient and modern, seem content to substitute erudition for charm.

John Lyly, for one, remarked on the inept drabness of the scholar:

MELIPPUS. *Well, thoght I, seeing bookish men are so blockish, and so great clarkes such simple courtiers. . . .*[29]

Campaspe, I, 3

One of the "bookish men" admits the truth of the stricture, and indeed amplifies:

MOLUS. *. . . we silly soules are only plodders at Ergo, whose wittes are claspt uppe with our bookes, and so full of larning are we at home, that we scarce know good manners when wee come abroad. Cunning in nothing but in making small things great by figures, pulling on with the sweate of our studies a great shooe upon a little foote, burning out one candle in seeking for an other, raw worldlings in matter of substaunce, passing wranglers about shadowes.*

Sapho and Phao, I, 3

A pedant, canting preacher, and a quack,
Are load enough to break one asses back. . . .

Farquhar's "New Prologue/In Answer to my very Good Friend, Mr. Oldnixon" to *The Constant Couple* (1699) contains another sneer at Doctor "B——re."
    [29] And Sir Francis Bacon for another. See *The Advancement of Learning,* Bk. I, Ch. 3, paragraph 8.

On the other hand, James Atkinson cheerfully admitted that "quackery is so pleasing, so natural, and so recondite a passion, that we may sometimes excuse it," and later he slyly defines a charlatan in medicine as: "A half concocted man; who, by puffing, advertising, false pretences, undue applications for business, impudence and falsehood, attempts unduly to cut the grass under the feet of his colleagues. Have you seen such an one? Yes. What, in your town? Yes. Quacks in all towns." [30]

A touch of quackery still remains the *sine qua non* of ante-mortem notoriety, if not of posthumous fame.[31] Just as the caricaturist seizes on an unusual feature, the satirist pounces on an unconventional attitude or way of life. Dr. Sydenham, "English Hippocrates" though he undoubtedly was, had absolutely no dramatic interest, and the lapse of many years was necessary before he could have a historical one. But Dr. Chamberlen, who manipulated his secret instrument under the cover of an obstetrical sheet and brought forth an infant before the curious eyes of the populace, was the type of man made to order for a dramatic allusion. Thus, if today Sydenham has a page in the history of medicine while Chamberlen has only a phrase, the male midwife at least had his day of dramatic notoriety; and no doubt he is still the more interesting figure to those who prefer the manner to the matter of life.

[30] *Medical Bibliography*, p. 181.

[31] It is a temptation here to list the names of some of our contemporary physicians and scientists whose pontifical words in the daily newspapers and popular magazines demonstrate that there is still quackery in high places. But the reader will be ready, and perhaps eager, to compile his own list. "Quacks in all towns?" Yes; and in all sciences.

6

The Virtuoso

SIR MARTIN. *I am sure, in all companies I pass for a vertuoso.*
MOODY. Vertuoso! *What's that too? is not vertue enough
without O so?*

—DRYDEN, *Sir Martin Mar-all*

ONE DAY SAMUEL PEPYS LIFTED HIS EYES FROM THE BUSY SCENE of London life and love and exclaimed: "But Lord! to see the absurd nature of Englishmen, that cannot forebear laughing and jeering at anything that looks strange" (*Diary,* November 27, 1662). Not very long after Pepys had scribbled that sentiment (which certainly is not peculiar to the Anglo-Saxon) into his diary, his countrymen had a priceless opportunity to prove the diarist's acumen.

In 1662 Charles II chartered the Royal Society, and under the monarch's careless patronage that scientific body displayed a meteoric rise. Among its charter members were bright stars in the firmament of English science—Boyle, Wallis, Wren, Oldenburg, Hooke—, nor has their light lessened with the passing years. They were known as "virtuosos"—amateurs of experiment, connoisseurs of science. Even the King was a virtuoso of sorts: he watched with high pleasure the dissection of two bodies, a man and a woman,[1] and he had a "little elaboratory, under his closet, a pretty place; and there [Pepys] saw a great many

[1] Pepys, *Diary,* May 11, 1663, records the event.

chymical glasses and things, but understood none of them." [2]

The inquisitive diarist himself pulled a few strings early in the game, and on February 15, 1664/65, "Mr. Pepys was unanimously elected and admitted" to the Royal Society. Although the good man was more at sea in the flood of philosophical terms than he ever was on a man-of-war, yet he found it "a most acceptable thing to hear their discourse, and see their experiments; which were this day upon the nature of fire, and how it goes out in a place where the ayre is not free, and sooner out in a place where the ayre is exhausted, which they [Hooke and Boyle] showed by an engine on purpose" (*Diary*, February 15, 1664/65). One can almost see the mixture of enthusiasm and obfuscation on the writer's face as he penned the words. Withal, he always found at Gresham College, where the Society met, "very noble discourse."

But other people, possessed not of keener sight but of better understanding, were not diddled by the word "Royal" and the patronage of the Merry Monarch and were inclined to snicker into their lace sleeves at mention of the Society. It must be admitted that in its early enthusiasm for putting every conceivable object and superstition to experimental test, the Royal Society often overstepped the bounds of the sublime and ended by making itself not a little ridiculous. There were learned papers on little shells adhering to trees, having within them little perfectly shaped birds, none of which were ever seen alive; on the production of young vipers from powdered liver and lungs of

---

[2] *Ibid.*, Jan. 15, 1668/69.

The following passage from a letter from Sir Henry Saville to Rochester, Aug. 15, 1676, reveals the enthusiasm of the King: "[come back] in to towne this beeing the criticall time . . . ke your fortune, for Mon[r] Rabell is soe . . . [fav]ourite of his Majty and your LP of Monr Rabell, that I doe not see you can ever have a better opportunity of doeing your businesse, now, your chymicall knowledge will give you entrance to a place where Manchester himselfe is kept out for his ignorance, which hitherto has carryed him through all, in a word the dayes of learning are coming upon us, and under a receipt for the wormes noe man will bee admitted soe farr as the privy chamber" (Johannes Prinz, *John Wilmot, Earl of Rochester, His Life and Writings, With his Lordship's private correspondence, various other documents, and a bibliography of his works and of the literature on him* [Leipzig, 1927], p. 291).

vipers; and on magnetic and sympathetic cures. The members invented quadrants, scales, beams, levels, augurs, buckets, diving-bells, thermometers, and instruments for improving hearing and the planting of corn. They investigated matters animal, vegetable, mineral, medical, mechanical, and optical; light, sound, color, motion, water, and heat.[3]

No one will now deny that the Royal Society was the greatest force leading to pure and applied science in Restoration and eighteenth-century England. But it is nonetheless impossible to ignore the fact that such an ambitious program in the hands of what were, after all, mainly talented amateurs, provided full justification for laughter when news of these naïve meetings at Gresham College got abroad. Even their patron the King "mightily laughed at [the College], for spending time only in weighing of ayre, and doing nothing else since they sat" (Pepys, *Diary*, February 1, 1663/64). As for the dramatists, their golden opportunity was here, and Thomas Shadwell, the most wide-awake journalist of them all, was not slow to avail himself of it.

The Royal Society listed among its members fourteen noblemen, barons, and knights; eighteen esquires; eighteen physicians; five doctors of divinity; two bishops "for prevention of these panick, causeless terrors"; and thirty-eight men of lesser degree. Shadwell scanned the list with a professional's contempt for the amateur and flexed his muscles in a preliminary assault in *The Sullen Lovers*, produced in 1668:

EMILIA. *Others after twenty or thirty years study in philosophy arrive no further than at weighing of carpe, the invention of a travailling wheel, or the poisoning of a cat with the oyle of tobacco; these are your wits and virtuosos.*

III

Indeed, for the "weighing of carpe," Thomas Sprat, the first historian of the Society, recorded in 1667 that "several accurate beams" had been developed under its aegis. One of these may have determined the weight of a carp with a pennyweight's more

[3] M. Ornstein, *Role of the Scientific Societies in the XVII Century* (Chicago, 1928), pp. 104 f.

accuracy than the cheating fishmonger's scales. As for the other discoveries, I shall let Pepys, who by this time is a valued member and is eventually to become president, speak for himself: "Lord Bruncker . . . and I to Gresham College to have seen Mr. Hooke and a new invented chariott of Dr. Wilkins . . ." (*Diary*, January 11, 1665/66). "I here saw my Lord Bruncker ride in [the chariot]; where the coachman sits astride upon a pole over the horse, but do not touch the horse, which is a pretty odde thing; but it seems that it is most easy for the horse, and, as they say, for the man also" (*Diary*, January 22, 1665/66).

If the whole business was rather odd to the credulous and partisan Pepys, it is no wonder that elsewhere it aroused a spark of dramatic contempt. The cat's demise (referred to above by Shadwell) was a more significant affair, for whereas the new chariot does not seem to have survived its one trial on the London streets, the poisoned animal was among the first of millions which have since been "sacrificed" to science. On May 3, 1665, Pepys went "to Gresham College, and saw a cat killed with the Duke of Florence's poyson, and saw it proved that the oyle of tobacco drawn by one of the Society do the same effect, and is judged to be the same thing with the poyson both in colour and smell and effect."

To satirizing scientific experiments—particularly those of the Royal Society—Shadwell devoted a full-length play. *The Virtuoso* was produced in 1676, but internal evidence points to the probability of a much earlier creation. In this play Shadwell drew a new dramatic type, a new "humor" in the Jonsonian sense; and since this Gresham College scientist was, to the playwrights, merely a new humor, it will not be amiss to define the word. According to Jonson, a humor was a bias of disposition, a warp, so to speak, in character by which

> . . . some one peculiar quality
> Doth so possesse a man, that it doth draw
> All his affects, his spirits, and his powers,
> In their confluctions, all to runne one way.
> This may be truly said to be a humour.
>   Every Man out of His Humour, Induction

Shadwell was an ardent disciple of Ben Jonson, and in painting the portrait of Sir Nicholas Gimcrack, the virtuoso, he was laying his colors on a background which the older dramatist had already sketched in. At the beginning of Jonson's *The New Inne*, produced in 1629, we find Lovel, "a complete gentleman, a soldier and a scholar," accused by the host of the inn of

> . . . drawing fleas
> *Out of my mattes, and pounding 'hem in cages*
> *Cut out of cards, & those rop'd round with pack-thred,*
> *Drawne therow birdlime! a fine subtilty!*
> *Or poring through a multiplying glasse,*
> *Upon a captiv'd crab-louse, or a cheese-mite*
> *To be dissected, as the sports of nature,*
> *With a neat Spanish needle! Speculations*
> *That doe become the age, I doe confesse!*
> *As measuring an ants egges with the silke-wormes,*
> *By a phantastique instrument of thred,*
> *Shall give you their just difference, to a haire!*
> *Or else recovering o' dead flyes, with crums!*
> *(Another quaint conclusion i' the physickes)*
> *Which I ha seene you busie at, through the key hole. . . .*
>
> I, 1

Surely Lovel is the very prototype of the amateur experimenter who later helped to make up the Royal Society! But literary sketches of this type of man are not rare and, indeed, date back to antiquity, for it was Aristophanes who created the first virtuoso in *The Clouds*, produced in 423 B.C. The object of his satire was Socrates and the Sophists, and the humble flea and lowly gnat served Aristophanes as they later served Jonson, Butler, and Shadwell.

DISCIPLE. *Lately, a flea bit Chærephon on the brow and then from there sprang on to the head of Socrates. Socrates asked Chærephon, "How many times the length of its legs does a flea jump?"*

STREPSIADES. *And how ever did he set about measuring it?*

DISCIPLE. *Oh! 'twas most ingenious! He melted some wax, seized the flea and dipped its two feet in the wax, which, when cooled, left them shod with true Persian buskins. These he slipped off and with them measured the distance.*

STREPSIADES. Ah! great Zeus! what a brain! what subtlety.

DISCIPLE. I wonder what then you would say, if you knew another of Socrates' contrivances.

STREPSIADES. What is it? Pray tell me.

DISCIPLE. Chærephon of the dome of Sphettia asked him whether he thought a gnat buzzed through his proboscis or through its rear.

STREPSIADES. And what did he say about the gnat?

DISCIPLE. He said that the gut of the gnat was narrow, and that, in passing through this tiny passage, the air is driven with force towards the breech; then after this slender channel, it encountered the rump, which was distended like a trumpet, and there it resounded sonorously.

STREPSIADES. So the rear of a gnat is a trumpet. Oh! what a splendid discovery! Thrice happy Socrates.[4]

For "great Zeus" substitute "what a Pox!" and one has Shadwell himself.

A philosopher later than Socrates was seduced by virtuosity and paid dearly for it. Aubrey was told that the cause of Sir Francis Bacon's death was trying an experiment, to wit,

> As he was taking the aire in a coach with Dr. Witherborne (a Scotchman, physitian to the King) towards High-gate, snow lay on the ground, and it came into my lord's thoughts, why flesh might not be preserved in snow, as in salt. They were resolved they would try the experiment presently. They alighted out of the coach, and went into a poore woman's house at the bottome of Highgate hill, and bought a hen, and made the woman exenterate it, and then stuffed the bodie with snow, and my lord did helpe to doe it himselfe. The snow so chilled him, that he immediately fell so extremely ill . . . that in 2 or 3 dayes . . . he dyed of suffocation.
>
> Brief Lives, I, 75

Thus the hen as well as the flea has an honorable place in the history of virtuosity (science, we call it now). The bird also

---

[4] Aristophanes, *The Eleven Comedies*, Black and Gold Library (2 vols. in 1; New York, n.d.), I, 305.

helped James Shirley hang another early virtuoso in effigy in 1633:

PHANSIE. *This grave man, some yeares past was a physitian,*
  A Galenist, and parcell Paracelsus,
  Thriv'd by diseases, but quite lost his practise,
  To study a new way to fatten poultry
  With scrapings of a carrot, a great benefit
  To th' commonwealth.

Triumph of Peace, p. 8

Shadwell's virtuoso, Sir Nicholas Gimcrack, was scornfully described as "A sot, that has spent 2000 l. in microscopes, to find out the nature of eels in vinegar, mites in cheese, and the blue of plums, which he has subtilly found out to be living creatures" (*The Virtuoso*, I). Here was a fit companion for Butler's Sidrophel, who:

  . . . *knew whats' ever's to be known,*
  But much more then he knew, would own.
  What med'cine 'twas that Paracelsus
  Could make a man with, as he tells us.
  What figur'd slates are best to make,
  On wat'ry surface, duck or drake.
  What bowling-stones, in running race
  Upon a board, have swiftest pace.
  Whether a pulse beat in the black
  List of a dappled louse's back:
  If systole or diastole move
  Quickest, when he's in wrath, or love;
  When two of them do run a race,
  Whether the gallop, trot, or pace.
  How many scores a flea will jump,
  Of his own length, from head to rump;
  Which Socrates, and Chærephon
  In vain, assay'd so long agon;
  Whether his snout a perfect nose is,
  And not an elephants proboscis;
  How many different specieses
  Of maggots breed in rotten cheese,

And which are next of kin to those,
Engendred in a chaundler's nose;
Of those not seen, but understood,
That live in vineger and wood.

Hudibras, Pt. II, Canto 3

Both Shadwell's and Butler's attacks were evidently provoked by the microscopical investigations of Robert Hooke, made before the Royal Society and summarized in 1665 in *Micrographia: or some physiological descriptions of minute bodies made by magnifying glasses*, which Pepys called "the most ingenious book that ever I read in my life" (*Diary*, January 21, 1664/65).

Mr. Hooke's experiments seem to have been the talk of the town, for in *The Man of Mode* Sir George Etherege alludes to the notorious flea, though with the conventional satiric undertone directed otherwise than at the virtuosos:

TOWNLY. Mr. Dorimant swears a flea or maggot is not made more monstrous by a magnifying glass, than a story is by his telling it.

II, 1

And Dr. Baliardo, the virtuoso of Aphra Behn's *The Emperor of the Moon*, conjures up "all his little devils with horrid names, his microscope, his horoscope, his telescope, and all his scopes" (I, 1), as the half-frightened, half-disgusted servingmaid avers.

The fact is that of all the new tools of seventeenth-century science the microscope made the deepest impression on the lay mind. As the urinal marked the physician, the magnifying glass symbolized the scientist.

Today the place of many of the seventeenth-century dramatic pieces would be partly filled by the magazine sections of the Sunday papers. Thus, when Elizabeth Sawyer of Edmonton was convicted of witchcraft and executed on April 19, 1621, the episode called forth *The Witch of Edmonton: a known true story* by Rowley, Dekker, and Ford. This play was produced with great popular acclaim at the Cockpit in Drury Lane during the autumn or winter of 1621.[5] A modern journalist could not have supplied the demand for news much more quickly.

[5] Montague Summers, *The History of Witchcraft and Demonology* (New York, 1926), p. 290.

Another case in point is *The Late Lancashire Witches,* ascribed to Heywood and Brome, produced at the Globe in 1634. The year before there had been a witch scare in Pendle Forest. Over eighteen suspected witches were tried at the Lancashire Assizes, and seventeen were convicted. The trial judge, dissatisfied with the evidence, obtained a reprieve, and later King Charles, scenting fraud, pardoned the lot. The play was produced immediately following the trial and before the King's pardon was granted. This is evident from the Epilogue, which begins:

> Now while the witches must expect their due
> By lawfull justice, we appeale to you
> For favourable censure; what their crime
> May bring upon 'em, ripenes yet of time
> Has not reveal'd. Perhaps great Mercy may
> After just condemnation give them day
> Of longer life. We represent as much
> As they have done, before lawes hand did touch
> Upon their guilt; but dare not hold it fit,
> That we for justices and judges sit,
> And personate their grave wisedomes on the stage
> Whom we are bound to honour. . . .

No better evidence of the dramatists' ability to convert news into timely literature can be found.

Thomas Shadwell was the ideal topical dramatist. His flair lay in an intuitive knowledge of the subjects in which his audience was most vitally interested at the moment. He also contributed a play based on the Lancashire trial, *The Lancashire Witches and Teague o Divelly, the Irish Priest,* in the preface to which he naïvely confessed: "For the magical part I had no hopes of equalling Shakespeare in fancy, who created his witchcraft for the most part out of his own imagination (in which faculty no man ever excell'd him), and therefore I resolv'd to take mine from authority."

It is this very lack of imagination which makes Shadwell so valuable a commentator on the Restoration scene. His characters, especially those with fantastic humors, are drawn with remarkable vigor;[6] his scenes are triumphs of photographic realism; his plays are full of bustle and rude, riotous fun. In a word, he transferred his England bodily to the stage. *The Virtuoso* admirably illustrates all these qualities, so distasteful to the criticaster but so invaluable to the social historian.[7]

Dramatic interest lies in the gallery of humors the genius of Shadwell improvised. A quartet of lovers who pursue a stereotyped path to connubial bliss in the last act; old Snarl, "a great admirer of the last age, and a declaimer against the vices of this, and privately very vicious himself," who keeps a strumpet to whip him into passion until the vagary is discovered in Act V; Sir Nicholas Gimcrack and his whore; Lady Gimcrack and her bravo; and "that immortal figure of sublime inconsequences and trivial eloquence," the Virtuoso's grandiloquent clawback Sir Formal Trifle, make up the *dramatis personae*. Sir Formal and the Virtuoso are unique, the glories of the piece, on which Langbaine delivers this just and judicious verdict:

> *I think there is no body will deny this play its due applause; at least I know, that the University of Oxford, who may be allowed competent judges of comedy (especially of such characters, as Sir Nicholas Gimcrack, and Sir Formal Trifle) applauded it: and as no man ever undertook to discover the frailties of such pretenders to this kind of knowledge, before Mr. Shadwell; so none since*

---

[6] So other dramatists agreed. Sir George Etherege, in a letter to Shadwell's intimate friend Jephson, wrote in March, 1687/88: "tho' I have given over writing plays I shou'd be glad to read a good one, wherefore pray lett Will. Richards send me M[r] Shadwell's [*The Squire of Alsatia*, produced at Drury Lane in May], when it is printed, that I may know what follies are in fashion; the fops I knew are grown stale, and he is likely to pick up the best collection of new ones" (Etherege, *Dramatic Works*, ed. H. F. B. Brett-Smith [Boston, 1927], I, lxiii).

[7] My brief and specialized treatment of Thomas Shadwell as a dramatist should be accompanied by an apology and a reference to Montague Summers' brilliant and entertaining, though sometimes eccentric and biased, Introduction to his edition of Shadwell's works (London, 1927, I, xvii–ccli). Ever since Dryden with malice aforethought libeled Shadwell with "dulness," Tom has been neglected and scorned. Dryden's harsh stricture has not only worked a grave injustice to a fine dramatist, but to prospective readers of Shadwell's highly amusing plays.

Mr. Jonson's time, ever drew so many different characters of humours, and with such success.[8]

So much for the play as literature.

The scientific satire begins full blast in the second act. Two young lovers, Bruce and Longvil, in order to meet the Virtuoso's two nieces, pretend to be philosophers and so secure an invitation to visit Sir Nicholas' laboratory to see "the dissection of a little animal, commonly called a Chichester Cock-Lobster; and afterwards to take a dish of meat, and discourse of the noble operation, and to sport an author over a glass of wine."

Having arrived at Sir Nicholas' house, they are told by Lady Gimcrack that the Virtuoso is occupied with his swimming-master, and that "he has a frog in a bowl of water, tied with a pack-thread by the loins; which pack-thread Sir Nicholas holds in his teeth, lying upon his belly on a table; and as the frog strikes, he strikes; and his swimming-master stands by, to tell him when he does well or ill." And surely enough, the next "Scene opens, and discovers Sir Nicholas learning to swim upon a table, Sir Formal and the swiming-master standing by."

SIR FORMAL. *In earnest, this is very fine. I doubt not, sir, but in a short space of time, you will arrive at that curiosity in this watery science, that not a frog breathing will exceed you, though I confess it is the most curious of all amphibious animals (in the art, shall I say, or rather nature of swiming.)*

SWIMMING MASTER. *Ah! well struck, Sir Nicholas; that was admirable, that was as well swom as any man in England can. Observe the frog, draw up your arms a little nearer, and then thrust 'em out strongly—Gather up your legs a little more—So, very well—Incomparable. . . .*

And so on. Sir Nicholas, Sir Formal, Longvil, and Bruce bandy about compliments, until finally Longvil asks:

Have you ever tri'd in the water, sir?
SIR NICHOLAS. *No, sir; but I swim most exquisitely on land.*

[8] *An Account of the English Dramatick Poets* (Oxford, 1691), p. 451.

BRUCE. *Do you intend to practise in the water, sir?*

SIR NICHOLAS. *Never, sir; I hate the water, I never come upon the water, sir.*

LONGVIL. *Then there will be no use of swiming.*

SIR NICHOLAS. *I content my self with the speculative part of swiming; I care not for the practick. I seldom bring anything to use; 'tis not my way, knowledge is my ultimate end.*

BRUCE. *You have reason, sir; knowledge is like vertue, its own reward.*

SIR FORMAL. *To study for use is base and mercenary, below the serene and quiet temper of a sedate philosopher.*

SIR NICHOLAS. *You hit it right, sir. I never studi'd any thing for use but physick, which I administer to poor people: you shall see my method.*

This pleasant nonsense is evidently based on the fact that the Royal Society had spent some time on diving. Sir Nicholas' flesh-and-blood colleagues had invented a bell, spectacles, and other instruments for underwater explorers. One must admit that Gresham College had no hesitation in turning its erudition to utilitarian ends.

But the visitors are not to let Sir Nicholas off thus easily and so deprive the audience of a full view of the follies of science. "Sir, I beseech you," asks Longvil ingenuously, "what new curiosities have you found out in physick?"

SIR NICHOLAS. *Why, I have found out the use of respiration, or breathing, which is a motion of the thorax and lungs, whereby the air is impell'd by the nose, mouth, and wind-pipe, into the lungs, and thence expell'd farther to elaborate the blood, by refrigerating it, and separating its fulaginous steams.*

BRUCE. *What a secret the rogue has found out.*

SIR NICHOLAS. *I have found too, that an animal may be preserved without respiration, when the wind-pipe's cut in two, by follicular impulsion of air; to wit, by blowing wind with a pair of bellows into the lungs.*

At a meeting of the Royal Society on October 24, 1667, Robert Hooke, whose duty it was as curator to perform the public experiments, and who fulfilled his task with an enthusiasm and versatility to which science and the college shall ever be in debt, originated Sir Nicholas' experiment of insufflating the lungs by a current of air.[9] In the history of physiology only Harvey's work was more epoch-making, for anciently the Greeks believed that the essential feature of respiration was the *movement* of the lungs. Hooke demonstrated that the fundamental process was ventilation with fresh air, however induced. In this instance Shadwell had trained his guns on an invulnerable position. But, after all, how was he to know, when even doctors disagreed?

When, in the play, Sir Nicholas has finished with respiration, with a flightiness worthy of a Gresham College virtuoso he continues along other lines: "Besides, tho' I confess I did not invent it, I have performed admirable effects by transfusion of blood; to wit, by putting the blood of one animal into another." And Sir Formal floridly amplifies:

> Upon my integrity he has advanc'd transfusion to the achme of perfection, and has the ascendant over all the virtuosi in point of that operation. I saw him do the most admirable effects in the world upon two animals; the one a domestick animal, commonly call'd a mangy spaniel; and a less famellick creature, commonly call'd a sound bull-dog. Be pleas'd, sir, to impart it.
>
> SIR NICHOLAS. Why, I made, sir, both the animals to be emittent and recipient at the same time, after I had made ligatures as hard as I could, for fear of strangling the animals, to render the jugular veins turgid, I open'd the carotid arteries, and jugular veins of both at one time, and so caus'd them to change blood one with another.
>
> SIR FORMAL. Indeed that which ensu'd upon the operation was miraculous; for the mangy spaniel became sound, and the sound bull-dog, mangy.
>
> SIR NICHOLAS. Not only so, gentlemen, but the spaniel became a bull-dog, and the bull-dog a spaniel.
>
> SIR FORMAL. Which considering the civil and ingenuous temper and education of the spaniel, with the rough and untaught savageness

[9] In 1555 Vesalius reported that, even though the chest wall be pierced, an animal may be kept alive if the lungs are continually aerated by means of a bellows. But he neglected to draw Hooke's impressive conclusions.

of the bull-dog, may not undeservingly challenge the name of a
wonder.

BRUCE. 'Tis an experiment you'll deserve a statue for.

For the facts of this remarkable case let us refer once more to
the ubiquitous Pepys:

> Dr. Croone told me, that, at the meeting of Gresham College to-
> night there was a pretty experiment of the blood of one dogg [a
> little mastiff] let out, till he died, into the body of another [a
> spaniel] on one side, while all his own run out on the other side.
> The first died upon the place, and the other pretty well, and
> likely to do well. This did give occasion to many pretty wishes, as
> of the blood of a Quaker to be let into an archbishop, and such
> like; but, as Dr. Croone says, may, if it takes, be of mighty use to
> man's health, for the mending of bad blood by borrowing from a
> better body.
>
> > Diary, November 14, 1666

> This noon I met Mr. Hooke, and he tells me the dogg which was
> filled with another dog's blood at the College the other day, is
> very well, and like to be so as ever, and doubts not its being
> found of great use to man.
>
> > Diary, November 16, 1666

> The late experiment of the dog, which is in perfect good health,
> may be improved for good uses to men.
>
> > Diary, November 28, 1666

Again the dramatist was wrong, and the diarist and his fellow
virtuosos right, for blood transfusion has long ceased to be
merely a spectacular lecture-room experiment. The prophecies of
Dr. Croone and Mr. Hooke cannot be set down and dismissed as
a lucky guess. The first-class scientist possesses an intuition which
enables him, from the mist of crude experimentation and fortuitous result, to discern the distant gleam of truth. Today we fancy
that the more complicated our apparatus and the more complex
our experimental conditions, the greater will be the resultant
discovery. But fundamental discoveries have arisen from the
simplest experiments, as the history of early science reveals.

The Royal Society, however, had not been the first to set its hand to the transfusion problem. In 1490 when Pope Innocent VIII lay dying of old age, a Jewish physician was summoned who transferred the blood from the veins of three young boys into the pontiff. Each boy received one ducat (less than two of our depreciating dollars) but the money did them even less good than our dollarettes do us. Soon after, the boys died; the physicians escaped; and the Pope did not recover, wrote an eye-witness.[10]

It is surprising then to learn of the Virtuoso's next step. Longvil, still baiting Sir Nicholas, remarks: "That was a rare experiment of transfusing the blood of a sheep into a mad-man." But Sir Nicholas is not to be outdone. "Short of many of mine," he asseverates.

> I assure you I have transfus'd into a humane vein 64 ounces, haver de pois weight, from one sheep. The emittent sheep dy'd under the operation, but the recipient mad-man is still alive; he suffer'd some disorder at first. The sheep's blood being heterogeneous, but in a short time it became homogeneous with his own. . . . The patient from being maniacle, or raging mad, became wholly ovine or sheepish; he bleated perpetually, and chew'd the cud; he had wool growing on him in great quantities, and a Northampton-shire sheepe tail did soon emerge or arise from his anus or humane fundament.

Old Snarl, who had entered in time to hear Sir Nicholas conclude, snorts in disgust: "I believe if the blood of an ass were transfused into a virtuoso, you would not know the emittent ass from the recipient philosopher, by the mass."

Nevertheless Shadwell, except for the delightful business of the cud, wool, and tail (which would have enchanted Gresham College beyond words), was reporting a sober fact. Such an experiment was indeed performed by Doctors Lower and King at Arundel House on November 23, 1667, before a distinguished gathering, including the Bishop of Salisbury (for prevention of those panic, causeless terrors?) and several members of Parliament. The subject's name was Arthur Coga, but opinion was

[10] J. A. Symonds, *The Renaissance in Italy* (New York [1935]), I, 204.

somewhat divided as to the extent of his madness. Pepys wrote
that Arthur was "a little frantic"; Dr. Wilkins that he was "poor
and a debauched man"; and Robert Boyle that "his brain was
sometimes a little too warm." But however mad he was, he was
exceedingly fortunate, for he survived an operation which might
easily have resulted in death. And not only did he survive, but he
prospered. "He found himself very well upon it, his pulse and
appetite being better than before, his sleep good, his body as
soluble as usual." A contemporary victim in France was not as
lucky: he died, and transfusion was promptly forbidden by
French law.

Why sheep's blood? "The blood of a lamb has a certain
symbolic link with the blood of Christ, because Christ is the
Lamb of God," said Coga himself.

Of course, Pepys took a keen interest in the case. A week after
the operation, he writes:

> But here, above all, I was pleased to see the person who had his
> blood taken out. He speaks well, and did this day give the Society
> a relation thereof in Latin, saying that he finds himself much
> better since, and as a new man, but he is cracked a little in his
> head, though he speaks very reasonably, and very well. He had
> but 20 s. for his suffering it, and is to have the same again tried
> upon him: the first sound man that ever had it tried upon him in
> England, and but one that we hear of in France, which was a
> porter hired by the virtuosos.
>
> Diary, November 30, 1667

Samuel Butler seized on the same experiment to express a
"pretty wish" of his own. He is probably writing of William
Lilly, his astrological *bête-noir:*

> Can no transfusion of the blood,
> That makes fools cattle, do you good;
> Nor putting pigs t' a bitch to nurse,
> To turn 'em into mungrel-curs,

[11] T. Birch, *History of the Royal Society* (London, 1756), II, 214–216.
"Sanguis ovis symbolicam quandam facultatem habet cum sanguine Christi, quia
Christus est Agnus Dei."

Put you into a way, at least,
To make your self a better beast?
Can all your critical intrigues,
Of trying sound for rotten eggs;
Your several new-found remedies
Of curing wounds and scabs in trees;
Your arts of fluxing them for claps,
And purging their infected saps;
Recov'ring shankers, crystallines,
And nodes and botches in the rinds,
Have no effect to operate
Upon that duller block, your pate?
But still it must be leudly bent
To tempt your own due punishment;
And, like your whimsy'd chariots draw
The boys to course you without law;
As if the art you have so long
Profest of making old dogs young,
In you, had virtue to renew
Not only youth, but childhood too.[12]

Sir Nicholas' researches into the social organization of the ant and the habits of the spider are likewise the objects of a fair amount of foolery in Act III. Needless to say, the Gresham College virtuosos had also maintained such questions of natural history on their list. One of the earliest experiments performed by the infant College was to place a spider within a circle of powdered unicorn's horn. The Duke of Buckingham promised the Royal Society a piece of unicorn's horn on June 6, 1661, and a month later kept his word. The virtuosos powdered a bit of this precious commodity and made a circle of it around a spider. The creature immediately hopped out and made off, much to the astonishment of all present.[13]

Science then as now had an arm as long as the World Health Organization's:

[12] "An Heroical Epistle of Hudibras to Sidrophel" in *Hudibras*, in Three Parts (London, 1726).

[13] D. Harwood, *Love for Animals and How It Developed in Great Britain* (New York, 1928), p. 80.

SIR NICHOLAS. *I keep a constant correspondence with all the virtuoso's*
in the north and north-east parts. There are rare phaenomena's in
those countrys. I am beholding to Finland, Lapland, and Russia
for a great part of my philosophy. I send my queries thither.
                                                              Virtuoso, III

This too was a part of the Royal Society's program. Thomas
Sprat, the historian of that body, wrote:

> *First they employ fellows to examine treatises, etc., of countries;*
> *they employ others to discourse with seasmen, travellers, trades-*
> *men and merchants; then they compose a body of questions*
> *about observable things. Then the fellows would start corre-*
> *spondence with the East Indies, China, St. Helena, Teneriff,*
> *Barbary, Morocco. . . .*[14]

Pepys listened to the report of one such scientific ambassador.
At Gresham College he "heard Sir Robert Southwell give an
account of some things committed to him by the Society at his
going to Portugall, which he did deliver in a mighty handsome
manner (*Diary*, March 12, 1667–68).

But there was nothing new in this. Ben Jonson years before
had received scientific intelligence from abroad:

CLERKE. *They write from Libtzig (reverence to your eares)*
    The art of drawing farts out of dead bodies,
    Is by the brotherhood of the Rosie Crosse,
    Produc'd unto perfection, in so sweet
    And rich a tincture. . . .
                                                   Staple of Newes, III, 2

Mr. Hooke had made for the college, under Robert Boyle's
direction, a vacuum pump. Into the glass chamber of this engine
they placed in turn a dog, a viper, a sparrow, a shrew-mouse, a
candle, and a kitling. As the air was pumped out, both candle
flame and animal life were extinguished. Once again we have an
experiment so simple and fundamental that genius is the only
word applicable to its originators. But why, wondered Shadwell,
driven in Act V by the spirit of promiscuous satire, stop with
animals? His hero does not:

[14] Quoted by Ornstein, *Role of the Scientific Societies*, p. 121.

LONGVIL. *Will stinking flesh give light like rotton wood?*

SIR NICHOLAS. *O yes; there was a lucid surloin of beef in the Strand, foolish people thought it burnt, when it only became lucid and crystalline by the coagulation of the aqueous juice of the beef, by the corruption that invaded it. 'Tis frequent. I myself have read a Geneva Bible by a leg of pork?*

BRUCE. *How, a Geneva Bibly by a leg of pork?*

SIR NICHOLAS. *O ay, 'tis the finest light in the world; but for all that, I could eclipse the leg of pork in my receiver, by pumping out the air; but immediately upon the appulse of the air let in again, it becomes lucid as before.*

Now this Disquisition on a Leg of Pork is not so foolish as it sounds. If the virtuosos actually performed the experiment, they are indeed to be congratulated; for reference to any modern textbook of biochemistry will show that phosphorescence and oxygen are not unrelated. Lack of oxygen extinguishes, and presence of the gas is necessary to, this form of cold light.

Sir Nicholas, as he told his admirers at the end of his swimming lesson, is a physician as well as a philosopher. The close of the fourth act finds him administering to his patients:

> Scene is the courtyard full of several
> lame and sick people.
> Enter Sir Nicholas, Sir Formal, Longvil, and Bruce.

SICK PEOPLE. *Heav'n bless your worship.*

SIR NICHOLAS. *Come, gentlemen, you must know I have studi'd all manner of cases, and have bills ready written for all diseases; that's my way, I give 'em advise for nothing.*

SIR FORMAL. *Not more resorted to the temple of Æsculapius; I am sure not so many found relief, as from my noble friend: You have reason, good languishing people to be trumpeters of his illustrious fame, whose indefatiguable care, for the good of feeble and distress'd mankind, with his transcendent skill, each day cures even incurable diseases.*

LONGVIL. *Your orators are very subject to that figure in speech call'd a bull.*

SIR NICHOLAS. *I still administer'd to the incurable in Italy, and never fail'd of success. Here are my bills. Where is the roll? Call it over.*

SIR FORMAL. *Gout.*

2 GOUT. *Here*—   [halting]
SIR NICHOLAS. *There's a bill for you two; take it betwixt you.*
SIR FORMAL. *Stone.*
2 STONE. *Here, sir.*
SIR NICHOLAS. *There's one for you two.*
SIR FORMAL. *Scurvy.*
4 SCURVY. *Here, sir.*
SIR NICHOLAS. *There's a bill for you four.*
SERVANT. *Go, pass by as you are serv'd.*
SIR FORMAL. *Consumption.*
2 CONSUMPTION. *Here.*
SIR NICHOLAS. *Take your bill.*
SIR FORMAL. *Dropsie.*
2 DROPSIE. *Here, sir.*
SIR NICHOLAS. *There's for you two.*
SIR FORMAL. *There is a mad-man I have set by for transfusion of blood.*
SIR NICHOLAS. *That's well. The truth on't is, we shall never get any but madmen, for that operation. But proceed.*
SIR FORMAL. *These are the last, but not the least—pox.*
                         [Enter a great number of men and women.]
ALL. *Here, here, here*—
SIR NICHOLAS. *There are three or four bills for you, you are so many.*
ALL. *Heav'n bless your worship*—
                                                [Exeunt omnes.]

Superficially this satire is as lighthearted as the rest of Shadwell's pleasantries, but fundamentally it is the most serious and thought-provoking of all. It was Dr. Benjamin Rush's proud boast that medicine was his wife and science his mistress, and this sort of vicarious adultery has become increasingly popular and prevalent as the decades pass. That an immense amount of valuable scientific work has been performed by practicing physicians is, of course, indisputable. One need only mention William Beaumont's celebrated experiments on digestion, sandwiched within the busy years of an active army-surgeon's life. But on the other hand, one wonders whether the laboratory man has any place in the clinic. The laboratory point of view cannot be carried over into the sick-room without grave injustice to the patient, for the physician's function is, after all, the healing of the sick, not the simultaneous performance of a scientific experiment and a course of treatment. The human animal, in some mysterious way, differs from the laboratory animal. To the same degree the art of medicine differs from medical science. The mark of the successful physician is not how many articles he has published in technical journals, but how many sick folk he has helped or cured.

At last Sir Nicholas pursued his final investigation and like great Bacon before him, in it met his death. His widow Elizabeth thus sadly relates the circumstances in a letter to Isaac Bickerstaff early in September, 1710:

> . . . *Upon Midsummer-Day last, as he was walking with me in the fields, he saw a very odd-coloured butterfly just before us. I observed, that he immediately changed colour, like a man that is surprised with a piece of good luck, and telling me that it was what he had looked for above these twelve years, he threw off his coat, and followed it. I lost sight of them both in less than a quarter of an hour; but my husband continued the chase over hedge and ditch till about sun-set; at which time, as I was afterwards told, he caught the butterfly as she rested her self upon a cabbage, near five miles from the place where he first put her up. He was here lifted from the ground by some passengers in a very fainting condition, and brought home to me about midnight. His violent exercise threw him into a fever, which grew upon him by degrees, and at last carried him off. . . .*
>
> The Tatler, No. 221

And so science lost the leading figure of his time. Even in death he remained the true philosopher, and as a tribute *The Tatler* published his will:

> *I Nicholas Gimcrack being in sound health of mind, but in great weakness of body, do by this my last will and testament bestow my worldly goods and chattels in manner following:*
>   *Imprimis, To my dear wife,*
>   *One box of butterflies,*
>   *One drawer of shells,*
>   *A female skeleton,*

A dried cockatrice.

Item, To my daughter Elizabeth,

My receipt for preserving dead caterpillars,
As also my preparations of winter May-dew,
and embrio pickle.

Item, To my little daughter Fanny,

Three crocodile's eggs,
And upon the birth of her first child, if she marries with her
mother's consent,
The nest of a humming-bird.

Item, To my little daughter Fanny,

lands he has vested in my son Charles, I bequeath
My last year's collection of grasshoppers.

Item, To his daughter Susanna, being his only child, I bequeath my

English weeds pasted on royal paper,
With my large folio of Indian cabbage.

Item, To my learned and worthy friend Dr. Johannes Elserickius, professor in anatomy, and my associate in the studies of
nature, as an eternal monument of my affection and friendship
for him, I bequeath

My rat's testicles, and
Whale's pizzle.

To him and his issue male; and in default of such issue in the
said Dr. Elserickius, then to return to my executor and his heirs
for ever.

Having fully provided for my nephew Isaac, by making over to
him some years since,

A horned scarabaeus,
The skin of a rattle-snake, and
The mummy of an Egyptian king,

I make no further provision for him in this my will.

My eldest son John having spoken disrespectfully of his little
sister whom I keep by me in spirits of wine, and in many other
instances behaved himself undutifully towards me, I do disin-
herit, and wholly cut off from any part of this my personal estate,
by giving him a single cockle shell.

To my second son Charles, I give and bequeath all my flowers,
plants, minerals, mosses, shells, pebbles, fossils, beetles, butter-
flies, caterpillars, grasshoppers, and vermin, not above specified:

*As also all my monsters, both wet and dry, making the said
Charles whole and sole executor of this my last will and testa-
ment; by paying, or causing to be paid, the aforesaid legacies
within the space of six months after my decease. And I do hereby
revoke all other wills whatsoever by me formerly made.*

The Tatler, No. 216

Though Shadwell's play remains the chief source of dramatic
allusion to the Royal Society, off the stage Samuel Butler castigated the virtuosos with all the vigor of his pen. Butler's *Characters*, written about 1668–1670, includes an unflattering portrait
of "A Virtuoso," and in his poetical remains there was found a
fragmentary satire upon the Royal Society. His fine satire in
Hudibrastic verse, *The Elephant in the Moon*, hits frankly at
the habitués of Gresham College. In fact, the pompous credulity
of the early scientists affected Butler so strongly that he rewrote
the latter tale, with additions, "in long verse."

The Elephant in the Moon tells of a group of virtuosos who
train their telescope on the moon and seem to see there a great
battle fought between two opposing hosts of creatures, the Pri-
volvans and Subvolvans. As the lunar struggle progresses they are
amazed to see an elephant race swiftly across the face of the
moon. This phenomenon, they think, deserves the solemn scientific report they forthwith compose. As they are engaged in their
writing, some footboys peep into the telescope and discover a
mouse. After much specious argument whether there be a mouse
within, the scientists resolve to dismantle the instrument to see
for themselves.

Montague Summers, a mine of information—trustworthy or
not—remarks that Shadwell's topical plays demand full annotation, and he supplies innumerable interesting notes to every play
but *The Virtuoso*. Perhaps to one not medically trained the task
of annotating this play may have seemed more difficult than it
actually is; or perhaps the lack of technical comment merely
indicated the deprecation of science by the church. But aside
from the problem of annotation, there are two questions which
Father Summers leaves unasked and unanswered.

The Virtuoso was produced in May, 1676, and published in

quarto the same year. But from an analysis of the play (first made by Carson S. Duncan, and later by Albert S. Borgman) one discovers that all of the lampooned experiments were performed between 1665 and 1667. It is this nine-year lapse between the events and the satire which seems strange. The other question affects the medical historian more directly: he cannot help wondering whether Sir Nicholas Gimcrack was drawn from the life or whether he was entirely a synthetic humor.

Before Shadwell turned playwright he had mingled long and intimately with the wits and poets, drunkards and coxcombs, lechers and *bona robas*, and every manner of eccentric of the time. When he came to turn the fruits of his observation to dramatic account, his memory (and his notebooks) swarmed with the elements of personal satire. In his first play, *The Sullen Lovers*, he transferred Edward and Sir Robert Howard and Sir Robert's mistress, Susanna Uphill, bodily to the stage under the transparent disguises of Ninny, Sir Positive At-all, and Lady Vaine. His third play, *The Humourists*, also contained a good deal of satire on particular persons which the author was forced to delete before the piece was allowed to proceed.

Thus between the years 1667 and 1669 Shadwell must have recorded a good many portraits drawn from the life and a good many episodes taken directly from the contemporary scene. Some of these (both personalities and episodes) were contributed by the newly founded Royal Society, for all of the experiments Shadwell burlesqued were performed by the Gresham College scientists and goggled at by Pepys between 1665 and 1667 when the dramatist was roaming the town with a critical and disrespectful eye.

That Shadwell made immediate record of the startling phenomena revealed at the College is indicated by the very tone of (for example) Longvil's remark: "That was a rare experiment of transfusing the blood of a sheep into a mad-man." This seems consistent, not with the year 1676 when the play was produced, but with 1667 when poor Arthur Coga was the talk of the town. Besides, we have noticed the tone before in Emilia's scornful characterization of "Wits and Virtuosos" in Act III of *The Sullen Lovers* (1668). Further to prove that Shadwell's animadversions on the Royal Society took form at the earlier date, there is a slap in *The Royal Shepherdess* (1668/69) and another in *The Humourists* (1670):

NEANDER. *Here I'm sure of something, I'm a lord,*
    And live with men. But to be turn'd a grazing
    In the Elizian-Fields (that men do talk of)
    Among philosophers, n'ere could make a legg.
ENDYMION. *Fie, fie, Neander! this is too prophane,*
    And relisheth far more of beast than man.
NEANDER. *My lord, I ask your pardon, I'd forgot*
    You are a virtuoso.

Royal Shepherdess, I

BRISK. *And be sure if your eye brows be not black, to black 'em soundly; ah your black eye-brow is your fashionable eye-brow. I hate rogues that wear eyebrows that are out of fashion.*
DRYBOB. *By the soul of Gresham a most phylosophical invention.*

Humourists, III

By 1676 the topical allusions to the virtuosos' experiments must have seemed, to those few denizens of the pit with long memories, decidedly behind the times.

We can hazard an explanation of the singular fact that a play which from its context appears to have been written about 1667 or 1668 was not produced until 1676. In his dedication of *The Virtuoso* to the Duke of Newcastle, Shadwell wrote:

> *That there are a great many faults in the conduct of this play, I am not ignorant. But I (having no pension but from the theatre, which is either unwilling or unable to reward a man sufficiently for so much pains as correct comedies require) cannot allot my whole time to the writing of plays, but am forced to mind some other business of advantage.*

This conventional but unnecessary apology may mean, in part, that the author fell back on notebook material collected years before and found in it the substance of which comedies of humors are made.[15] Moreover, in the Prologue of *The Virtuoso* Shadwell had written:

> For wit, like china, should long buri'd lie,
> Before it ripens to good comedy. . . .

This play's nine-year gestation brought forth ample wit.

We have seen that Shadwell once placed the Howards on the stage in a none-too-flattering and all-too-recognizable light, and before the censor took the sting out of *The Humourists*, others of the dramatist's acquaintance were certainly lampooned. Having been in trouble twice for his ability to project his fellows cinematographically onto the stage, Shadwell seems a little anx-

---

[15] There is still another possibility to consider. In a letter to Anthony Wood on October 26, 1671, John Aubrey wrote: "I am writing a comedy for Thomas Shadwell, which I have now almost finished since I came here, et quorum pars magna fui. And I shall fit him with another, *The Countrey Revell*, both humours untouch, but of this, mum! for 'tis very satyricall against some of my mischievous enemies which I in my tumbling up and downe have collected" (*Brief Lives*, ed. Clark 1898, I, 52). There is now no trace of Aubrey's first play, although fragments of the second remain (see ch. 8, below). We know that Aubrey wanted very much to join the Royal Society but was never invited; he never forgot the insult. His *Brief Lives* contains a great deal of material of medical, chemical, and general scientific interest; he was obviously interested in virtuosity. For example, concerning F. Potter's method for transfusion of blood (see n. 16, below), Aubrey has a sneer at Lower and possibly at the Royal Society as well. Thus it is possible that Shadwell was indebted to Aubrey for much of *The Virtuoso*, especially those humors of Sir Nicholas and Sir Formal which Oxford University so commended. That Shadwell's other plays contain jibes at the virtuosos hardly controverts the above hypothesis; for the satire of *The Virtuoso* aside, Shadwell's other fleers at Gresham College might have been penned by many another dramatist—Dryden, Etherege, Lacy, Wilson—as our parallel allusions show.

In *Thomas Shadwell, His Life and Comedies* (New York, 1928), Albert S. Borgman dealt with Robert Hooke's being Shadwell's model for Sir Nicholas Gimcrack. In Professor Borgman's footnotes on pp. 169 ff., he quotes from an unpublished dissertation at the University of Chicago by Carson S. Duncan, "The New Science and English Literature in the Classical Period." On p. 101 of that dissertation, Duncan lists the articles in *Philosophical Transactions of the Royal Society* that were used by Shadwell in *The Virtuoso* (1676). Borgman also indicates on p. 171 in his own book exactly where "eels in vinegar, the blue of plums, and sining flesh" come from and when the papers were presented to Hooke [editor].

ious in the Prologue to *The Virtuoso* to make his present position clear:

> Yet no one coxcomb in this play is shown,
> No one man's humour makes a part alone,
> But scatter'd follies gather'd into one.

Of course, this equivocation may have been intended to refer to the character of Sir Formal Trifle, or old Snarl, but with the Virtuoso himself in mind certain facts gathered together lead to an interesting conclusion.

As curator of the Royal Society it was Robert Hooke's duty to perform the public experiments, no matter by whom originally devised. Hooke himself was directly responsible for the experiment on artificial respiration, and Sir Nicholas introduces the subject by saying, "I have found, too, that an animal may be preserved without respiration. . . ." On the other hand, blood transfusion was first done by Richard Lower,[16] and concerning this the Virtuoso remarks, "Besides, tho' I confess I did not invent it, I have performed admirable effects by transfusion of blood. . . ." When the announcement of the first successful transfusion of blood by Lower at Oxford was transmitted to the Royal Society by Dr. Wallis, Hooke was instructed on August 22, 1666, to make preparations for the repetition of these experiments.

Then, too, it was Hooke who constructed Boyle's air pump and demonstrated its use. Moreover, he was the well-known

---

[16] Lower's experiment seems to have been anticipated, even in England. John Aubrey writes: "Memorandum that at the Epiphanie, 1649, when I was at his house, he [Francis Potter (1594–1678)] then told me his notion of curing diseases, etc. by transfusion of bloud out of one man into another, and that the hint came into his head reflecting on Ovid's story of Medea and Jason, and that this was a matter of ten yeares before that time. About a yeare after, he and I went to trye the experiment, but 'twas on a hen, and the creature to little and our tooles not good: I then sent him a surgeon's lancet. Anno. . . . I received a letter from him concerning this subject, which many yeares since I shewed, and was read and entred in the bookes of the Royal Societie, for Dr. Lower would have arrogated the invention to himselfe . . ." (*Brief Lives*, I, 166–167). To this account Aubrey annexes Mr. Potter's letter, "in perpetuam rei memoriam," and a diagram of the apparatus employed.

author of *Micrographia,* which dealt with "Eels in Vinegar, Mites in Cheese, and the Blue of Plums." In a word, Mr. Hooke was connected directly with each bit of this scientific satire.

Robert Hooke was also a physician of sorts and at one time had served under the celebrated Thomas Willis at Oxford. It is not difficult to imagine this demon experimenter dealing with his patients in just such an efficient and scientific manner as Sir Nicholas Gimcrack. He must have been a fairly successful practitioner, in any event, for in 1691 the Archbishop of Canterbury granted Mr. Hooke the degree of Doctor of Physick—"in nomine Domine," according to the empowering act of 1531. Perhaps it would be unkind to mention in passing that the seventeenth-century Archbishops of Canterbury were notorious for the light-heartedness with which they dispensed medical licenses to great men and quacks alike.[17]

In his personal characteristics, too, Mr. Hooke was apparently at the mercy of a satirical pen. Even Pepys, whose admiration for the scientist was unbounded, admitted to his diary that Mr. Hooke "is the most, and promises the least, of any man in the world that ever I saw" (February 15, 1664/65). Another contemporary description of the virtuoso makes the diarist's wonder clear:

> As to his person he was but despicable, being very crooked, tho' I have heard from himself, and others, that he was straight till about 16 years of age when he first grew awry, by frequent practicing with a turn-lath, and the like incurvating exercises, being but of a thin weak habit of body, which increas'd as he grew older, so as to be very remarkable at last: This made him but low of stature, tho' by his limbs he shou'd have been moderately tall. He was always very pale and lean, and latterly nothing but skin and bone, with a meagre aspect, his eyes grey and full, with a sharp ingenious look whilst younger; his nose but thin, of a moderate height and length; his mouth meanly wide, and upper lip thin; his chin sharp, and forehead large; his head of a middle

---

[17] William Lilly, the astrologer, was also made Doctor of Medicine, being granted a license to practice by Archbishop Sheldon on Oct. 11, 1670, at the instigation of Elias Ashmole.

size. He wore his own hair of a dark brown colour, very long and hanging neglected over his face uncut and lank. . . . He went stooping and very fast (till his weakness a few years before his death hindred) having but a light body to carry and a great deal of spirits and activity, especially in his youth.[18]

Mr. Hooke was said to have a soul as irritable and disputatious as his body was crooked. "His temper was melancholy, mistrustful and jealous, which more increas'd upon him with his years." A deformed, ill-tempered man fanatically performing farcical experiments before a crowd of excited dilettanti and awe-struck sightseers (or so it must have appeared to a cynical layman) was surely a fair target for satire. It is surely not beyond the bounds of probability that, in drawing the Virtuoso, Shadwell had the demonstrator of the Royal Society in the forefront of his mind, a conclusion also arrived at by Professor Albert S. Borgman.[19]

The battle between Shadwell and the seventeenth-century scientists was a drawn one. If the dramatist was too disparaging, the virtuosos were too enthusiastic. But the Royal Society soon lost its early exuberance, while Shadwell's son became a physician and F.R.S. and was knighted for it. Honors even again.

[18] Richard Waller's "Life of Hooke" in *Posthumous Works* (London, 1705), quoted by W. S. Middleton, "The Medical Aspect of Robert Hooke," *Annals of Medical History,* IX (1927), 242.

[19] Needless to say, it would have been Mr. Hooke the virtuoso, and not the private citizen, that Shadwell had in mind. Hooke was a bachelor and probably as innocent of a whore as of a wife. Nor does the fact that Sir Nicholas Gimcrack was a knight invalidate the hypothesis that Hooke was the original of the portrait. Shadwell himself (also no knight) was satirized as Sir Barnaby Whigg in D'Urfey's play of the same name (produced in 1681). Such gratuitous ennobling merely heightened the jest.

7

The French Disease

A poxe of his Bedlem purity.
—Ben Jonson, *Bartholomew Fayre*

Syphilographers running a professional eye down the prose or blank verse of the old plays risk having their moral sense scandalized by the number of poxes called down on innocent heads. For the seventeenth century saw the full flowering of those syphilitic seeds scattered abroad by Columbus' returning seamen; the pox occupied a much more massive position both in medicine and in life than it does today. Perhaps not everyone in England actually had the French Disease, but beyond all doubt everyone who had an articulate enemy in the world was at some time or another visited with Middleton's pious wish: "A pox search you . . . the very loins of thee." Or Otway's comprehensive curse: "Now poverty, plague, pox, and prison fall thick upon the head of thee!"

In the twentieth century there are laws which make the mere imputation of syphilis tantamount to libel. Thanks be to the patron saints of the pox, no such legislative or judicial curbs existed three hundred years ago. The plays would have been far duller reading if they had.

Compared with the pocky literary output of the seventeenth century we have today a disease-free literature; at least, the currently fashionable diseases are mental and moral. But it would be difficult to maintain that syphilis was more widespread in earlier centuries than in the Penicillin Age. If any one generalization on the subject be truer than another, it is that the pox has been driven from literature into life. As the disease diffused through the populace, the theater audience's relish for seeing a mirror held up to its bald, saddle-nosed, and rosoleate countenance sensibly diminished. A changing morality may have freed the drama of the syphilitic taint, but not the bloodstream.

Yet, there were a few plays written in the late nineteenth or early twentieth century dealing with the then-forbidden subject of venereal disease. These are notably Ibsen's *Ghosts* and Brieux's *Les Avariés*.[1] Ibsen's theme is in part the conspiracy of silence about the disease which permits the evil to grow. A less well-known and equally apt example of the changed attitude toward syphilis is found in Brieux's play. It was received with scant enthusiasm in the France of 1905, and numberless diatribes appeared in the French newspapers denouncing Brieux as a corrupter of public morals and a menace to the purity of youth. Shadwell's *The Humourists* was produced two hundred and thirty-five years earlier, and with correspondingly little applause. But the reasons for Shadwell's lack of success were theatrical, not moral: there had been drastic last-minute alterations at rehearsal; the actors were imperfect in their lines; a clique composed of the author's enemies roundly damned the play.

Both Brieux and Shadwell dealt with syphilis. In *Les Avariés*, a syphilitic young man marries in spite of his doctor's orders; his children are born with congenital lues; a wet-nurse is infected through the nursling and, with high peasant purity, brings the whole structure of the young man's outwardly respectable life down on the head of his innocent family.

The Humourists, on the other hand, is remarkable for the comic character, Crazy: "One that is in pox, in debt, and all the misfortunes that can be, and in the midst of all, in love with most women, and thinks most women in love with him." It

[1] Rendered in English by John Pollack as *Damaged Goods* in *Three Plays by Brieux* (New York, 1913).

cannot be too strongly emphasized that Crazy was intended, and was received, as a legitimate figure of comedy. To Shadwell and his audience the pox was not a malady but a humor, and as we proceed to trace Crazy's pocky progress through the several acts of the piece, the old attitude toward syphilis will stand clearly revealed.

The play begins with a ribald rush as Crazy appears on the stage in a nightgown and cap, lamenting his misfortune: "Oh this surgeon! this damn'd surgeon! will this villanous quack never come to me? Oh this plaister on my neck! It gnaws more than Aqua-Fortis: this abominable rascal has mistaken sure, and given me the same caustick he appli'd to my shins, when they were open'd last." Now enters Mrs. Errant, a bawd. "Good morrow sweet Mr. Crazy," she greets him.

CRAZY. *Good morrow Mrs. Errant.*

ERRANT. *How does the pain in your head?*

CRAZY. *Oh I am on the rack: no primitive Christian under Diocletian ever suffer'd so much as I do under this rascal: this villain, that like a hangman destroys mankind, and has the law for't. Oh abominable quacks! that devour more than all the diseases would do, were they let alone, which they pretend to cure.*

ERRANT. *Ay, but sir, yours is a French surgeon, and who so fit to cure the French Disease as a French-surgeon?*

CRAZY. *Yes, as one poyson expels another; but if this rogue should cure me, he can cure me of nothing but what he has given me himself; 'twas nothing, when I put my self into his hands; he brought it to what it is, and I think I must deal with him as they do that are bitten with a viper, crush the rogues head and apply it to the part, for if I do not kill him, he'l be the death of me.*

ERRANT. *It may be sir, he favours the disease for his countrey's sake.*

CRAZY. *A curse on these French cheats, they begin to be as rife amongst us, as their countrey disease, and do almost as much mischief too: no corner without French taylors, weavers, milliners, strong-water-men, perfumers, and surgeons: but must I be such a fantastick sot as to be cheated by them? Could not I make use of my own countreymen, that are famous all over the world for cheating one another?*

ERRANT. *I am heartily sorry sir, for you could not have been ill in so unseasonable a time.*

CRAZY. *Oh! why Mrs. Errant, what's the matter?*

ERRANT. *Do you think he could not mend you, and patch you up to hold together a little for the present?*

CRAZY. *Why Mrs. Errant? Oh death! what's this I feel?*

ERRANT. *I was with Mrs. Striker the habberdashers wife, this morning, to sell some of my little French toys, as fans, points, that had been worn a little, and jessamine gloves; but chiefly a man of honours old gown, that fitted her to a hair; and a delicate white manteu: and a pair of the neatest little shoes that had been worn two or three days by a countess, that bewitched the very heart of her.*

CRAZY. *Well! and how does my dear Striker? Does she not desire to see me poor heart. . . . Oh what a twinge was that?*

ERRANT. *She does most impatiently wait the good hour, that she may steal from her husband and give you a meeting at the White-Hart at Hammersmith.*

CRAZY. *Alas! dear soul! I know she loves me entirely. Oh my shinne! 'tis there now: sweet Mrs. Errant sit down, and do me the favour to chafe it a little.*

[She sits down and rubs his shins, he makes sowre faces.]
[Enter RAYMUND, "a gentleman of wit and honour."]

RAYMUND. *Ha, ha, ha! this is pleasant, 'faith; this itinerant habberdasher of small wares, is a ranger of the game, a very bawd-errant . . . chafing of his shins too! ha, ha, ha . . . but how could I think any of that profession could be otherwise, procuring lies so in their way, they cannot avoid it.*

CRAZY. *She is a most delicate person. I love her infinitely, and I believe she has no unkindness for me.*

RAYMUND. *Ah brave Crazy! do'st thou hold up thy humour still? Art thou still in love with all women?*

CRAZY. *'Faith Raymund I cannot but have an affection, nay a veneration for the whole sex yet.*

RAYMUND. *I'll swear all women ought to believe thou lov'st 'em, for thou hast suffer'd more for them than all knight errants in romances ever did. I'll say that for thee, and thou hast as much passive-valour as to pill and bolus, as any man in Christendom.*

ERRANT. *It shews him to be a person of much generosity and honour.*

CRAZY. *Perhaps there is not a truer lover of the sex than my self among mankind. . . . Oh my shoulders!*

RAYMUND. *Thou hast reason, witness that twinge else; well certainly so much love and pox never met together in one man since the creation. Nor 'faith do know which is the more tolerable disease of the two.*

CRAZY. *Prethee Raymund no more of this raillery.*

ERRANT. *Do not scandalize Mr. Crazy so; the venom of his disease is all gone; this is but a rheum, a meer rheum.*

RAYMUND. *Why thou villain Crazy, wilt thou never leave wheedling women thus?*

CRAZY. *Prethee leave off; I tell thee 'tis no more.*

RAYMUND. *Why what impudence is this? If thou goest on in this, thou art not fit to go loose; I will have a red cross set upon thy door: Why don't I know thou hast taken bushels of pills and bolus's enough to purge all the corporations in the King's dominions.*

CRAZY. *You make good use of your time, to get drunk so soon in a morning.*

RAYMUND. *Hast thou not rais'd the price of sarsaperilla, and guiacum all over the town. The drugsters are very ungrateful fellows, if they do not give thee a pension for the good thou hast done to their trade.*

CRAZY. *Mind him not Mrs. Errant, he's lewdly drunk.*

ERRANT. *I protest, sir, he's the least in my thoughts.*

RAYMUND. *Why thou sot thou, dost talk of love, and say thou hast no pox? Why, I will not give six moneths purchase for an estate during the term of thy natural nose! I shall live to see thee snuffle worse than a Scotch bagpipe that has got a flaw in the bellows.*

CRAZY. *Let him alone, let him alone! This is a way he has with him.*

ERRANT. *He's a very uncivil man, let me tell you that.*

RAYMUND. *Why hast thou not for these seven years observ'd thy seasons, like the swallow or the cuckoo: with them thou stir'st abroad in the summer, and with them retir'st in the winter: why, thou art a kind of vegetable, that peep'st out thy head at the coming of spring, and shrink'st it in again at the approach of the winter; while we that drink Burgundy, like bay-trees, are green, and flourish all the year.*

CRAZY. *Why, hast thou the confidence to compare wine to beauty?*

ERRANT. *Ay, I thought what a proper man you were.*

CRAZY. Wine, that makes you swell'd like trumpetters with pimpl'd faces; and eyes staring like pigs half roasted, prominent bellies, perish'd lungs, tainted breaths, parch'd livers, decay'd nerves, perpetual feavers, dropsies, gouts, palsies, and a complication of more diseases than you drink healths.

RAYMUND. With what ease can I return upon thee: women, that bring you to sore eyes, weaken'd hamms, sciatica's, falling noses, and rheums, Crazy.

ERRANT. Now out upon you for a base man, to revile women thus.

RAYMUND. But then wine, the bond of human society, that makes us free as absolute princes, rich without covetousness, merry, valiant, witty, generous, and wise without allay; that inspires us far above the level of humane thoughts, and affords us diviner raptures than the deities of old did to their prophets in their extasies.

CRAZY. But then beauty, heaven's brightest image, the thing which all the world desires and fights for; the spur to honour and all glorious actions, without which, no dominion would have been priz'd, or hero ever heard of; the most gentle, sweet, delicate, soft thing—

ERRANT. O, dear Mr. Crazy! Go thy ways, thou art a sweet man.

[She claps CRAZY on the shoulders.]

CRAZY. O Death! What have you done? You have murder'd me; oh, you have struck me just upon a callous node, do you think I have a body of iron?

ERRANT. Sir, I beg your pardon, I had quite forgot it, this rheum is very violent.

CRAZY. Oh, oh.

RAYMUND. The most sweet, delicate, gentle soft thing, go on Crazy.

CRAZY. The most delicate, sweet, gentle, soft—Oh Devil what do I endure?

[Enter PULLIN the French Surgeon.]

PULLIN. Good morr, Good morre.

CRAZY. Oh, oh.

PULLIN. Tis ver wel, come to our business; ve vil proceed to de operation.

CRAZY. Oh my neck and shoulders.

PULLIN. Yes, yes, I vas ver vel assure of dat; it vil put you to de pain indeed; but if dere be such tinge in Englande for draw, den I am no syrigin indeed.

CRAZY. Oh you damn'd eternal son of a whore quack!

PULLIN. Cacque morbleu! Vat is cacque? I know ver vel vat is son for a whore, but vat is cacque vertu-bleu I can no tell.

RAYMUND. 'Tis a certain rascal that cheats a man both of his money and health.

CRAZY. Just such a rascal as you are.

PULLIN. Begar, you are mistake, cacque is no French vard; it is for the damn'd syrigin-English. Mais vat is de matre vid you?

RAYMUND. Damn'd English surgion! Why you impudent villain, did not you when you came first into England, ride upon a milch ass, and did not you maintain your self by selling her milk to people in consumptions, till you set up for an abominable barber, but for the damn'd roughness of your hand, and the filthy noisomness of your breath, could get no customers; and then were fain to set up with six penny worth of diaculum and a collection of rotten pippins, and pretended only to the cure of broken heads; and had you any other customers for a year together, than the cudgel-players of Moor-fields, or now and then a drawer that was wounded with a quart pot.

PULLIN. I am amaze, vat is de businesse?

ERRANT. Sir, I must make bold to take my leave.

CRAZY. Your servant sweet Mrs. Errant, present my service to Theodosia, and let her know I have a passion for her, you understand me.

Errant. Fear it not, sir—   [Exit ERRANT.]

PULLIN. Ver vel, you make de jest of me.

RAYMUND. Was not the next thing you arriv'd at, the inestimable secret of brimstone and butter for the cure of the itch, and had you any one receipt more?

PULLIN. 'Tis ver vel indeed Mr. Crazy! I am come to be abuse.

CRAZY. Why, have you the impudence to deny this? Good Mounseur Pullin, do not I remember when you first set up for the cure of this disease you pretend to, with only two pound of turpentine and a little china, a few hermodactyles, a pound or two of sarsaparilla, and guiacum; two glyster-bags, and one syringe: could all thy wealth arrive at more materials than these?

RAYMUND. I must confess, since, you have learn'd some little experience, by marrying an unsound English strumpet, that was pepper'd by some of your ambassadors footmen; she, by the many courses she has gone therow, has taught you something.

PULLIN. *Tete bleu, dat I shoule be dus affronte.*

RAYMUND. If you had been good for any thing, there were diseases enough in your own country, to maintain you, without coming to us, with a pox to you.

PULLIN. *O Jernie, vat is dis? I have cure ten thousand gentlemen of de clappe in Paris, and to be abuse!*—

CRAZY. Am not I oblig'd to you then, that you would not cure one in England? For Raymund, now there is not a woman here, I confess to you, he has not wholly cur'd me; but on my conscience I can do a woman no hurt.

PULLIN. *I am assure dat all de operators for de clapp in England, can no do so much as I do to cure you.*

RAYMUND. Why, hast thou not been longer in curing him than a Chancery suit is depending?

CRAZY. Did not I put my self into your hands when it was first a gonorrhea virulenta? Did not you by your damn'd French tricks, your styptick-injections, and your turpentine-clysters, suffer me to be chorde, to come to caruncles, to the phymasii, caries, pubii, bubones, herniae.

RAYMUND. Nay, have you not driven his enemy out of the open field, where he might have been easily conquer'd, into his strong holds and garisons.

PULLIN. *Ver vel, ver vel.*

CRAZY. Is there any one symptome which I have not had?—Oh—have I not had your carbuncula, acbrocordones, mermecii, thymi, all sorts of ulcers superficial and profound, callous, cancerous, fistilous.

RAYMUND. Hey-brave Crazy! Thou hast terms enough to set up two reasonable mountebanks.

CRAZY. Have I not had your pustulae, crustatae, and sine crustis verucae, cristae, tophi, ossis, caries, chyronya, telephia, phagaenia, disepulotica.

RAYMUND. What art thou going to raise the devil with these hard words?

PULLIN. *Vel! and have I no cure all dese? Have I no given you de sweate, not in a damned English tub or hot-house, but I have taught you to sweat in de cradle, and vid spirit of vine in de Pape lanthorn, a la Francois, and taught you de use of de Baine d'Alexandre.*

CRAZY. And has all this done any thing but driven him to his winter quarters, where he domineers as much as ever? Oh I have him here.

RAYMUND. You have given him so many bolus's in gold-leaf, that the loathsomeness of 'em, has made his stomach turn at a twenty shillings piece, and that's the reason he never carries any in his pocket.

CRAZY. Do you hear that rascal? I have been cheated enough by you; but I'll bilk your cribbidge for you.

PULLIN. But assure de law will give de remede.

CRAZY. And that thou mayst be curst sufficiently for this, mayst thou be as long in law as I have been in physick.

RAYMUND. Prethee curse him to purpose, may he be choak'd with bolus's, drown'd in dyet-drink, or smother'd in a privy-house, that he may die by that excrement by which he liv'd.

PULLIN. Diable, no curse me, give de madiction to the dam whore.

CRAZY. O impudence! I protest to you Raymund, she is as pretty a civil young lady, and between you and I, a person of honour?

RAYMUND. She was a very pocky person of honour.

CRAZY. And on my conscience and soul, loved me as passionately as any young lady in England.

RAYMUND. Besides, if she were a whore, his calling [To PULLIN] is to give it, and yours to cure it, sirrah.

CRAZY. Shall I suffer so excellent, so virtuous a person, to be traduc'd by your foul mouth, you rascal: get you gone, you dogge.— [Kicks him.]

PULLIN. O vat is dis? Elp. Elp—vel, vel, dere is de law for do me justice—   [Exit PULLIN.]

Poor Crazy's misfortunes mount in the second act, when he is arrested by bailiffs:

CRAZY. Arrest me! at whose suit? Hold, hold, hands off. Oh you hurt my callous node.

BAYLIFF. Do not tell us of this and that, I arrest you at the suit of Monsieur Pullin the French surgeon. Come away.

Throughout the play the unfortunate man continually suffers blows and accidental knocks on his tender lesions. We can almost hear the audience guffaw at Crazy's yells of pain as, for example, in Act V, when he comes on the stage, stumbles, and falls:

> *Murder, murder. O Heaven! What shall I do? I have hurt my self*
> *just upon the shin-bone, that was exfoliated: I have spoil'd my*
> *arm: I fell just upon that part of my arm, where is a callous node*
> *upon the* Periostium. . . . *'Sdeath, I have spilt my bottle of diet-*
> *drink in my pocket.* . . .

The play closes in a double hoax. Crazy has married Lady
Loveyouth for her money, and too late it is discovered that she
had previously been tricked into signing away her fortune to her
niece.

"Am I thus cozen'd and abus'd?" the Lady wails, and Crazy
echoes the protest with "'Tis I am cozen'd and abused." But
"I'le be reveng'd of her," he says to himself, and aloud: "I must
tell you, madam, you are not less disappointed than I am; for I
must ingeniously confess I am very much visited with the pox."
"O Heaven," moans her ladyship. "I am undone for ever; this is
a most unspeakable disappointment to a lady! O miserable
woman that I am."

Crazy is far from a unique figure, nor are heroes with the
French disease characteristic only of dissolute Restoration days
Don John, the principal personage in Beaumont and Fletcher's
The Chances (produced about 1623), is described by his land-
lady as

> . . . *ne'r without a noise of sirynges*
> *In's pocket, those proclaim him; birding pills,*
> *Waters to cool his conscience, in small viols.* . . .
>
> III, 3

In the first act of the play Frederick wanders over the stage
seeking Don John. "Sure," he mutters:

> . . . *he has encountred*
> *Some light o' love or other, and there means*
> *To play at in and in for this night. Well Don John,*
> *If you do spring a leak, or get an itch,*
> *Till ye claw off your curl'd pate, thank your night-walks.* . . .
> . . . *if he be a bobbing,*
> *'Tis not my care can cure him: To morrow morning*

I shall have further knowledge from a surgeon's—
Where he lyes moor'd, to mend his leaks.

I, 4, 7

Eventually the two friends meet:

JOHN.   *This night*
    This bawdy night.
FRED. *I thought no less.*
JOHN. *This blind night,*
    What dost think I have got?
FRED. *The Pox it may be.*

II, 1

At no time during the century was the presence on the stage
of the pox sufficient to turn comedy into tragedy. Rather the
reverse. How is it then that Brieux wrote on a tragic theme
tragically, and the seventeenth-century dramatists on the same
theme lightsomely? Syphilis was equally as dread a disease two
hundred and fifty years ago as in Brieux's period. The times had
changed, one concludes; not the pox.

But even in the seventeenth century, it was the dramatists, not
the medical men, who laughed at the disease and the sufferers
from it. There is no humor, for instance, in Dr. Sydenham's
account of the course of the pox in his time, and this grimness is
not entirely owing to that great physician's singular lack of
humor. Sydenham writes:

> *The patient is afflicted with an unusual pain in the genitals*
> *. . . A spot, about the size and colour of a measle, appears on*
> *some part of the glans . . . A discharge appears from the*
> *urethra . . . The aforesaid pustule becomes an ulcer. . . .*
> *Great pain during erections, pathognomic of the disease. . . .*
> *Ardor urinae. . . . Buboes in the groin. . . . Pain in the head,*
> *arms and ankles. . . . Crusts and scabs appear on the skin.*
> *. . . The bones of the skull, the shin-bones, and the arm-bones,*
> *are raised into hard tubers. . . . The bone becomes carious and*
> *putrescent. . . . Phagedaenic ulcers destroy the cartilage of the*
> *nose. This they eat away; so that the bridge sinks in and the nose*

flattens. . . . At length, limb by limb perishing away, the lacer-
ated body, a burden to earth, finds ease only in the grave.[2]

And the cure, as those poor devils who had experienced both
observed fervidly, was quite as bad as the disease. Once again
one wonders how the old poets could write so unconcernedly of
so terrible a plague, when a modern author in the days of an
attenuated virus and an easy specific cannot touch on the subject
without morbidity and an atmosphere of impending doom. A
comprehensive review of the seventeenth-century allusions will
answer the question without a commentator's aid.

Syphilis in the seventeenth century was both an old and a new
disease. It was new in the sense that it had been unknown (as
such) to the ancient world, for all laymen and most physicians
believed the disease to have been imported by the sailors of
Columbus from the New World in 1493. One of those smug
nineteenth-century English travelers called it "the terrible disorder with which the Aborigines of America avenged themselves
on their European invaders." [3] Two centuries before, Webster in
The Devils Law-case had termed it the "Indian Pox" (III, 3).
His fellow dramatists were all agreed that it was a "new disease,"
and I think this popular attribution of novelty to the disorder is
important enough to call for chapter and verse:

widow. . . . *they are not gentlemen, that with their secret sins
increase our surgeons, and lie in foraign countries, for new
sores. . . .*
BEAUMONT and FLETCHER, *Wit with-out Money*, III, 1

*The new disease (otherwise called the Great Pox) with all its
appendices, [is cured] in few dayes; with herbs which I gather in
the woods, and gums of trees.*
WILSON, *Cheats*, II, 2

The disease was old in that over a century had elapsed between its European introduction and 1600, and its course had

---

[2] *Works*, trans. Dr. Greenhill (London, 1848), II, 35 ff.
[3] *Narrative of an Excursion from Corfu to Smyrna* (London, 1827), p. 179.

changed from its first acute manifestations to the more chronic form we now know.

The controversy still rages, but in a mild and endemic manner, whether the pox was actually a New World disease or whether it had belonged to antiquity under a different name and perhaps a different train of signs and symptoms. We are not concerned here with paleopathological evidence, or medical works of doubtful date, or medical writers of doubtful descriptive ability. But germane to the general thesis of this book is the insufficiently appreciated observation that any disease striking enough to cause a flood of medical discussion can be counted on to precipitate a shower of lay comment as well. In the case of the pox the medical historian Daniel LeClerc perspicaciously reasoned:

> Si cette honteuse maladie avoit eu anciennement course en Grèce ou en Italie, se pourroitil que dans tant d'écrits satiriques qui nous ont restez des poëtes de ce tems-là, il n'y eut pas un seul trait piquant, lancé contre quelcun, soit homme, ou femme qui auroit été atteint d'un pareil mal? Le silence des poëtes à cet égard me paroit du moins d'un aussi grand poids pour la preuve du fait dont il s'agit, que celui des médecins.[4]

> [If this shameful malady had formerly run its course in Greece or in Italy, could it be that in so many of the satiric writings which have come down to us from the writers of that time, there would not be a single biting portrait drawn of someone, be it man or woman, who had been disfigured by such an evil? The silence of the writers in this respect would appear to me to be at least as significant in connection with the subject under consideration as that of the physicians.]

A few years later the syphilographer Jean Astruc considered in greater detail certain allusions from Greek and Latin authors which those who believed in the antiquity of the pox twisted to support their thesis. Horace, Martial, Juvenal, Suetonius, Tacitus, Lucian, Eusebius, Palladius, and Ausonius were examined

---

[4] *Histoire de la Médicine* (new ed.; La Haye, 1729), pp. 788–789.

and adjudged innocent of any knowledge of the French Disease.[5]

This absence of satirical reference to the pox before 1495 seems to me almost the only incontrovertible evidence that before that date the disease was unknown in Europe. The majority of medical historians have also reached that conclusion from more technical evidence—and the lack of it. At any rate, we owe it solely to the wave of seventeenth-century European nationalism that syphilis is not known to this day and forever as the American Disease.

In 1494 the French army under Charles VIII invaded Italy and laid seige to Naples, defended by the Spaniards. The Spanish saw themselves beaten by force and hence fell'back on strategy. The Spanish contingent, like all armies of that era, was accompanied by an ancillary brigade of harlots. Thanks to the sailors of Columbus who had taken service with Spain, this brigade was well polluted with the pox. The passage which follows is a free translation from *De Morbo Gallico* by Fallopius, the illustrious sixteenth-century anatomist:

> *The Spanish knew very well how dangerous and easily communicable the disease was, and at the same time they were not ignorant of the Frenchman's susceptibility to feminine wiles; so they sent their debauched women into the ranks of the French army. The strategem succeeded. The Frenchman lost no time in meeting the harlots and incidentally in catching their disease. Soon all the army was infected, and it was thus that the malady began to make itself known throughout Italy, both as to name and as to effect.*

When the French army disbanded shortly thereafter and the mercenaries dispersed to their homes throughout Europe, the pox accompanied them in ever-widening waves. It is only fair to say that, however attractive Fallopius' hypothesis of the spread of the disease may seem, it lacks sufficient evidence to raise it to the full dignity of an established fact.

[5] *Treatise of Venereal Diseases* (London, 1754), Bk. I, Ch. 3.

Thus the varied terminology was born. The disgruntled Italians and Spanish called the malady the "French disease." The French, in a vain attempt to recover from the scurvy trick played them by their penchant for petticoats, retaliated with the "Neapolitan disease" and the "Spanish sickness." German soldiers of fortune returned home, and with a spiteful glance over their eastern border spoke of the "Polish pocks." The Poles had equally hard things to say about the "German pox." Maritime Italian traders learned to their sorrow of the "Turkish disorder" or the "Persian fire." Each nationality tried enthusiastically to saddle the disease on its nearest neighbor. In the congress of nations, the French were outvoted; and in the seventeenth century the pox—*mal franzoso, morbus gallicus,* the French Disease —was one of France's chief claims to fame.

Needless to say, the dramatists were more than occasionally intrigued by this matter of calling a spade by a less direct name. Middleton's *Any thing for a Quiet Life* contains a scene of spirited surgical satire and a bit of syphilitic fun:

BARBER. *So friend, Ile now dispatch you presently: Boy, reach me my dis-membring instrument, and let my cauterize[r] be ready; and hark you Snipsnap!*

BOY. *I sir.*

BARBER. *See if my l[i]xi[v]ium, my fomentation be provided first, and get my rowlers, bolsters, and pleggets arm'd.*

RALPH. *Nay good sir dispatch my business first; I should not stay from my shop.*

BARBER. *You must have a little patience sir, when you are a patient; if prepu[t]ium be not too much perisht, you shall loose but little by it, believe my art for that.*

RALPH. *What's that sir?*

BARBER. *Marry if there be exulceration between prepu[t]ium and glan[s], by my faith the whole penis may be endanger'd as far as os pub[i]s.*

RALPH. *What's that you talk on, sir?*

BARBER. *If they be gangren'd once, Testiculi, Vesica, and all may run to mortification.*

RALPH. *What a pox does this Barber talk on?*

BARBER. *O fie youth, pox is no word of art, Morbus Gallicus, or Neopolitanus had bin well. . . .*

II, 3

Pox may have been no word of art, but it was a word of universal understanding.

Other names for the ubiquitous disease were legion. There were as many synonyms for the pox as there were for the whores, and to list them in space would dwarf even the Mithridatian formula. One of the strangest was "the goose," a singularly apt name for any venereal swelling. "Winchester goose" was an accepted Elizabethan phrase, for within the Bishop of Winchester's liberties stood the notorious stews of the Bankside. Thus Pettifog deposes:

> *Ile tell you how he was served: this informer comes into Turnbull-street to a victualling-house, and there falls in league with a wench. . . . Had belike some private dealings with her, and there got a goose. . . . Now sir, this fellow in revenge of this, informs against the bawd that kept the house, that she used cannes in her house; but the cunning jade comes me into th' court, and there deposes that she gave him true Winchester measure.*
>
> WEBSTER, *Cure for a Cuckold*, IV, 1

English medical books of the day, catering more to the sufferer than the doctor, spoke on their title pages of the French Pox, Pest, or Disease. It was otherwise across the channel: with singular unanimity the French authors substituted "venereal" for "French," while in all Europe around them treatises called *De Morbo Gallico* appeared. Of course, others besides Frenchmen realized that it was not quite fair to identify the word with the deed. Witness Ben Jonson:

PUNTARVOLO. *Methinkes, Carlo, you looke verie smooth! ha?*
CARLO. *Why, I come but now from a hot-house; I must needs looke smooth.*
PUNTARVOLO. *From a hot-house!*
CARLO. *I, doo you make a wonder on't? Why it's your only physicke.*

> Let a man sweate once a weeke in a hot-house, and be well rub'd,
> and froted, with a good plumpe juicie wench, and sweet linnen:
> hee shall ne're ha' the poxe.

PUNTARVOLO. *What, the French poxe?*

CARLO. *The French poxe! our poxe. S'bloud we have 'hem in as good
forme as they, man: what?*

Every Man out of His Humour, IV, 3

Nevertheless, the English dramatists never missed the chance to score off their hereditary enemies and their acquired disease at one blow. One Timorous Cornet, speaking of young English fops whose farthest travel is into France, "Where they learn to swear Mor-blew, Mor-dee," has the burden of his complaint amplified:

FRIENDLY. *And tell you how much bigger the Louvre is than White-
hall; buy a suit a-la-mode, get a swinging clap of some French
marquise, spend all their money, and return just as they went.*

APHRA BEHN, *Widow Ranter*, II, 2

Thomas Nashe had said much the same thing, almost a century earlier: "What is there in Fraunce to bee learned more than in England, but . . . to esteeme of the pox as a pumple, to weare a velvet patch on their face, and walke melancholy with their arms folded" (*Unfortunate Traveller*, p. 95). And others wrote:

BOULT. . . . *But, mistress, do you know the French knight that
cow'rs i'the hams?*

BAWD. *Who, Monsieur Verollus?*

BOULT. *Ay, he. He offered to cut a caper at the proclamation; but he
made a groan at it, and swore he would see her to-morrow.*

BAWD. *Well, well; as for him, he brought his disease hither: here he
does but repair it. . . .*

SHAKESPEARE, *Pericles*, IV, 2

Enter Raph [from the French wars] being lame.

WIFE. *Trust mee I am sorrie Raph to see thee impotent, Lord how
the warres have made him sunburnt: the left leg is not well, 'twas
a faire gift of God, the infirmitie took not hold a little higher,
considering thou camst from France, but let that passe.*

DEKKER, *The Shoemakers' Holiday* [6]

---

[6] *Dramatic Works* (London, 1873), I, 40.

MEG. *Whate'er we get by strangers,*
    The Scotch, the Dutch, or Irish,
  Or, to come nearer home,
    By masters of the parish;
  It is concluded thus,
    By all and every wench,
  To take of all their coins,
    And pay 'em back in French.
                  MIDDLETON, *Faire Quarrell*, IV

For though Chineses go to bed,
And lye in, in their ladies stead,
And for the pains they took before,
Are nurs'd, and pamper'd to do more:
Our green-men do it worse, when th' hap
To fall in labour of a clap
Both lay the child to one another,
But who's the father, who the mother,
'Tis hard to say in multitudes
Or who imported the French goods.
              BUTLER, *Hudibras*, Pt. III, Canto 1

You're no such fools as first to mount a wall,
Or for your king and country venture all.
With such like grinning honour 'twas perchance,
Your dull, forefathers first did conquer France.
Whilst they have sent us, in revenge for these,
Their women, wine, religion, and disease.
         APHRA BEHN, *Young King*, Prologue

Compare Mrs. Behn's last couplet with the English traveler's remark. The pox was an instrument of national as well as personal vengeance.

No respecter of geographical lines, the pox transcended social boundaries as well. Ben Jonson called it "the punques evil," [7]

---

[7] Nightingale sings (*Bartholomew Fayre*, II, 4):
  Heare for your love, and buy for your money.
  A delicate ballad o' the ferret and the coney.
  A preservative again' the punques evill.
  Another of goose-greene-starch, and the devill.

Wycherley, the "modish distemper," [8] and between these two extremes of society the disease ran riot. We are somewhat surprised, nevertheless, to learn that the upper classes were even harder hit than their humbler sisters.

> There was about 1644 a pamphlet (writt by Henry Nevill, esq. anonymous) called The Parliament of Ladies, 3 or 4 sheets in 4to, wherein Sir Henry Blount was first to be called to the barre for spreading abroad that abominable and dangerous doctrine that it was far cheaper and safer to lye with common wenches than with ladies of quality.
>
> AUBREY, Brief Lives, I, 109

On two separate occasions Thomas Shadwell enunciated Blount's doctrine on the stage. Old Tope in Act II of *The Scowrers* thus meditates on the subject before he attempts to lay aboard Lady Maggot: "So now have at her, pray Heaven she be sound—she's of quality—hah! may be ne're the sounder for that neither—Hail solitary damsel." And in Act III of *Bury-Fair* Lord Bellamy comments in the same vein: "Your fine women, are a company of proud, vain, fops and jilts, abominably daub'd and painted; and I had rather kiss a blackamoor, with a natural complexion, than any such: and, besides, many of them are so unsound, that making love is become as dangerous as making war; and the wounds and scars are dishonorable to boot."

Nor was this disrespectful attitude toward noble ladies a fruit of the Restoration, for back in 1619 Beaumont and Fletcher knew of the dangers lurking beneath gentle plackets:

LEONTIUS. *Here's one has served now under Captain Cupid,*
And crackt a pike in's youth: you see what's come on't.
LIEUTENANT. *No, my disease will never prove so honourable.*

---

[8] *Mrs. Martha.* Besides, they say, he has the modish distemper.
   Sir Simon Addleplot. He can cure it with the best (French) chyrurgion in town.

                              (*Love in a Wood*, IV, 2)

Sir Simon's remark recalls Sudhoff's contention that the French Disease was so called because the French surgeons were so skillful in curing it. The quotations in this chapter effectively dispose of such a piece of whitewashing. The French Disease received its name because one caught it from Frenchmen or Frenchwomen. Furthermore, quackish clap-surgeons in the plays were almost always French— and far from skillful, as Crazy and many another infected character could testify.

LEONTIUS. *Why, sure, thou hast the best pox.*
LIEUTENANT.   *If I have 'em,*
   I am sure I got 'em in the best company;
   They are pox of thirty coats.
                    Humourous Lieutenant, I, 1

Be the unsoundness of the upper-class women as it may have been, references in the plays to the perils in punks' petticoats would fill a chapter in themselves. One nondramatic example, from *The Fire-Ships*, 1691,[9] must suffice here, for queans and their evils are linked in half the plays I shall quote:

> *Permit me now dear Strephon, to relate,*
> *The tricks and wiles of whores of second rate*
> *The play-house punks, who in a loose undress,*
>   *. . . sell their rotten ware:*
> *Tho' done in silence and without a cryer,*
> *Yet he that bids the most, is still the buyer;*
> *For while he nibbles at her am'rous trap,*
> *She gets the mony, but he gets the clap.*

To demonstrate that in this respect literature only mirrored life, John Aubrey describes two lives, one high and one low, with a common pocky touch. Eleanor Ratcliffe, Countess of Sussex, was:

> . . . *a great and sad example of the power of lust and slavery to it. She was as great a beautie as any in England and had a good witt. After her lord's death (he was jealous) she sends for ——— (formerly) her footman, and makes him groom of the chamber. He had the pox and shee knew it; a damnable sot. He wuz not very handsom but his body of an exquisit shape. . . . His nostrills were stufft and borne out with corkes in which were quills to breathe through. About 1666 this countess dyed of the pox.*
> Brief Lives, II, 198

---

[9] The author gives his solemn word that he *did not* invent *The Fire-Ships*, although he is now unable to locate the source of his notes. He pleads guilty only to a unique lapse in that aspect of scholarship called "chapter-and-versification." In fact, he wishes he *had* invented *The Fire-Ships*, and he apologizes to his present readers for not having had wit enough to do so.

Elizabeth Broughton, too,

> . . . was a most exquisite beautie, as finely shaped as nature
> could frame; and had a delicate witt. She was soon taken notice
> of at London, and her price was very deare—a second Thais.
> Richard, earle of Dorset, kept her (whether before or after Vene-
> tia [Stanley, who afterwards married Sir Kenelm Digby] I know
> not, but I guesse before). At last she grew common and infamous
> and gott the pox, of which she died.
>
> Brief Lives, I, 127

Fashionable men were no less unsound than ladies of quality
and even gloried in their disability, although we shall do well to
take Duffett's satirical epilogue to *The Spanish Rogue* with a
grain or two of salt:

> Poets, from France, fetch'd new intrigue, and plot,
> Kind women, new French words, and fashions got:
> And finding all French tricks so much did please,
> T'oblige ye more, they got—ev'n their disease,
> That too did take—and as much honour gets
> As breaking windows, or not paying debts.
> O 'tis so gente! So modish! and so fine!
> To shrug and cry, Faith Jack! I drink no wine:
> For I've a swinging clap this very time. . . .

Tom D'Urfey and Charles Sedley have some similar lines, and
one is forced to conclude that so much smoke must have arisen
from some small burning in the privy parts of young blades who,
flaunted the proof of their deviltries.

> The stages ruine unconcern'd you see,
> And dam th' original of gallantry.
> Shou'd we leave off then, we shou'd hear you say,
> Dam 'em what drones are there, why don't they play?
> 'Sblud I shall never leave this wenching vein,
> Jack, my last swinging clap's broke out agen.
> And if we do play—then you censure raise,
> And to encourage us, dam all our playes.
>
> D'URFEY, Madam Fickle, Prologue

Proclaim your drunken fray's three benches round
What claps y'have met with, and what punks are found
Who are the bully-rocks: and who gives ground.

SEDLEY, Bellamira, Prologue

The virtuous Pepys, who in some miraculous manner kept himself from taint, also voiced his indignation at conditions above him: Mr. Pickering, "though he be a fool, yet he keeps much company, and will tell all he knows or hears, and so a man may understand what the common talk of the town is. . . . He tells me plainly of the vices of the court, and how the pox is so common there, and so I hear on all hands that it is as common as eating and swearing" (*Diary*, September 2, 1661).

"Who took care of your education there [at the court]?" Vanbrugh's anachronistic Æsop asks a beau.

BEAU. *A whore and a dancing-master.*
ÆSOP. *What did you gain by them?*
BEAU. *A minuet, and the pox.*

ÆSOP, Part II

The seventeenth century had male counterparts of its female fire-ships, and it was no secret that they were equally unsound. Three such inmates of a male stews come on the stage in Fletcher and Massinger's *The Custom of the Country*. One was a Frenchman:

Alas, he's all to fitters,
And lyes, taking the height of his fortune with a syringe.

III, 3

The next a Dane:

He's foul i'th' touch-hole; and recoils again,
The main spring's weaken'd that holds up his cock,
He lies at the sign of the sun, to be new breech'd.

The third an Englishman:

Drink, and their own devices, have undone 'em.

Obviously three such wrecks were of no use in the trade, and one Rutilio becomes the reigning inmate. At last he too is worn to skin and aching bones, and when his predecessors appear on

the stage "with night-caps very faintly" Rutilio's jeering changes
to a plea to relieve him of his place:

RUTILIO.   Good gentlemen;
  You seem to have a snuffing in your head sir,
  A parlous snuffing, but this same dampish air—
2 GENTLEMAN. *A dampish air indeed.*
RUTILIO. *Blow your face tenderly,*
  Your nose will ne're endure it: mercy o' me,
  What are men chang'd to here? is my nose fast yet?
  Me thinks it shakes i'th' hilts: pray tell me, gentlemen,
  How long is't since you flourisht here?
3 GENTLEMAN. *Not long since.*
RUTILIO. *Move your self easily, I see you are tender,*
  Nor long endured.
2 GENTLEMAN. *The labour was so much sir,*
  And so few to perform it—
RUTILIO. *Must I come to this?*
  And draw my legs after me like a lame dog?
  I cannot run away, I am too feeble:
  Will you sue me for this place again gentlemen?
1 GENTLEMAN. No truly sir, the place has been too warm for our
complexions.

                  IV, 1

If male punks were unsound, panders were no less so. Lodovico knew. "I have been a pander," he tells Jaques in Rowley's
All's Lost by Lust, "knowst thou what a pander is?" "In briefe a
knave; more at large thus," sings Jaques in reply:

  Hee's a thing that is poore,
  He waits upon a whore,
  When shee's sick, hee's sore,
  In the streets he goes before,
  At the chamber waits at doore,
  All his life a runs o'th score,
  This I know, and know no more.

"All this Ile adde to it," carols Lodovico:

  He weares long locks,
  And villainous socks,

Many nights in the stocks,
Endures some knocks,
And a many of mocks,
Eates reversions of cocks,
Yet lies in the flocks,
Thrives by the smocks,
And dies with the pox.

V, 3

The seventeenth century may not have known "how the venereal contagion began" (and no more do we), but it knew very
well how it was propagated. Toward the middle of the previous
century a Florentine syphilographer observed that "the infection
of the French Disease has never been observed to be communicated by means of the air." [10] The author, Vidus Vidius, was
making no mere sardonic inference. Both popular and medical
minds fought as long as possible against the idea that the pox
was venereally transmitted. "For which reason the physicians
. . . in general believed . . . that this new disease was epidemi-
cal, like other pestilential distempers, and owing to an external
and common cause, which some of them thought to be a malig-
nant influence of the stars, or the bad aspect of the planets, and
others an unwholesome disposition of the air, brought on by
rains and inundations." [11]

Long before 1600, however, men—and women—learned that
the pox traveled from an unsound man or woman to his or her
sound paramour; that syphilitic mothers had pocky children;
that an infected child could pox its wet-nurse and vice versa. In
the case of adults, indeed, the vulgar mind satirically denied the
probability of innocent infection, and medical experience apparently corroborated the cynics. "So Fallopius, *Tractatu de Morbo
Gallico*, Cap. 13, laughs at some particular persons, who 'in
order to defend the chaste matrons, said that they were infected
by the blessed water; but that infection, says he, I know owed its
origin to a certain sprinkling.' " [12]

[10] Astruc, *Treatise of Venereal Diseases* (London, 1754), p. 119.
[11] *Ibid.*, p. 117.
[12] *Ibid.*, p. 121.

The dramatists, too, knew what that certain sprinkling was. "Come away," commands a bawd to a courtesan under her protection; "Poverty's catching." "So is the pox, good matron, of which you can afford good penniworth's," retorts the moneyless customer (Aphra Behn, *The Rover*, Pt. II, I, 1).

Here are some variations on the theme:

AMOROUS. *Suppose I trade with some of her aunts the bawds, and get the pox and give it her. Why then, the venom of her own nature will relieve it, and I alone am wretched.*
D'URFEY, Love for Money, III, 2

GALLIARD. *And what's this high-priz'd lady's name, sir?*
SIR SIGNAL BUFFOON. *La Silvianetta,—and lodges on the Corso, not far from St. James of the Incurables—very well situated in case of disaster—hah.*
APHRA BEHN, Feign'd Courtezans, III, 1

MERRYMAN [to Cuningham]. *. . . a wench may starve that has had to do with you; no man will venture upon her, who has any reverence for his nose: nor have you anything to give 'em but the pox.*
SEDLEY, Bellamira, I, 2

SIR ALEXANDER WENGRAVE. *Art sure of this?*
TRAPDORE. *As every throng is sure of a pick-pocket, as sure as a whoore is of the clyents all Michaelmas tearme, and of the pox after the tearme.*
MIDDLETON, Roaring Girle, III

HECCATE. *Hail! hail! hail! you less than wits and greater!*
  Hail fop in corner! and the rest now met here,
  Thou you'l ne're be wits—from your loins shall spread,
  Diseases that shall reign when you are dead.
DUFFETT, The Empress of Morocco, Epilogue [13]

One would suppose that, with all the wenching that went on in those days, virtuous wives lay in the greatest danger from their husbands' unlawful loves. But even kept women feared the

---

[13] EPILOGUE./Being a new Fancy after the old,/and most surprising way/OF/MACBETH,/Perform'd with new and costly/MACHINES,/ . . . Printed in the Year 1674. [Affixed to his farce *The Empress of Morocco*.]

wages of sin. Such a one was Betty Flauntit, who belonged to Sir
Timothy Taudrey, the town fop of Mrs. Behn's play. Her contempt for a pair of common whores is almost beyond words.
"Lord," she exclaims, "how they stink of paint and pox, faugh."
And when she catches Sir Timothy in their company she berates
him with all the outraged virtue of a churched woman: "'Tis
here you spend that which should buy me points and petticoats,
while I go like no body's mistress; I'd as live be your wife at this
rate, so I had: and I'm in no small danger of getting the foule
disease by your lewdness" (*Town-Fop*, IV, 1).

A story is told of Francis I that he desired the wife of a
Parisian tradesman, but she refused him. After consulting the
court lawyers the King determined to exert the royal prerogative;
and the woman, hearing of this, acquired a syphilitic infection
with the aid of her husband and a pocky whore. In due time
Francis caught the pox and, it is said, died of it.[14]

Sir Charles Sedley's epigram on "Scilla" is in order here:

> Storm not, brave friend, that thou hadst never yet
>   Mistress nor wife that others did not—,
> But like a Christian, pardon and forget,
>   For thy own pox will thy revenge contrive.[15]

And this tale from Aubrey's *chroniques scandaleuses*:

> Anno. . . . (as I remember, 1635) there was a maried woman
> in Drury-lane that had clapt [i.e., given the pox to] a woman's
> husband, a neighbor of hers. She complained of this to her

---

[14] When the Earl of Southesk discovered the intrigue of his wife with the Duke
of York, the accidental discovery ". . . broke off a commerce which the Duke of
York did not much regret; and indeed it was happy for him that he became
indifferent; for the traitor Southesk meditated a revenge, whereby, without using
either assassination or poison, he would have obtained some satisfaction upon
those who had injured him, if the connection had continued any longer.

"He went to the most infamous places, to seek for the most infamous disease,
which he met with; but his revenge was only half completed; for after he had
gone through every remedy to get quit of his disease, his lady did but return him
his present, having no more connection with the person for whom it was so
industriously prepared" (Anthony Hamilton, *Mémoirs of Count Grammont*, ed.
with notes by Sir Walter Scott [London, 1876], pp. 179–180.

[15] In *Poetical and Dramatic Works*, ed. V. De Sola Pinto (London, 1928), I,
62.

neighbour gossips. *So they concluded on this revenge, viz. to gett
her and whippe her and [to shave all the haire off her pu-
denda];* [16] *which severities were executed and put into a ballad.
'Twas the first ballad I ever cared for the reading of: the burden
of it was thus:—*
Did yee ever heare the like
    Or ever heare the same,
Of five woemen-barbers
    That lived in Drewry lane?* [17]

Brief Lives, II, 73

There was no Wassermann reaction to safeguard prospective
seventeenth-century inamorata, and prudent lovers sometimes
refused to take good health on faith. Thus Evanthe, to whom a

[16] The words between brackets are represented by a series of dots in Clark's
(1898) edition of *Brief Lives*. The ballad must thus have seemed pointless to
many a reader before John Collier's edition (New York, 1931) supplied the
missing phrase.

[17] Aubrey's remembrance of the date of the ballad is a little off. In Act IV,
scene 3 of Richard Brome's *The Court Beggar*, which had been produced in
1632, there is an amusing reference to those same women-barbers.
Strangelove and her suitors resolve to be revenged on a doctor who had a
lunatic patient, and "who thought to have cur'd his patient (who has bin a
notable Gamester at *In* and *In*) between my Ladies legs." Cit-wit says the erring
doctor should "be presently hang'd out o' the way." Court-wit suggests "First,
opening the pericranion, then take out the cerebrum; wash it in albo vino, till it
be throughly clens'd; and then—" But Swaynwit, the third suitor, objects that
they must not be guilty of the death of even a dogleech. He himself recommends
filling the doctor's "belly full of whey, or buttermilke, put him naked into a hogs-
head, then close up the vessell and roll your garden with it."
Widow Strangelove rejects all these proposals, and just then a sow-gelder's horn
is heard off-stage. "Fetch in that minister of justice," orders the humorous dame,
and as the implication strikes home to the others they burst into applause.
"But you will not see the execution madam?" asks Court-wit. She replies:

Why not as well as other women have
Seene the dissections of anotamies,
And executed men rip'd up and quarter'd?
This spectacle will be comicall to those.

Then, while the sow-gelder "*whets his knife and all in preparation, Linnen,
Bason, &c.*," the terror-stricken doctor pleads for his manhood. The widow relents
at the last possible moment. "Would I ha' seene you guelt dee think?" she
laughs. "That would have renderd mee more brutish then the women barbers."

king is making unwelcome advances, asks the bawd, his embassadress:

> . . . *but canst thou tell me,*
> *Though he be a king, whether he be sound or no?*
> *I would not give my youth up to infection.*
> CASTRUCCIO. *As sound as honour ought to be, I think, lady.* . . .
>   BEAUMONT AND FLETCHER, *Wife for a Month*, IV, 1

And Lady Thrivewell, in Brome's *Mad Couple Well Match'd* (III, 1), demands, "Is the man found true?" To which Careless replies, "I defy surgeon, or the potecary can come against mee." Evidently Careless was not all his name implied.

One of the tricks considered fair in seventeenth-century courting was to impute the pox to a rival. One lover of the day bribed a lady's maid to further his suit. Said he:

> ELDER LOVELESS. *I shall not need to teach you how to discredit their beginning, you know how to take exception at their shirts at washing, or to make the maids swear they found plasters in their beds.*
>   BEAUMONT AND FLETCHER, *Scornful Lady*, III

To be discovered with a bottle of diet-drink in one's pocket or a plaster or a tub in one's chamber was to be caught *in flagrante delicto*, as it were.

The men were quite as cautious as the women—when time allowed. Witness Lysimachus in a bawdy-house:

> LYSIMACHUS. *How now? How a dozen of virginities?*
> BAWD. *Now the gods to bless your Honour!*
> BOULT. *I am glad to see your Honour in good health.*
> LYSIMACHUS. *You may so; 'tis the better for you that your resorters stand upon sound legs. How now, wholesome iniquity? Have you that a man may deal withal and defy the surgeon?*
> BAWD. *We have here one, sir, if she would—but there never came her like in Mytilene.*
> LYSIMACHUS. *If she'd do the deed of darkness, thou wouldst say.*
> BAWD. *Your Honour knows what 'tis to say well enough.*
>   SHAKESPEARE, *Pericles*, IV, 6

The old substitute for the Wassermann reaction is evident from Valerius' song in Heywood's *The Rape of Lucrece:*

> Pompie *I will show thee, the way to know*
> *A daintie dapper wench.*
> *First see her all bare, let her skin be rare*
> *And be toucht with no part of the French* . . .
>
> II, 5

There may have been cases of innocent infection in life, but not on the boards. Thus Gondarino vows, forswearing women: "when I [meddle] with them, for their good, or their bad; may time [call] back this day again, and when I come in their companies, may I catch the pox, by their breath, and have no other pleasure for it" (Beaumont and Fletcher, *Woman Hater*, V, 2). And the clever valet, Scapin: "If any man puts a trick upon me without return, may I lose this nose with the pox, without the pleasure of getting it" (Otway, *Cheats of Scapin*, III).

Of all the symptoms and manifestations of the French disease, summarized by Dr. Sydenham a few years before Scapin's remark, the two which intrigued the playwrights above all others were flattening of the nose and falling out of the hair. Syphilitic baldness, popularly known as the "French crown," was a favorite literary *double entendre*, especially in the earlier years of the century. The reasons for this nasal and hirsute emphasis are readily apparent. Noses and hair are prominent features, and any accident to either of them cannot be effectively hidden from the curious bystander. A noseless or a bald man thus became the symbol of a combatant who had been disastrously defeated in Venus's wars. It would be hard to say whether there were more "pocky-nosed rascals" on the stage or on the streets, for the plays abound in allusions to the syphilitic "saddle-nose":

FEESIMPLE. . . . But Mr. Wel-tri'd, *if they be not very valiant, or dare not fight, how come they by such cuts and gashes, and such broken faces?*

WELTRI'D. *Why their whores strike 'em with cans, & glasses, and quart pots, if they have nothing by 'em, they strike 'em with the*

poxe, and you know that will lay ones nose as flat as a basket hilt
dagger.

FIELD, Amends for Ladies, III

2 KNIGHT. *I am a knight, Sir Pock-hole is my name,*
  And by my birth I am a Londoner,
  Free by my copy, but my ancestors
  Were Frenchmen all, and riding hard this way,
  Upon a trotting horse my bones did ake,
  And I faint knight to ease my weary limbes,
  Light at this cave, when straight this furious fiend,
  With sharpest instrument of purest steel,
  Did cut the gristle of my nose away,
  And in the place this velvet plaster stands,
  Relieve me gentle knight out of his hands.

BEAUMONT AND FLETCHER, Knight
of the Burning Pestle, III, 1

This is the sad tale of a man fallen first into the arms of a harlot
and then into the hands of a barber-surgeon.

In another play a maid named Calipso has had her nose hewn
off with a dagger, and laments that there is

  . . . no bridge
Left to support my organ, if I had one:
The comfort is, I am now secure from the crincomes.
I can lose nothing that way.

MASSINGER, Guardian, IV, 3

"Grinkcomes," says Taylor, the self-styled "water poet," "is an
Utopian word, which is in English a P. at Paris." [18]

PRIGG. *Love! Ay, if a man gets a clap, 'twill take him down.*
YOUNG MAGGOT. *May it take down your nose, you unthinking animal.*

SHADWELL, True Widow, I

DON JOHN. *I could find it in my heart to cut your rascals nose off, and*
  save the pox a labor.

SHADWELL, Libertine, I

---

[18] John Taylor, *Works* (London, 1630), p. 111.

CAMILLO. *Let in those ladies, make 'em room for shame there.*
TONY. *They are no ladies, there's one bald before 'em,*
    A gent. bald, they are curtail'd queans in hired clothes.
    They come out of Spain I think, they are very sultry.
MENALLO. *Keep 'em in breath for an ambassadour.*
    Me thinks my nose shakes at their memories. . . .
            BEAUMONT AND FLETCHER, *Wife for a Month*, II, 1

CLOWN. *Why, masters, have your instruments been at Naples, that*
    they speak i' th' nose thus?
                SHAKESPEARE, *Othello*, III, 1

Naples was France's most formidable rival in the geographical
attribution of the pox: "Morbus Gallicus, or Neopolitanus had
bin well."

In Brome's *The Weeding of the Convent Garden*, Nick Rooks-
bill, a roaring boy, teases Gabriel Crossewill, a precisian, with:

> . . . we are brethren, sir, and as factious as you, though we differ
> in the grounds; for you, sir, defie orders, and so do we; you of the
> Church, we of the Civil Magistrate; many of us speak i' th' nose,
> as you do; you out of humility of spirit, we by the wantonnesse of
> the flesh; now in devotion we go beyond you, for you will not
> kneel to a ghostly father, and we do to a carnal mistresse.
>
>   IV

Lorenzo required only one thing of his mistress: good health.
As he put it:

> *I leave the choice to you; fair, black, tall, low,*
> *Let her but have a nose. . . .*
>   DRYDEN, *Spanish Fryar*, I, 1

A more hot-blooded spark in Shadwell's *Epsom-Wells*, about to
venture on a masked lady, had less rigid requirements:

BEVIL. *I like thy shape and humour so well, that gad if thou'lt satisfie*
    my curiosity; I'll not repent, though you want that great orna-
    ment of a face, called a nose.

                                                I

Such nasal fancies were not at all the product of the literary
imagination. The Pseudo-Aristotle tells us, for example, that the

planet Venus governs the nose, "which by the way, is one reason that in all unlawful venereal encounters, the nose is too subject to bear the scars which are gotten in those wars." [19] The poor nose suffered in strickly marital battles as well.

Sir Thomas Browne, the Norwich physician, in writing of the regenerative faculty of the organs of certain animals, says: "were it communicated unto animals . . . we might abate the art of Taliacotius, and the new in-arching of Noses" (*Pseudodoxia Epidemica*, Bk. 3, Ch. 9).

The famous "art of Taliacotius" merits a digressive sentence here.[20] Casper Tagliacozzi (1546–1599) of Bologna was the author of a Latin treatise on the engrafting of noses and ears, and so miraculous were the reported results of his operations that his book was condemned by the church and his body exhumed and reburied in unconsecrated ground. No wonder that he captured the imagination of later poets:

> So learned Taliacotius from
> The brawny part of porter's bum,
> Cut supplemental noses, which
> Would last as long as parent breech:
> But when the date of nock was out,
> Off dropt the sympathetick snout.
>
> BUTLER, *Hudibras*, Pt. I, Canto 1

As for the "new in-arching of Noses," some of the poets themselves spoke from first-hand experience, and others from direct observation of their colleagues. Sir William Davenant was one of these pocked poets, and Sir John Suckling one who took literary advantage of his fellow knight's misfortune. From "A Session of the Poets" (in *Fragmenta Aurea*, 1646) comes the following:

> Will Davenant, ashamed of a foolish mischance
> That he had got lately travelling in France,
> Modestly hoped the handsomeness of's muse

[19] *The Works of Aristotle, in Four Parts* . . . A new edition (London, 1792), p. 98.

[20] See Appendix: Isaac Bickerstaff's dissertation upon noses, *The Tatler*, No. 260.

HUNT LIBRARY
CARNEGIE-MELLON UNIVERSITY

Might any deformity about him excuse.
                    And
Surely the company would have been content,
If they could have found any precedent;
But in all their records either in verse or prose,
There was not one laureat without a nose.

There seems, however, to have been some disagreement over the source of Will's infection. It was domestic and not imported, according to Aubrey, who reports that Davenant "gott a terrible clap of a black handsome wench that lay in Axe-Yard, Westminster, whom he thought on when he speakes of Dalga in Gondibert, which cost him his nose, with which unlucky mischance many witts were too cruelly bold: e.g. Sir John Menis, Sir John Denham, etc." (*Brief Lives*, I, 206).[21]

Suckling himself seems to have been the laureate of the pox, for he expressed satirical sympathy for the equally unlucky mischance of another poet, Thomas Carew:

Troth, Tom, I must confess I much admire
Thy water should find passage through the fire:
For fire and water never could agree:
These now by nature have some sympathy:
Sure then his way he forces, for all know
The French ne'er grants a passage to his foe.
If it be so, his valour I must praise,
That being the weaker, yet can force his ways;
And wish that to his valour he had strength,
That he might drive the fire quite out at length;
For, troth, as yet the fire gets the day,
For evermore the water runs away.[22]

The reader will recall that *ardor urinae* was one of the particularly unpleasant consequences of the venereal disease.

Sir Richard Blackmore, the poet-physician, wrote a "Satire against Wit" with the avowed intention of raising the moral

[21] In Buckingham's *The Rehearsal*, produced in 1671, Bayes is Dryden, but the incident at the end of Act II where he injures his nose and appears "*with a papyr on his nose*," is a sharp bob at Davenant's nasal misfortune.

[22] "Upon T. C. Having the Pox" in *Works*, ed. A. H. Thompson (London, 1910), p. 10.

tone of contemporary drama. If the success of his efforts had entailed the reduction of the stage to the level of his own incredible dullness, it is fortunate that he failed. Nevertheless, the poets did not take the attack lying down, and Sir Charles Sedley led the charge:

> A grave physician, us'd to write for fees,
> And spoil no paper, but with recipe's,
> Is now turn'd Poet. . . .
> It is a common pastime to write ill;
> And doctor, with the rest, e'en take thy fill;
> Thy satyr's harmless: 'Tis thy prose that kills,
> When thou prescrib'st thy potions and thy pills.
> Go on brave doctor, a third volume write,
> And find us paper while you make us S——.[23]

Blackmore's stolidity of temper, or perhaps his self-esteem, rendered him absolutely impenetrable to such shafts of ridicule, but Sedley's verses were answered on the doctor's behalf by an unidentified author of *Discommendatory Verses, etc.*, 1700, thus:

> A P–x on rhymes and physick, S–dly cry'd
> (And he had sense and reason on his side;)
> For both of rhimes and physick h'had his fill,
> And swallow'd more than ev'ry verse a pill.
> A doctor coming by, and loath to lose
> A knight so famous for his P—— and Muse,
> Offer'd him means to give his knighthood ease,
> And make the radicated torments cease.
> Vile quack, said he, go patch up Mother Q——les,
> Sir Richard turn prescriber to Sir Ch——ls?
> It shall not be, jog homeward if you please,
> I'll have no paper spoil'd on my disease.
> The doctor cry'd, 'Tis true, th' infection's such,
> 'Twill certainly discolour't with a touch:
> But I'll affirm, and so withdrawing smil'd,
> My papers may, but thou cans't ne'er be spoiled.[24]

[23] "Upon the Author of the Satyr Against Wit" in Sedley's *Works*, I, 46–47.
[24] "To the Poetical Knight, who would have no Body Spoil Paper but Himself," quoted in Sedley's *Works*, I, 288.

Even Dryden was gratuitously poxed. "The Epistle to the Tories," prefixed to the anonymous satire *The Medal of John Bayes* (i.e., John Dryden), 1682, snarls: "His prostituted muse will become as common for him, as his mistress Revesia was, upon whom he spent so many hundred pounds; and of whom (to shew his constancy in love) he got three claps. . . ." Revesia was, of course, Anne Reeve, the actress, who was kept by Dryden.

Sir George Etherege and Sir John Denham, as we shall see later, were also poets afflicted with the pox. It has also been said that as Anacreon died by the pot, so George Peele died by the pox.

Not only the dramatists, as so many of the allusions show, but the seventeenth-century medical men as well, confused the clap with the pox. Dr. Sydenham, for example, believed the clap to be an early stage of syphilis, and the clap striking inward to the blood produced the confirmed pox.[25] This was the common view. This confusion lasted well into the nineteenth century, having gathered overwhelming support from the bold experiment of John Hunter (1728–1793). This courageous spirit inoculated himself with the "virus" of gonorrhea, and ultimately the symptoms of syphilis appeared. But it was of angina pectoris that he died.

Whether the burning in the following two case reports was due to the clap or the pox I leave to the reader to resolve:

SYRACUSE DROMIO. *Master, is this Mistress Sathan?*
SYRACUSE ANTIPHOLUS. *It is the devil.*
SYRACUSE DROMIO. *Nay, she is worse, she is the devil's dam! And here she comes in the habit of a light wench; and thereof comes that the wenches say 'God damn me!' That's as much to say, 'God make me a light wench!' It is written, 'They appear to men like angels of light.' Light is an effect of fire, and fire will burn; ergo, light wenches will burn. Come not near her!*
                        SHAKESPEARE, Comedy of Errors, IV, 3

PRINCE. *For the women?*
FALSTAFF. *For one of them, she's in hell already, and burns poor*

[25] "Treatise on the Venereal Disease" in Sydenham's *Works*, II, 34 *passim.*

souls. For th' other, I owe her money; and whether she be
damn'd for that, I know not.
SHAKESPEARE, *Henry the Fourth*, Part II, II, 4

One of the more appropriate synonyms for the pox was, in fact,
the "brenning" or burning disease. Thus, to be "fir'd" meant to
be poxed, and many a punning playwright took advantage of the
term.

The remainder of the symptoms described by Dr. Sydenham
are scattered fulsomely throughout the old plays. Baldness was
prevalent:

LUCIO. *Behold, behold, where Madam Mitigation comes!*
1 GENTLEMAN. *I have purchas'd as many diseases under her roof as
come to—*
2 GENTLEMAN. *To what, I pray?*
LUCIO. *Judge.*
2 GENTLEMAN. *To three thousand dolours a year.*
1 GENTLEMAN. *Ay, and more.*
LUCIO. *A French crown more.*
SHAKESPEARE, *Measure for Measure*, 1, 2

BRACHIANO. *O but her jealous husband.*
FLAMINEO. *Hang him, a guilder that hath his braynes perisht with
quicke-silver is not more could [cold] in the liver. The great
barriers moulted not more feathers then he hath shed haires, by
the confession of his doctor.*
WEBSTER, *White Divel*, I, 2

BRACHIANO.   *Where's this whore?*
FLAMINEO. *What? what doe you call her?*
BRACHIANO. *Oh, I could bee mad,*
  Prevent the curst disease shee'l bring mee to;
  And teare my haire of[f].
White Divel, IV, 2

The plays were full of characters who disguised themselves in
wigs, only to tear them off at the dénouement. When they did,
there were always punsters ready with a quip:

GREENEWIT [disguised]. *Nay gentlemen, seeing your woemen are so
hote, I must loose my haire in their company I see.*

MISTRESSE OPENWORKE. *His haire sheds off, and yet he speaks not so much in the nose as he did before.*

GOSHAWK. *He has had the better chirurgion.* . . .

MIDDLETON, *Roaring Girle,* IV

PARENTHESIS. *Looke you, your schoole-maister has bin in France, and lost his hayre.* . . .   [takes off his wig.]

DEKKER, *West-ward Hoe,* V, 1

QUINCE. *Some of your French crowns have no hair at all. And then you will play barefaced.*

SHAKESPEARE, *Midsummer Night's Dream,* I, 2

Other symptoms of syphilis found on the stage include aches and pains in the bones:

THERSITES. . . . *After this, the vengeance on the whole camp! or rather the Neapolitan bone-ache! for that methinks is the curse dependent on those that war for a placket.* . . .

SHAKESPEARE, *Troilus and Cressida,* II, 3

1 GENTLEMAN. *Thou art always figuring diseases in me; but thou art full of error—I am sound.*

LUCIO. *Nay, not (as one would say) healthy, but so sound as things that are hollow. Thy bones are hollow; impiety has made a feast of thee.*

1 GENTLEMAN [to Bawd]. *How now? Which of your hips has the most profound sciatica?*

SHAKESPEARE, *Measure for Measure,* I, 2

Phagedenic ulcers:

> *For Hebrew roots, although th'are found*
> *To flourish most in barren ground*
> *He had such plenty, as suffic'd*
> *To make some think him circumcis'd:*
> *And truly so he was perhaps,*
> *Not as a proselyte, but for claps.*
>
> BUTLER, *Hudibras,* Pt. I, Canto I

Premature senility:

> *—You everlasting grievance of the boxes,*
> *You wither'd ruins of stum'd wine and poxes;* . . .
> *Your fevers come so thick, your claps so plenty,*

Most of you are threescore at five and twenty.
APHRA BEHN, *False Count*, Epilogue

Shakespeare gives a professional summing-up in *Timon of Athens*:

TIMON.   Consumptions sow
In hollow bones of man; strike their sharp shins
And mar men's spurring. Crack the lawyer's voice,
That he may never more false title plead
Nor sound his quillets shrilly. Hoar the flamen,
That scolds against the quality of flesh
And not believes himself. Down with the nose—
Down with it flat; take the bridge quite away—
Of him that, his particular to foresee,
Smells from the general weal. Make curl'd-pate ruffians bald,
And let the unscarr'd braggarts of the war
Derive some pain from you. Plague all;
That your activity may defeat and quell
The source of all erection. There's more gold.
Do you damn others, and let this damn you,
And ditches grave you all!
IV, 3

Literary detectives who bridge a hiatus in a poet's life by quotations from his works should note these allusions well, for on them they can build a case that Shakespeare speaks with more feeling than a mere observer of the ravages of the disease might be expected to show.[26] All their indefatigable research ought to

---

[26] It will be very instructive here to follow Shakespeare's lines with the parallel speech in Shadwell's adaptation of *Timon of Athens* (produced in 1677):

Sow your consumptions in the bones of men;
Dry up their marrows, pain their shins and shoulders;
    [crack the lawyer's voice, that he
May never bawl, and plead false title more.
Entice the lustful and dissembling priests,
That scold against the quality of flesh,
And not believe themselves; I am not well.
Here's more, ye proud, lascivious, rampant whores.
Do you damn others, and let this damn you;
And ditches be all your death-beds and your graves.

Where Shadwell cannot touch the pox lightly, he apparently will not touch it at all. But Shakespeare, though he will pun on the French Disease with any man, reveals in *Timon of Athens* a depth of feeling about it.

bring to light an apothecary's bill for a diet-drink made out to
"W. Shakespere," or a surgeon's reckoning for a mercury sweat.
It would be the discovery of the century.

High living in youth brings its pains in old age. The ancient
idea that gout arose from venereal indiscretion early in life was
carried into the seventeenth century. About 300 B.C., the poet
Hedylus wrote: "The daughter of limb-loosening Bacchus and
limb-loosening Venus is limb-loosening gout." Dr. Sydenham
agreed: "Gouty patients are, generally, either old men, or men
who have so worn themselves out in youth as to have brought on
a premature old age—of such dissolute habits none being more
common than the premature and excessive indulgence in venery,
and the like exhausting passions." [27] And the poets went even
further than the scientific doctor:

HORNER. *As gout in age, from pox in youth proceeds;*
    So wenching past, then jealousy succeeds:
    The worst disease that love and wenching breeds.
                                        WYCHERLEY, *Country-Wife*, I

COURTWELL. *There are ladies Ned, who consider not the man, but his*
    pockets, half a pence for a clean pair of sheets, half a crown for a
    thrice retayl'd bottle of rhenish, and—
LOVECHANGE. *The pox into the bargain.*
COURTWELL. *The pox in others will be but the gout in me.*
                                        DOVER, *The Mall*, I, 1

But an etiology directly the opposite was advanced by another
dramatist. Said Wat in Brome's *The Damoiselle*:

I know from whence the pocks is now descended.
The gout begets it.

                                                    III, 1

There is no medical evidence to support either contention,
but Falstaff's impatient oath in the second part of *Henry the
Fourth* settles the confusion nicely: "A pox of this gout! or, a
gout of this pox!" (I, 2).

The Professor of Medicine in Gresham College, Dr. Henry

[27] "Treatise on the Gout" in Sydenham's *Works*, II, 129.

Paman, asked his good friend Dr. Sydenham to summarize the
current cure of the pox:

> As it is, its treatment is now with the quacks, barber-surgeons,
> and mountebanks; and as such men, partly from want of skill and
> partly from want of honesty, protract the cure, the expense and
> the trouble become so great, that the miserable patient, under
> the hands of his tormenters, becomes sick of life, and thinks
> worse of the cure than the complaint. . . . To suffer at the
> hands of God is enough; no need that the physician torture him
> as well.[28]

But in the eyes of the satirical dramatists, the quacks were not
the only healers who profited from the French Disease. Crack
sang:

> Then let us be freinds, and most freindly agree.
> The pimp and the punck and the doctor are three,
> That cannot but thrive, when united they be.
> The pimp brings in custom, the punck she gets treasure,
> Of which the physitian is sure of his measure,
> For work that she makes him in sale of her pleasure.
> For which, when she failes by diseases or paine,
> The doctor new vamps and upsets her againe.
>
> BROME, City Wit, III, 1

And here is the "new Vamping" process in prose, in full and
scandalous detail:

JOLLY. . . . There is a friend of ours (that for the present shall be
nameless) has got a small mischance:—You may guess what I
mean.

DOCTOR MOPUS. Well sir—I apprehend you, and will set him right
again.

JOLLY. Then you take it for granted, it must be a man:—Suppose it
be a woman? Does that alter the case?

DOCTOR MOPUS. Sir, I'll deal plainly with you—If your friend be a
man, I'll cure him for five pieces; but if a woman, I shall not take
her in hand under twenty.

JOLLY. Why this difference?

[28] *Ibid.*, II, 30.

DOCTOR MOPUS. *O sir, not without reason:—The sooner you cure a man, the sooner you have him again—He's a constant termer—But a woman—Ah sir, she brings grist to mill;—cure her once, and she growes cunning, you'll hardly ever hear of her more, . . . I shall not bate any thing of twenty pieces to cure her: but this I'll do with you, I'll patch her up against term, for forty shillings.*

WILSON, Cheats, III, 1

The surgeon also benefited, as the experienced Falstaff well knew:

FALSTAFF. *If the cook help to make the gluttony, you help to make the diseases, Doll. We catch of you, Doll; we catch of you. Grant that, my poor virtue, grant that.*

DOLL. *Yea, joy—our chains and our jewels.*

FALSTAFF. *Your brooches, pearls, and ouches. For to serve bravely is to come halting off: you know, to come off the breach with his pike bent bravely, and to surgery bravely; to venture upon the charg'd chambers bravely—*

SHAKESPEARE, Henry the Fourth, Pt. II, II, 4

So too did John Chapman, who in *All Fooles* rained pocky puns down on surgeon and France alike:

Enter Page and [Fraunces] POCK [a surgeon].

POCK. *God save you Signior Darioto.*

DARIOTO. *I know you not sir, your name I pray?*

POCK. *My name is Pock sir; a practitioner in surgery.*

DARIOTO. *Pock the surgeon, y' are welcome sir, I know a doctor of your name maister Pocke.*

POCK. *My name has made many doctors sir.*

RINALDO. *Indeede tis a worshipfull name.*

VALERIO. *Mary is it, and of an auncient discent.*

POCK. *Faith sir I could fetch my pedigree far, if I were so dispos'd.*

RINALDO. *Out of France at least.*

POCK. *And if I stood on my armes as others doe.*

DARIOTO. *No doe not Pock, let others stand a their armes, and thou a thy legs as long as thou canst.*

POCK. *Though I live by my bare practise, yet I could show good cardes for my gentilitie.*

VALERIO. *Tush thou canst not shake off thy gentry Pock; tis bred i' th bone.*

III, 1

Amateurs of medicine, of course, also pitted their skill against the course of the French Disease. Nowadays almost everyone will undertake to prescribe for your cold. The seventeenth-century equivalent of these dabblers in physic was Sir John Brute, who in Vanbrugh's *The Provok'd Wife* is hauled drunk and disguised as a parson before a justice of the peace:

JUSTICE. *Hyccop? Doctor Hyccop. I have known a great many country parsons of that name, especially down in the fenns. Pray where do you live, sir?*
SIR JOHN. *Here—and there, sir.*
JUSTICE. *Why, what a strange man is this? Where do you preach, sir? Have you any cure.*
SIR JOHN. *Sir—I have—a very good cure—for a clap, at your service.*

IV, 3

Another such healer, a real life one, was Sir John Menis, one of those who had poked cruel fun at poor Davenant. Said Pepys: "Up, and with Sir J. Minnes [Menis] by coach to St. James. . . . Thence home with him again, in our way he talking of his cures abroad, while he was with the King as a doctor, and above all men the pox. And among others, Sir J. Denham he told me he cured, after it was come to an ulcer all over his face, to a miracle." (*Diary*, August 15, 1664).

But Menis's cure, like many a later therapeutic miracle, helped the "doctor" rather than the patient. A letter written two years later than Pepys' entry recounts that

> . . . *Sir John Denham is now mad, which is occasioned (as is said by some) by the rough striking of [Valentine] Greatrakes upon his limbs; for they say that formerly having taken the fluxing pills in Holland, and they not working, they rubbed his shins with mercury: but that neither causing him to spit they supposed it lodged in the nerves till the harsh strokes caused it to sublimate . . . so Sir Denham did not die, but is fallen violently mad, and is likely to continue: He is now at one Dr. Lentall's house at the Charter House. The doctor is one that pretends to*

*cure those in this condition, and to him Dr. Fraisier and the rest
sent him: What that means you can safely imagine.*[29]

But apparently Dr. Lentall succeeded, in spite of the raised
eyebrows of Dr. Fraisier and his colleagues, for Denham recovered and Samuel Butler dashed off a satirical "Panegyric upon
Sir John Denham's Recovery from his Madness."

The reader will remember that Denham was one who had also
laughed at Davenant's nose. I think that must have been before
Sir John Menis had occasion to perform his miraculous cure.

Thus we come to the cure of syphilis, for luckily there was a
cure. Not "hangman's physic," however, although the French
doctor in Aphra Behn's *Sir Patient Fancy* disdained any less
radical remedy for the disease:

MONSIEUR TURBOON. *Verily, I have not kill'd above my five or six this
week.*

BRUNSWICK. *How, sir, kill'd?*

MONSIEUR TURBOON. *Kill'd, sir! ever whilst you live, especially those
who have the grand Verole [the pox]; for 'tis not for a man's
credit to let the patient want an eye or a nose, or some other
thing. I have kill'd ye my five or six dozen a week—but times are
hard.*

V, 1

The first appearance of the pox in epidemic form in Europe
confronted a medical profession completely baffled. Authority
had no weapon against a disease which had followed Galen's
death by almost thirteen hundred years. As a general measure
the first clap-doctors sweated their patients in bagnios. Then,
considering the pocky eruptions and pustules, they bethought
themselves of mercurial fumigations and inunctions, for mercury
had long been used by the Arabians against vermin and the itch.
Thus, happily led by a specious reasoning, the physicians discovered the first specific for the disease.

Later, in 1517, guaiacum came from the New to the Old
World in partial repentance for the aboriginals' revenge. This

<hr />

[29] Quoted by J. R. Clemens, "Notes on English Medicine (Henry VIII–George
IV)," *Annals of Medical History*, n.s. III (1931), 311.

drug had a tremendous vogue and was the main ingredient of most of the quack remedies for the pox. We find Dr. Drench threatening his orthodox colleagues:

> . . . and I must tell you I shall spoil the benefit you get by that disease; for I'l advise every man to plant a guaicum-tree in his orchard, and a leaf of that at any time will cure infallibly, and that's one of the secrets I will reveal to the world, to spoil the practice of mountebanks, clap doctors and bill men.
>
> LACY, Dumb Lady, V

It is true that guaiacum was kinder to the patient than was mercury, but it was also kinder to the spirochaetes.

China contributed China-root toward the cure of the plague, and America (about 1535) sarsaparilla and sassafras. These so-called drying-woods were offered as a substitute for the harshness of mercury, and by some medical miracle they apparently cured —or so thought the men about town:

> TOPE. . . . Love, ha, ha, ha.
> WILDFIRE. I am convinc'd, a man will certainly have it er'e he dyes, as the small pox; look to it, Jack, yet.
> TOPE. Heav'n send me the great ones, rather, without the help of sarsa, guyacum or mercury.
>
> SHADWELL, Scowrers, V

Infusions of the drying-woods were common ingredients of the "dyet-drinks" prescribed by the barber-surgeons for the poxed. Nicholas Culpeper's formula, for example, called for lignum vitae (guaiacum) and its bark, sassafras, sarsaparilla, juniper berries, coriander-seeds, cinnamon, and liquorice. Such drinks must have had a characteristic taste, for when Lysander gives Bro a bottle of wine the good woman remarks:

> I like your bottle well. . . .
> Doctor Verolles bottles are not like it;
> There's no guaicum here, I can assure you.
>
> CHAPMAN, Widdowes Teares, IV, 1

And the phrase furnished one more circumlocution for the "pox":

CRAZY. *Know you this mad doctor? Or do you owe any doctor any thing?*

TICKET. *I know him not, nor do I owe any doctor any thing; I onely owe my barber-surgeon for a dyet-drink.*

BROME, *City Wit*, V, 1

In less euphemistic language, Ticket had the pox.

Turpentine was another favorite remedy for the French Disease. Beantosser, the strumpet in Duffett's farce, cries: "O save the syring and the pot of turpentine-pills for my sake" (*Mock-Tempest*, I, 1). And apparently taking turpentine pills was as fashionable as taking snuff, for Bruce in *The Virtuoso* disgustedly paints the fops of his day as

> *Such as come drunk and screaming into a play-house, and stand upon the benches, and toss their full periwigs and empty heads and with their shrill unbroken pipes, cry, Dam-me, this is a damned play: Prethee let's to a whore, Jack. Then says another, with great gallantry, pulling out his box of pills, Dam-me, Tom, I am not in a condition; here's my turpentine for my third clap; when you would think he was not old enough to be able to get one.*
>
> I

But such pills had been in use for many decades, as we see from a play by Massinger and Dekker:

SPUNGIUS. . . . *we are justly plagued therefore for running from our mistres.*

HIRCIUS. *Thou did'st, I did not; yet I had run too, but that one gave me turpentine pils, and that staid my running.*

Virgin-Martir, III

But protean syphilis changed its shape, and the bark of roots and trees lost its efficacy. Only mercury, accompanied by purging and fasting, remained. The seventeenth-century physicians sweated, purged, and fasted their patients to the point of exhaustion, no less. Under properly regulated mercury treatment the patient spat four pints in twenty-four hours. His gums ulcerated, his teeth fell out, and he shrank into a dessicated skeleton; but the pox was gone. All the patient had now to do was recover from his cure. That took a long time.

One may appreciate the sad state of those undergoing mercurial treatments from Merryman's jibe at Cuningham in Sedley's *Bellamira*: "Thou may'st well be active, thou hast no more flesh upon thy back, than a flea, and thy bones have as much quicksilver in 'em, as ten bales of false dice: They will scarce lie still when thou art dead" (V, 1). This conceit also occurred to the pocky valet Dufoy in Etherege's comedy:

SIR FREDERICK. *Haste, Dufoy, perform what I commanded you.*
DUFOY. *I vil be ver quick begar; I am more den half de Mercurié.*
Comical Revenge, V, 5

Dufoy's creator was said by a contemporary enemy to have been "curs'd with loss of mony, pox, & wife." [30] Another satirist speaks of "fluxing George his sharp mercurial wit," a clear reference to the valet's retort above. Certainly, whatever effect the French Disease had on the poets' noses, it did not diminish their brilliant wit.

Like the man without a nose, the tub was a symbol of the French Disease, for it was in a tub that the pocky sweated out his disease. Cornelius Agrippa, the sixteenth-century alchemist and physician, was vulgarly credited with the invention of the sweating treatment, and his memory was kept green by the constant use of "Cornelius tubs." Nashe wrote in *The Unfortunate Traveller* (pp. 25–26): "This sweating sicknes, was a disease that a man then might catch and never goe to a hothouse. . . . Mother Cornelius tub why it was like hell, he that came into it, never came out of it." And John Webster characterized "A Phantastique," or an improvident young gallant, as "A scholer he pretends himselfe, and saies he hath sweate for it: but the truth is, hee knowes Cornelius farre better than Tacitus.[31]

Lazarillo, a character created by Middleton, said: "the commodities which are sent out of the Low Countries, and put in vessels called mother Cornelius' dry-fats [casks or boxes for hold-

[30] William Oldys in his MS notes on Langbaine (*Dramatick Poets*) says, "He went ambassador to Rothisbone [Ratisbon] as the punsters called it." Etherege represented the King at Ratisbon.
[31] In *Complete Works*, ed. F. L. Lucas (Boston, 1928), IV, 32.

ing dry things], are most common in France" (*Blurt, Master Constable*, I, 2). Lazarillo's high-flown fancies, translated into the vernacular, would read: Pocky whores abound in France.

Eventually, "Cornelius" became redundant. Reference to the "tub" sufficed. Said a dying philanthropist:

DIEGO. *I give to fatal dames, that spin mens threads out,*
    And poor distressed damsels, that are militant
    As members of our own afflictions,
    A hundred crowns to buy warm tubs to work in. . . .
            FLETCHER and MASSINGER, *Spanish Curate*, IV, 5

In D'Urfey's *A Fond Husband; or, The Plotting Sisters*, Cordelia and Sir Roger visit young Sneak in his lodgings and find him in a nightgown with an apothecary in attendance. The lady, moreover, discovers that a sweating-chair is part of his furniture. "Tis a mathematical engine they use at Cambridge," blusters Sir Roger, trying to pass it off.

As a general thing, however, such incriminating engines could not be passed off. Pepys recounts a case from real life which proves that it was much harder to be secret about a tub than about a course of antibiotics:

> Mr. Lowder is come to use the tubb, that is to bathe and sweat himself; and that his lady is come to use the tubb too, which he [Batten] takes to be that he hath, and hath given her the pox, but I hope it is not so, but, says Sir W. Batten, this is a fair joynture, that he hath made her, meaning by that the costs the having of a bath.
>
>   Diary, May 15, 1667

Beaumont and Fletcher's *The Knight of the Burning Pestle* is full of syphilitic jokes. In the third act Rafe, the grocer's boy turned knight-errant, descends upon a barber's shop, knocks down the proprietor, and liberates the inmates of his booth. One had just been shaved; another had had his nose dressed by the barber, having lost it by the pox; others, said the surgeon:

> *Prisoners of mine, whom I in diet keep,*
> *Send lower down into the cave,*

And in a tub that's heated smoking hot,
There may they find them and deliver them.

"Run Squire and Dwarf," commands Rafe; "deliver them
with speed." In a moment the two attendants re-enter, one
leading a man with a glass of lotion in his hand, the other
conducting a woman clutching her ration of diet-bread and
drink.

DWARF. *Here be these pined wretches, manfull knight,*
   That for this six weeks have not seen a wight.
RAFE. *Deliver what you are, and how you came*
   To this sad cave, and what your usage was?
MAN. *I am an errant knight that followed arms,*
   With spear and shield, and in my tender years
   I strucken was with Cupids fiery shaft,
   And fell in love with this my lady dear,
   And stole her from her friends in Turne-ball street,
   And bore her up and down from town to town,
   Where we did eat and drink and musick he[a]re;
   Till at the length at this unhappy town
   We did arrive, and coming to this cave,
   This beast us caught, and put us in a tub,
   Where we this two months sweat, and should have done
   Another month if you had not relieved us.
WOMAN. *This bread and water hath our dyet been,*
   Together with a rib cut from a neck
   Of burned mutton, hard hath been our fare;
   Release us frim this ugly gyants snare.
MAN. *This hath been [all] the food we have receiv'd,*
   But only twice a day for novelty,
   He gave a spoonful of his hearty broth
                                      [Pulls out a siringe.]
   To each of us, through this same [sl]ender quill.
RAFE. *From this infernall monster you shall go,*
   That useth knights and gentle ladies so.

The joke takes on a sharpened point when one recalls that
Turne-ball or Turnbull Street was a resort of whores.
   Sweating, starving, and purging make their appearance in this
play, but in Etherege's *The Comical Revenge; or, Love in a Tub*

(aptly named for the century!) satire becomes hilarious farce.

The French valet Dufoy, who made his bow a few pages back, becomes the butt of a practical joke which must have delighted a Restoration audience:

LETTICE. *What hast thou done to the French-man, girl? He lies yonder neither dead nor drunk; no body knows what to make of him.*

BETTY. *I sent for thee to help make sport with him; he'l come to himself, never fear him: have you not observ'd how scurvily h'as look'd of late?*

LETTICE. *Yes; and he protests it is for love of you.*

BETTY. *Out upon him for a dissembling rascal; h'as got the foul disease; our coachman discover'd it by a bottle of diet drink he brought and hid behind the stairs, into which I infus'd a little opium.*

LETTICE. *What dost intend to do with him?*

BETTY. *You shall see.*

IV, 6

A coachman enters, carrying "a tub without a bottom, a shut at the top to be lock'd, and a hole to put one's head out at, made easie to be born on ones shoulders."

COACH-MAN. *Here's the tub; where's the Frenchman?*

BETTY. *He lies behind the stairs; haste and bring him in, that he may take quiet possession of this wooden tenement; for 'tis neer his time of waking.*

They bring in Dufoy and put him into the tub. There is great fun when the valet awakens:

BETTY. *Good-morrow, monsieur; will you be pleas'd to take your pills this morning?* . . .

LETTICE. *Will you be pleas'd to drink, monsieur? There's a bottle of your diet-drink within.*

And so on. The poor valet had fallen not only into the hands of quacks, but into the remorseless grasp of two worldly-wise seventeenth-century chambermaids as well. Let us leave him to their tender mercies.

Every one of these old allusions to syphilis is touched with satire. This satire is rarely if ever bitter; on the contrary, it is almost always gay. Yet we have examined medical testimony that the pox was truly a terrible disease and that its cure was quite as unpleasant as the malady itself. Returning once more to Dr. Paman's letter to Dr. Sydenham, we find a paragraph which seems to strike a nineteenth-century note:

> We have read often of the so-called venereal disease, an ailment so disgraceful that the nations of Europe deny its origin among themselves, and in order to throw a shade over its rise and progress, make it over to the distant Indies. The scourge of the lecherous,[32] the punishment of the fornicator, it is slow in progress, perhaps, for the sake of giving time for repentence.

Yet there was precious little repentance shown in the plays; and, after all, the plays were a truer reflection of seventeenth-century life than were the puritanical Dr. Paman's pious sentiments. Compare the good doctor's balderdash to this sermon by Shadwell:

RAINES. Let 'em lye and preach on, while we live more in a wekk, than those insipid-temperate fools do in a year.
BEVIL. We like subtile chymists extract and refine our pleasure; while they like fulsom Galenists take it in gross.
RAINES. I confess, a disorder got by wine in scurvy company, would trouble a man as much as a clap got of a bawd; but there are some women so beautiful, that the pleasure would more than ballance the disaster.

Epsom-Wells, I

And to those who, like the ass and the two bales of hay, are torn between desire on the one hand and danger on the other, Etherege's song from *Love in a Tub* offers this out-of-date advice:

PALMER. He that leaves his wine for boxes and dice,
    Or his wench for fear of mishaps,

---

[32] When, in Webster's *The Devils Law-case* (II, 1), Ariosto is berating Julio for his whoring, "O yong quat [pimple], incontinence is plagued/In all the creatures of the world," the latter retorts: "When did you ever heare, that a cockesparrow/Had the French poxe?" Dr. Paman would have answered, "Syphilis is not transmittable to avian species."

May he beg all his days, cracking of lice,
And die in conclusion of claps.

II, 3

The difference between Dr. Paman's attitude toward the pox and Shadwell's is a paradox. To the physician, the French Disease was a question of morals; to the poet, it was a matter for the physician.

One can hardly deny that Sir George Etherege, Sir John Suckling, Sir William Davenant, Sir Charles Sedley, Tom Carew, and many others had as intimate a knowledge of the pox as Dr. Sydenham who treated it. Neither the physician's treatment nor the dramatists' attitude has withstood the cultural, moral, and intellectual advances of the following centuries. But the fault in the first case lay with the doctor's therapeutics; in the second, with the poets' descendants. To the impartial judge, Suckling's admirable conclusion to a letter to Tom Carew contains the germ of truth. Sir John . . . "did conclude at last, that Horsely air did excell the waters of the Bath, just so much as love is a more noble disease than the pox." [33]

Nor would Mrs. Behn, the century's lady-playwright, have disputed Suckling's contention. Divine Astrea sprinkled her pages well with the virus, and neither villain nor hero was immune. If further proof is needed that a touch of pox was no social handicap in the old days, here it is. The play is *The City Heiress*, and the hero (if modern sensibilities will accept the word in connection with the character to be revealed) is one Tom Wilding, a Tory blessed with the pox, an angry uncle, a discontented mistress, and an urgent desire for the person and purse of the city heiress.

Tom's uncle refuses to be beguiled further by his nephew's eloquence. He refuses to hear another word:

No, I have heard you out too often, sir, till you have talkt me out of many a fair thousands; have had ye out of all the bayliffs, serjeants, and constables clutches about town; have brought you

[33] *Works*, p. 336.

out of all the surgeons, apothecaries, and pocky doctors hands,
that ever pretended to cure incurable diseases.

I, 1

Mrs. Clacket, a bawd who has been attending to his amorous
business, reproaches him after this fashion:

Have I been the confident to all your secrets this three years, in
sickness and in health, for richer, for poorer; conceal'd the nature
of your wicked diseases, under the honest name of surfeits; call'd
your filthy surgeons, Mr. Doctor, to keep up your reputation.
. . .

II, 1

And Diana, his mistress, scorns his love in these words:

Love me! what if you do? how far will that go at the Exchange
for point? Will the mercer take it for current coin?—But 'tis no
matter, I must love a wit with a pox, when I might have had so
many fools of fortune: but the Devil take me, if you deceive me
any longer.

II, 2

In the end Wilding tricks his uncle into withdrawing his
disinheritance and into marrying the cast-off Diana, while he
himself snares the city heiress. Obviously the pox affected neither his eligibility nor his brain.

Before sentimentality corrupted both the stage and the audiences there was no moral stigma attached to the French Disease. In an age of strong stomachs and strong heads the pox was
an "unlucky" or a "foolish mischance." It was the unfortunate
price one occasionally paid for one's pleasures, but only a Puri-
tan would deny a pleasure because it was followed by a pain. As
men rode horses and took the risk of broken legs or neck; as they
fought duels and stood the chance of being run through the guts;
so, too, men went wenching and ran the hazard of the pox.
Cause and fortuitous effect were similar in each case, and the
softened manners of a later day were not without fundamental
unreality in their characteristic reaction to what was once "the
modish distemper."

In the seventeenth century the pox deformed the body; in Brieux's day the concern was not so much with what it did to the body as what it did to the psyche. Therein lies the difference between Brieux and the older dramatists. To Frenchmen of Brieux's time syphilis is no longer a disease; it is a moral cataclysm. But to Shadwell and his fellow poets, and to Etherege and his fellow knights, it was simply the French or the Spanish or the Neapolitan Itch. To them, pain was pain, deformity was deformity, death was death. The cause or the terminology made no difference in the end. As one of "the refin'd Witts of the Age" wrote:

> To be in oyl or roses drown'd
> Or water, wher's the difference found?
> Both bring one death, and death will be
> Unwelcome any way to me.[34]

[34] *Covent Garden Drollery*, ed. Montague Summers (London, 1927), p. 56.

8

Science and Satire

Here you see . . . a velvet physician [bowing low] to a
threadbare chemist . . . whilst they can hardly hold their
solemn false countenances.
—WYCHERLEY, *The Plain Dealer*

THE MOSAIC PORTRAIT OF SEVENTEENTH-CENTURY MEDICINE
composed from these jagged dramatic fragments may be crudely
painted, but from a distance the image appears fairly well-
rounded and complete. Perhaps from the popular literature of
no other age would an equally coherent picture emerge. The
fruits of modern printing presses must be ruled out, not because
our books by and about physicians, nurses, and patients are only
occasionally literature or photography, but because at the moment we have no integrated iatric system comparable in authority or extent to that which dominated countless generations of
medical men until after the seventeenth century came to a close.
Of course, in more recent books one finds newer medical and
scientific truth, but medicine itself has grown so unwieldy that
even its practitioners are lost outside their specialties; our lay
literature cannot be expected to reflect a comprehensive logic
and simple order when they do not exist in medicine itself.

In comparison with today all was lucid order in seventeenth-
century England. Biochemists and biophysicists, psychiatrists
and the devotees of a dozen other modern sciences were still
merely spermatogonia in Aesculapius' gonads. It is no wonder

that the simple physician's only fear was his patient's ghost, and that even a dramatist could comprehend the system under which his ills were sometimes cured.

It cannot be said, of course, that every medical truism of the time has been embalmed in some comedian's speech, or that the technical procedure of the physician and surgeon is set out in full in the stage directions. What one does see most clearly is medicine, doctor, and patient in the life of the day.

On the other hand, when one stops to consider the omissions rather than the inclusions of the dramatists, one is forced to conclude that, though medicine was a truly vital force, science was rather completely divorced from the life of the common man. Except for *The Virtuoso* there is only the rarest mention of contemporary science, and this in a century when anatomical, physiological, and chemical discoveries appeared every month.

The greatest discovery of the century, by all agreement, was William Harvey's unequivocal demonstration of the circulation of the blood. Dr. Harvey (1578–1657) was graduated M.D. at Padua in 1602 and in 1618 in his lectures on anatomy at the Royal College of Physicians (London) first began to teach his developing doctrine. In his lecture notes of April 17, 1616, Harvey had already convincingly argued his case, although not until 1628 was his *Exercitatio anatomica de Motu Cordis et Sanguinis in Animalibus* published in quarto at Frankfort.

Harvey's colleagues in the College of Physicians were familiar with his views, of course, even before the appearance of the *De Motu Cordis*. The profession at large, from the publication of James Primrose's *Exercitationes et Animadversiones in Librum Gulielmi Harvaei de Motu Cordis et Circulatione Sanguinis* (1630) on, argued for and against the doctrine in print. Nevertheless, so far as I am aware, it was not until 1668—forty years after—that cognizance of the great discovery was taken in a play.

Six years after Harvey's death, in 1663, Walter Charleton published his *Chorea Gigantum: Or, The Most Famous Antiquity Of Great Britain, vulgarly called Stone-henge, Standing on Salisbury-Plain, Restored to the Danes*, to which were prefixed some verses by John Dryden "To my honor'd friend Dr. Charleton." The lines relating to Harvey are well known:

> The circling streams, once thought but pools, of Blood
> (Whether life's fuel, or the body's food,)
> From dark oblivion Harvey's name shall save:[1]

It is in Dryden's *An Evening's Love; or, The Mock-Astrologer* (1668) that the first dramatic reference appears:

BELLAMY. *For that, madam, you may know as much of me in a day as you can in all your life: all my humours circulate like my blood, at farthest, within 24 hours.*

V

Now Dryden was, as poets go, a learned man, and moved as well in scholarly as literary circles. His scientific enlightenment may thus have proceeded, not from the *Zeitgeist*, but from one of Dr. Charleton's learned discourses. But when the comedian John Lacy, whose *The Dumb Wife; or, The Farriar Made Physician* was produced in 1669 (published 1672), recognized Harvey's doctrine, we may be sure that the newer physiological knowledge was on its way to becoming popular knowledge as well. In Act IV of Lacy's play the keepers of a madhouse explain how they whip the inmates out of a frenzy into stark madness and then whip them till they come round to their senses again. The wondering Dr. Drench comments: "That plainly shews the circulation of the blood. . . ."

The process of popular penetration was carried one step further in a song from *Covent Garden Drollery*, 1672, "Written by the refin'd Witts of the Age/And Collected by A[lexander]. B[rome]." The first verse runs:

> Since tis now become a fashion,
> To court all with equal passion
> And admirers now do prove,
> There is as well in love
> As in blood, a circulation[2]

---

[1] *Chorea Gigantum: . . .* (2nd ed., London, 1725).
[2] *Covent Garden Drollery*, ed. Montague Summers (London, 1927), p. 47.

To convert a physiological fact into a labored conceit for a love song is to pay science the highest compliment. But though physiologists may be proud of the tortured effort of this one of the refined wits, versifiers will appreciate the aptness of Norman Douglas's complaint that "It is the worst of writing poetry that you are apt to be torn between respect for truth and the exigencies of scansion." [3]

Perhaps this is why I have come across only one more allusion to Harvey's discovery from 1672 to the end of the century. It occurs in Farquhar's *Love and a Bottle* (1699)—and it is in prose:

LUCINDA. *Have you any bus'ness with me, sir?*
ROEBUCK. *Yes, madam, the bus'ness of mankind; To adore you.—My love, like my blood, circulates thro' my veins, and at every pulse of my heart animates me with a fresh passion.*

III

The Galenical doctrines may have been farther from the truth, but apparently they were far more amenable to the demands of poesy.

The English wits seem to have accepted the newer knowledge of the circulation without question. But in France, M. Diafoirus, one of the physicians in *The Hypocondriac* [*Le Malade Imaginaire*], produced in 1673, boasts that his son:

> . . . pursues his argument into the most retir'd recesses of logick; but the thing in which he pleases me most, and in which he follows my example, is his blind affection to the opinions of the ancients, and that he would never comprehend or so much as hearken to the reasons and experiments of the pretended discoveries of our age, concerning the circulation of the blood, and other opinions of that kind.

II, 5

And in corroboration son Thomas asseverates: "I have maintain'd a thesis against the gentlemen that are for the circulation."

[3] *Together* (New York, 1923), p. 85, n. 1.

It would not have been surprising had Dr. Harvey himself, as well as his doctrine, appeared on the stage, for the great anatomist was as vigorous and humorous a personality as any dramatist could desire. John Aubrey has left us a vivid portrait of the man: "He was not tall; but of the lowest stature, round faced, olivaster complexion; little eie, round, very black, full of spirit; his haire was black as a raven, but quite white 20 yeares before he dyed." He was a choleric old gentleman who "in his younger dayes wore a dagger [and] would be apt to drawe out his dagger upon every slight occasion." Nor did age much modify his humor, for "he was wont to say, that man was a great mischievous baboon," and he sent young Aubrey in no dispassionate manner to the fountain-head of Aristotle and Avicenna, "and did call the neoteriques [moderns] shitt-breeches." His opinion of chemists and women was equally epithetical, though for the latter Aubrey remembered "he kept a pretty young wench to wayte on him, which I guesse he made use of for warmeths-sake as King David did, and tooke care of her in his will, as also of his man servant" (*Brief Lives*, I, 299–302). Harvey has so often and piously been served up to us as the model of "calmness of mind and abnegation of self which we associate with the true philosopher" [4] that we are apt to forget another fact equally true: that the author of *De Motu Cordis* was a very human and humorous old fellow who might have lived within the pages of one of Ben Jonson's plays.

John Aubrey, who listened with respectful admiration to the old doctor's reminiscent monologues (perhaps over a dish of the coffee to which Harvey was devoted), "heard him say, that after his booke of the circulation of the blood came-out, that he fell mightily in his practize, and that 'twas beleeved by the vulgar that he was crack-brained; and all the physitians were against his opinion, and envyed him." Nevertheless, continued Aubrey, "All his profession would allow him to be an excellent anatomist, but I never heard of any that admired his therapeutic way. I knew severall practisers in London that would not have given 3*d.* for

---

[4] E. A. Parkyn, introduction to Harvey's *Motion of the Heart and Blood in Animals* (London [1923]), p. xv.

one of his bills [prescriptions]; and that a man could hardly tell by one of his bills what he did aime at."

Shadwell found dramatic material in a lesser virtuoso with no more justification.

It is a pity that Aubrey's fragmentary play, *The Countrey Revell, or the Revell at Aldford,* was never finished and produced, for in it Dr. Harvey comes vicariously to life. The play dates from 1671, when Aubrey was dodging the bailiffs for debt, so that twenty years after their conversations Harvey's words still echoed in his old friend's mind. The admiring reflections of the Sowgelder below reveal a phase of the great doctor's personality as no scientific treatise could:

SOWGELDER. *To see, Sir John, how much you are mistaken; he that marries a widowe makes himself cuckold. Exempli gratia, to speake experimentally and in my trade, if a good bitch is first warded with a curre, let her ever after be warded with a dog of a good straine and yet she will bring curres as at first, her womb being first infected with a curre. So, the children will be like the first husband (like raysing up children to your brother). So, the adulterer, though a crime in law, the children are like the husband.*

SIR JOHN FITZ-ALE. *Thou dost talke, me thinks, more understandingly of these matters than any one I have mett with.*

SOWGELDER. *Ah! my old friend Dr. Harvey—I knew him right well— he made me sitt by him 2 or 3 hours together discoursing. Why! had he been stiffe, starcht, and retired, as other formall doctors are, he had known no more than they. From the meanest person, in some way, or other, the learnedst man may learn something. Pride has been one of the greatest stoppers of the advancement of learning.*[5]

By all people but the Italians (who in 1876 accorded the honor and a commemorative statue to Andreas Caesalpinus), it has been taken for granted that Dr. Harvey was the discoverer of the systemic circulation. But according to Dr. John W. Wainwright, who lovingly investigated the medical knowledge of Wil-

---

[5] Fragments of this comedy have been printed as Appendix II to *Brief Lives,* ed. A. Clark (Oxford, 1898), II, 333–339.

liam Shakespeare, the poet's lines "indicate a knowledge of the circulation of the blood in anticipation of Harvey. The play of Hamlet was first printed in 1603 while Harvey made known his discovery of the circulation of the blood in 1628." [6]

Now this is an astounding thesis to maintain, but before we too hastily substitute Shakespeare's statue for Harvey's in the Royal College of Physicians, let us consider Dr. Wainwright's evidence. Here it is:

BRUTUS. *You are my true and honourable wife,*
  As dear to me as are the ruddy drops
  That visit my sad heart.

Julius Caesar, II, 1

MENENIUS. . . . *But, if you do remember,*
  I [i.e., the belly] send it [food] through the rivers of your blood
  Even to the court, the heart, to th' seat o' th' brain,
  And, through the cranks and offices of man,
  The strongest nerves and small inferior veins
  From me receive that natural competency
  Whereby they live. . . .

Coriolanus, I, 1

GHOST. *Upon my secure hour thy uncle stole,*
  With juice of cursed hebona in a vial,
  And in the porches of my ears did pour
  The leperous distilment; whose effect
  Holds such an enmity with blood of man
  That swift as quicksilver it courses through
  The natural gates and alleys of the body,
  And with a sudden vigour it doth posset
  And curd, like eager droppings into milk,
  The thin and wholesome blood.

Hamlet, I, 5

The reasonable conclusion, of course, is that Dr. Wainwright has confused his enthusiasm for Shakespeare's poetry with his perception as a medical historian. He does not recognize flagrant Galenism flaunted before his eyes. To the Greeks blood ebbed

[6] *The Medical and Surgical Knowledge of William Shakspere* (New York, 1915), p. 61.

and flowed within the veins, entering and leaving the heart in a periodic tidal flow. Even Shakespeare knew this:

KING JOHN. . . . *if that surly spirit, melancholy,*
   Had bak'd thy blood and made it heavy, thick,
   Which else runs tickling up and down the veins. . . .

King John, III, 3

And so firmly was the belief ingrained in common knowledge that in 1677 Mrs. Behn was still affirming it:

ANGELICA. *Does not thy guilty blood run shivering thro' the veins? . . .*
WILLMORE. *Faith, no child, my blood keeps its old ebbs and flows still, and that usual heat too, that cou'd oblige thee with a kindness, had I but opportunity.*

Rover, Pt. I, V, 1

It is not surprising to find Aphra Behn, poor untutored woman that she was, scientifically half a century behind the times. But to discover John Dryden, who only in 1663 had penned a panegyric on the circulation, in 1694 reviving the ancient tidal doctrine:

ALPHONSO. . . . *I feel my vital heat*
   Forsake my limbs, my curdled blood retreat.

Love Triumphant, IV, 1

leads one to conclude that truth alone is powerless to overcome tradition: Time is necessary as well.

Before we reassign the credit for medicine's greatest discovery where it rightfully belongs, we must dispose of three more claimants to the honor, and I do not mean Michael Servetus, Realdus Columbus, or Caesalpinus! The three were, like Shakespeare, all laymen. One was a Mr. Prothero; the second, a mathematician and philosopher named Walter Warner; the third, a dramatic poet. It is Aubrey to whom we owe these complications to the history of physiology.

> Mr. Warner did tell Dr. Pell, that when Dr. Harvey came out with his circulation of the blood, he did wonder whence Dr. Harvey had it: but coming one day to the earle of Leicester, he

found Dr. Harvey in the hall, talking very familiarly with Mr.
Prothero . . . to whom Mr. Warner had discoursed concerning
this exercitation of his De Circulatione Sanguinis, and made no
question but Dr. Harvey had his hint from Prothero.

Brief Lives, II, 291

To this Aubrey adds the following memorandum: "Dr. Pell
sayes that Mr. Warner rationated demonstratively by beates of
the pulses that there must be a circulation of the blood."

The third story reaches us in a roundabout manner. The
Bishop of Winchester told Isaac Walton (who relayed the news
in a letter to Aubrey) that the Bishop knew Ben Jonson, and
that the poet "saide he first found out the cerculation of the
blood, and discover'd it to Doᵉ Harvie (who said that 'twas he
[himself°] that found it), for which he is so memorably famose"
(*Brief Lives*, II, 16).

However much we admire Ben Jonson, it is clear that he is
boasting in his cups. To give Shakespeare his due, there is no
record that, under the influence or not, he ever announced his
discovery of the circulation of the blood. Nor was it Shakespeare
who designed *Hamlet* as a preliminary report to the *De Motu
Cordis*; but rather his later acolytes who consider the play not
only a psychiatric case history but a physiological milestone as
well.

From the conclusions of the Bardolaters (of whom Dr. Wainwright is perhaps the saddest medical example) we are led to a
matter of more serious import: How much dependence may the
historian place on a poet's words, and how much scientific truth
does poetic license afford? Norman Douglas, in his charming
study of the fauna of the Greek anthology, has this to say:

> We must be on our guard with these poets, and not only in the
> matter of plants. Exigencies of versification are responsible for
> some little botanical and zoological confusion in nearly all po-
> etry, and one really cannot expect these charming people to be
> meticulous about such trifles; they have enough to do avoiding
> hiatuses and minding their quantities.[7]

[7] *Birds and Beasts of the Greek Anthology* (New York, 1929), p. 23.

In another place he speaks of the zoological accidents which "are liable to happen to the best of us, when we try to stretch Natural History upon the Procrustean couch of the sonnet form." And when the subject is medicine, such accidents are likely to be as plentiful as the doctors' mistakes.

The whole question of taking poets' words as scientific fact becomes acute and critical in dealing with Shakespeare. This is not so much owing to this poet's actual words as to their interpretation by generations of adulatory critics who read into innocent phrases all the knowledge of the ancient and modern world. Shakespeare's plays are said to contain over five hundred medical allusions and a gallery of pathological portraits which have been made the basis of studies ranging from the most somber scholarly tome to the joyous glow of amateur discovery. The bibliography cited by one of the sanest discoverers that Shakespeare knew as much medicine as the average literate man of his day lists fifty-three books and almost two hundred articles dealing with one aspect or another of Shakespeare the Physician.[8] Obviously this torrent of adulation (for very little of it is valid medico-historical criticism) has been called forth by men who, like Dr. Wainwright, confused the poet's remarkable powers of observation and felicity of expression with a *technical* knowledge of the healing art.

The Bardolatry which has awarded Shakespeare a physician's license would, by the same requirements for graduation, be forced to issue an M.D. to Ben Jonson and a Ch. M. to John Webster, both *magna cum laude*, for in point of erudition Shakespeare cannot compare with the former, nor in his technical grasp of surgical matters can he match the truly remarkable knowledge of the latter. The fact is, Shakespeare merely shared the Elizabethan and Jacobean dramatists' large fund of medical information; but that is no sign, as physicians will agree, that he had digested the medicine of the past, practiced the medicine of his time, and anticipated the medicine of the future.

---

[8] I. I. Edgar, "Shakespeare's Medical Knowledge with Particular Reference to his Delineation of Madness," *Annals of Medical History*, n.s. VI (1934), 150.

Pliny scolded Sophocles for his falsehoods concerning amber, and so led Lynn Thorndyke to remark:

> It may seem surprising that he should expect strict scientific truth from a dramatic poet, but Pliny, like many medieval writers, seems to regard poets as good scientific authorities. In another passage he accepts Sophocles' statement that a certain plant is poisonous, rather than the contrary view of other writers, saying "the authority of so prominent a man moves me against their opinions." He also cites Menander concerning fish and, like almost all the ancients, regards Homer as an authority on all matters.[9]

Professor Thorndyke notwithstanding, it does seem that in our search for the absolute the poets are quite as likely to surprise one with "scientific truth" as is Pliny. The appeal is not to dramatic or philosophical authority, but (to speak as grandiloquently as Sir Formal Trifle) to experiment; and in the absence of experiment, a dramatist is probably a more valid signpost of contemporary belief than a philosopher or an encyclopedist. Certainly there is as much scientific truth in the seventeenth-century popular literature (discounting satire, euphuism, and "the exigencies of versification") as there is in the relevant portions of seventeenth-century medical works. For one must watch one's step when marching with scientists as well as with poets.

But I have wandered from the title of this chapter—although not so far as at first glance it might appear.

The medical satire in early English drama is almost entirely incidental. There was no Molière in seventeenth-century England whose personal grievances led him to pillory a whole profession because one of its number played him a scurvy trick. Nevertheless, there are scores of allusions in the English plays as trenchant as any of the Frenchman's. Not all, perhaps none of these thumbnail satires originated in the seventeenth century. The Greek and Latin poets dipped their pens into the same ink

[9] *History of Magic and Experimental Science during the First Thirteen Centuries of Our Era* (New York, 1929), I, 49.

which ever since, regardless of language, has served those who have been intrigued by the intimate relationship between the physician, fees, and death. There is little difference in feeling between Callicter's couplet, "Feeling slightly feverish, I happened to remember the name of Doctor Pheidon; and straightway died"[10] and Le Sage's thrust two thousand years later, "Don Gonzales is old, and a good deal shaken in constitution; so that a very little fever, in the hands of a very great doctor, would carry him to a better place." (*Gil Blas*, Bk. IV, Ch. 7).

Let us not pause too long, however, over the evolution and continuity of medical satire. That intriguing subject must wait for another day and another writer.

The seventeenth century abounded in metaphysical poets: Donne, Herbert, Vaughan, Crashaw, and others, who were preoccupied with thoughts of mortality. In this they typified the temper of the times. It was this morbid inclination, conscious or otherwise, which perhaps accounts for the mordant medical satire and the ever-present link between the physician and death. Here is what the dramatists thought of that notorious partnership:

MOSCA. *He ha's no faith in physick: he does thinke,*
 Most of your doctors are the greater danger,
 And worse disease, t'escape. I often have
 Heard him protest, that your physitian
 Should never be his heire. . . .[11]
   No, sir, nor their fees
 He cannot brooke: he sayes, they flay a man,
 Before they kill him. . . .
   And then, they doe it by experiment;
 For which the law not onely doth absolve 'hem,
 But gives them great reward: and, he is loth
 To hire his death, so.

[10] Quoted by Douglas, *Birds and Beasts of the Greek Anthology*, p. 198.
[11] A piece of prudence voiced earlier by John Lyly in *Campaspe* (Act V, scene 4):
 Alexander. If one be sick, what wouldest thou have him do?
 Diogenes. Be sure that he make not his phisition his heire.

CORBACCIO.   *It is true, they kill,*
   With as much licence, as a judge.
MOSCA.   *Nay, more;*
   For he but kills, sir, where the law condemnes,
   And these can kill him, too.
CORBACCIO.   *I, or me:*
   Or any man.

JONSON, Volpone, I, 4

The quintessence of all medical satire is here.

The barbed inventions of the dramatists would overflow the limits of space, and perhaps of the reader's patience, were they detailed here; but a few of the more ingenious conceits may entertain: [12]

ROMELIO. *I pray attend me: I am a phisician.*
2 SURGEON. *A phisician? where doe you practise?*
ROMELIO. *In Rome.*
1 SURGEON. *O then you have store of patients.*
ROMELIO. *Store? who looke you, I can kill my 20. a month*
   And worke but i' th forenoons: (you will give me leave
   To jest and be merry with you). . . .

WEBSTER, Devils Law-case, III, 2

MR. AYMWELL. *. . . doe not trust thy body with a physitian, heele make thy foolish bones goe without flesh in a fortnight, and thy soule walke without a body a seavennight after.*
MR. MANLY. *These are no doctors?*
MR. AYMWELL. *Doctor! art a Parisian, a Paduan, or a Leaden doctor?*
   How many and be true to us hast thou kild the last
   Spring, will it puzzel thy arithmeticke, my pretious
   Rectifier of nature, the wrong way. . . .

SHIRLEY, Wittie Faire One, III

[12] Other literary variations on the theme of death and the physician appear in Webster's *The Devils Law-case*, II, 3 (Romelio); Fletcher and Massinger's *The Spanish Curate*, II, 1 (Lopez); Massinger and Dekker's *The Virgin Martir*, IV (Antoninus); Dekker's *Old Fortunatus*, II, 2 (Shadow); Brome's *A Joviall Crew*, I, 1 (Hearty); Butler's *Hudibras*, Part I, canto 2, lines 316–320; Wycherley's *The Country-Wife*, I (Harcourt); Sedley's *The Mulberry Garden*, Epilogue; Farquhar's *The Constant Couple*, II (Sir Harry Wildair), and *Love and a Bottle*, II (Bullfinch).

There's but the twinckling of a star
Between a man of peace and war,
A thief and justice, fool and knave,
A huffing officer and a slave,
A crafty-lawyer and pick-pocket,
A great philosopher and a block-head,
A formal preacher and a player,
A learn'd physitian and man-slayer.

BUTLER, *Hudibras*, Pt. II, Canto 3

FOURBIN. *Truely Sir David, if, as you say, the man must be well murder'd without any remorse for mercy; betwixt Turk and Jew, 'tis honestly worth two hundred pounds.*
SIR DAVY DUNCE. *Two hundred pounds! why I'l have a physitian shall kill a whole family for half the money.*

OTWAY, *Souldiers Fortune*, IV

Aphra Behn, unfortunately for her later welfare, once spoke too disparagingly of the profession:

LAURA LUCRETIA.—*Come, sir, we must deal with him, as physicians do with peevish children, force him to take what will cure him.*
FILLAMOUR. *And like those damned physicians, kill me for want of method.*

Feign'd Courtezans, III, 1

With a dramatic justice the authoress must have been the last to appreciate, the doctors had their revenge. "Here I must draw to an end," sadly wrote Mrs. Behn's biographer, "for tho' considerable trusts were repos'd in her, yet they were of that import, that I must not presume here to insert 'em; but shall conclude with her death, occasion'd by an unskilful physician, on the 16th of April, 1689." [13]

Medical satire on the Continent was equally devastating. *Don Quixote*, it is true, does not afford many examples, for primarily Cervantes' noble work is a study of character and not of manners. Indeed, one of Sancho's shrewd proverbs, "A doctor gives his advice by the pulse of your pocket," contains the harshest

[13] "Life and Memoirs of Mrs. Behn" in *Plays, Histories and Novels* (London, 1871), V, 72.

stricture in the entire book, and that, though a perennial blow beneath the belt, is here amiable enough.

Yet Le Sage, with a pen as sharp as Dr. Sangrado's lancet, pricks medicine in a hundred vulnerable points. *Gil Blas* is a pure comedy of manners, and it is in literature of this genre that medical satire abounds. Chapters 3, 4, and 5 of the first book, wherein the hero enters into Dr. Sangrado's service and ends by becoming a famous if unauthorized practitioner himself, deserve a place near the top of the medical *Index Expurgatorius*. In fact, none of the twelve books of Le Sage's masterpiece is without its share of gay and graceful allusions to the folly of contemporary physic and physicians. Here are a few of them:

> Doctor Sangrado was sent for; the Hippocrates of Valladolid . . . a tall, withered, wan executioner of the sisters three, who had done all their justice for at least these forty years!
>
> Bk. 2, Ch. 2

> Don Vincent was a very rich old nobleman, who had lived many years unencumbered with lawsuits or with a wife. The physicians had removed the last plague out of the way, in their attempts to rid her of a cough, which might have lasted a great while longer, if the remedies had not been more fatal than the disease.
>
> Bk. 4, Ch. 1

> Don Alphonso was taken ill. . . . By the greatest mercy in the world, the place was not beset by a single physician, and I got clear off without any harm but my fright.
>
> Bk. 6, Ch. 3

> The warden, who took a lively interest in my recovery, fancying in his unmedical head that physicians cured fevers, brought me a double dose of death in two of that doleful diety's most practised executioners.
>
> Bk. 9, Ch. 8

And so forth. The medical satire in *Gil Blas* really merits a chapter in itself, but the reader will want to undertake his own explorations.

To the student of medical satire Molière with his medical

lampoons is the most significant single figure.[14] His jokes and
jeers at the expense of the Paris Faculté are notorious,[15] though
the reason for his peculiar asperity toward the physicans is not
entirely clear. It is said that medical mismanagement led to the
death of his only son; again that the dramatist himself was
troubled with a consumption the doctors could not cure. But
where the English poets castigated the physician, it was the art
of medicine itself which received the full volume of the Frenchman's scorn:

ARGAN. *Your Molière with his comedies is a sawcy fellow, let me tell
    you, to offer to expose such worthy gentlemen as the physicians.*
BÉR[ALDE]. *He does not expose physicians, but the ridiculousness of
    Physick.*
                    The Hypocondriack [Le Malade Imaginaire], III, 3

As a further example of Molière's distaste for the healing art
one should read Act III, Scene 1 of *Don John: Or, The Libertine*
[*Don Juan*]. This universal heretic calls medicine "one of [the]
greatest errors that are amongst men," and the libertine's creator
makes a hearty amen. Nevertheless, whether by chance or by
design, the poor practitioner himself comes in for the major part
of Molière's attack:

LYS[ETTA]. *What do you mean to do, sir, with four physicians? Is not
    one enough to kill any one body?*
                    Love the Best Physician [L'Amour Médecin], II, 1

ARG[AN]. . . . *Dr. Purgon is a person that has good 8000 livres a year.*
TOIN[ETTE]. *Lord! What a world of people must he have kill'd to get
    such an estate!*
                    The Hypocondriack, I, 5

SGAN[ARELLE] [*the physician*]. *I find, after all, [medicine] 'tis the
    best of trades; for whether we do well or ill, we're sure to be paid*

[14] Molière's "medical" plays are *Le Médecin Malgré Lui, L'Amour Médecin,
Le Malade Imaginaire, Le Médecin Volant,* and *Monsieur de Pourceaugnac;* see
introduction to my translation, "The Flying Physician," *Medical Life,* 44 (New
York, 1937), 342–348.

[15] The relations between the dramatist and the doctors has been entertainingly
treated by J. W. Courtney, "Molière and the Faculty," *Annals of Medical
History,* V (1923), 309.

alike. *The ill effects are never laid to our charge, and we cut out as we please the stuff we work upon. A shoemaker cannot spoil a piece of leather, but he's made to pay sauce for't; but here we may spoil a man, and 'tweill cost us nothing. The error is never ours, but his that dyes. In short, the good of this profession is, that there's a certain generosity, an unparalel'd discretion, among those that dye; and they never lay their deaths at the physician's door.*

The Forced Physician [*Le Médecin Malgré Lui*], III, 1

Let us see now what John Lacy made of Sganarelle's paean in *The Dumb Lady.* Said Dr. Drench:

[*Medicine*] *is the securest cloak for ignorance of all arts: other professions are liable to miscarriages and questionable: but the physician may kill from the fool to the senator, from the beggar to the bloud-royal, and ne'er be call'd in question; the dead was never so uncivil yet, as to come out o' the other world to complain of the physician.*

III

If the speech lost force in crossing the Channel, it also lost a certain bitterness.

Whatever the purpose behind Molière's attacks, the results are often excruciatingly funny. The pomposity of the Paris Faculté lent itself admirably to satire, and the "pedantic formalism and complacent ineptitude of the French internist of the period," in Fielding Garrison's words, needed little exaggeration to become ridiculous. The burlesque consultation of physicians in *L'Amour Médecin* (Act II) and the travesty of the Bachelor's initiation into the Faculté in *Le Malade Imaginaire* (*Troisième Interméde*) are immortal examples of Molière's genius. If Medicine had existed for no other purpose than to stimulate the production of these precious scenes, it would have been "une des grandes bénédictions qui soient parmi les hommes."

The burlesque consultation in *L'Amour Médecin* found an English counterpart in *Sir Patient Fancy,* that study of another hypochondriac which owes its comic elements not so much to the French dramatist as to Aphra Behn's observation of London life. The scene (and it is a long one) is worth a full transcription.

In Act V, Scene 1, Sir Patient, the hypochondriac, has summoned a full supply of physicians in an attempt to guide his footsteps back onto the road to health. There are Monsieur Turboon, whom we have met before, a Fat Doctor, doctors from Amsterdam, Leyden, and Brunswick, and finally Sir Credulous Easy disguised as a physician: six god-sons of Hippocrates, any one of whom can singlehandedly slay his man. The sick man greets them all:

SIR PATIENT. *You're welcome, sir,—Pray sit; ah.—Well, sir, you are come to visit a very crazy sickly person, sir.*

BRUNSWICK. *Pray let me feel your pulse, Sir;—what think you gentlemen, is he not very far gone?—*

[Feels his pulse, they all feel.]

SIR CREDULOUS. Ah, far, far.—Pray, sir, have you not a certain wambling pain in your stomach, sir, as it were, sir, a—a pain, sir.

SIR PATIENT. *Oh very great, sir, especially in a morning fasting.*

SIR CREDULOUS. *I knew it by your stinking breath, sir—and are you not troubled with a pain in your head, sir?*

SIR PATIENT. *In my head, sir?*

SIR CREDULOUS. *I mean a—kind of a—pain,—a kind of a vertigo, as the Latins call it; and a whirligigigoustican, as the Greeks have it, which signifies in English, sir, a dizzie-swimming kind—of a do ye see—a thing—that a—you understand me.*

SIR PATIENT. *Oh intolerable, intolerable!—why this is a rare man!*

FAT DOCTOR. *Your reason, sir, for that?* [To Sir Credulous.]

SIR CREDULOUS. *My reason, sir? why, my reason, sir, is this, Haly the Moore, and Rabbi Isaac, and some thousands more of learned Dutchmen, oh—serve your dull wall eye and your whir—whirligigiusticon, to be inseparable.*

BRUNSWICK. *A most learned reason!*

FAT DOCTOR. *Oh, sir, inseparable.*

SIR CREDULOUS. *And have you not a kind of a—something—do ye mark me, when you make water, a kind of a stopping—and—a— do ye conceive me, I have forgot the English term, sir, but in Latin, 'tis a strong-gullionibus.*

SIR PATIENT. *Oh, sir, most extremely; 'tis that which makes me desperate, sir.*

SIR CREDULOUS. Your ugly face is an infallible sign; your dysurie, as the Arabicks call it, and your ill-favour'd countenance, are constant relatives.

ALL. Constant, constant.

SIR CREDULOUS. Pray how do you eat, sir?

SIR PATIENT. Ah, sir, there's my distraction. Alas, sir, I have the weakest stomach—I do not make above four meals a-day, and then indeed I eat heartily—but alas, what's that to eating to live? —nothing. Sir, nothing.—

SIR CREDULOUS. Poor heart, I pity him.

SIR PATIENT. And between meals, good wine, sweet-meats, caudles,— cordials and mirabilises, to keep up my fainting spirits.

SIR CREDULOUS. A pox of his aldermanship; an the whole bench were such notable swingers, 'twould famish the city sooner than a siege.

AMSTERDAM. Brothers, what do you think of this man?

LEYDEN. Think, sir? I think his case is desperate.

SIR CREDULOUS. Shaw, sir, we shall soon rectify the quiblets and quillities of his blood, if he observes our directions and diet, which is to eat but once in four or five days.

SIR PATIENT. How, sir, eat but once in four or five days? Such a diet, sir, would kill me; alas, sir, kill me.

SIR CREDULOUS. Oh no, sir, no; for look ye sir, the case is thus, do ye mind me—so that the business lying so obvious, do ye see, there is a certain method, do ye mark me—in a—Now, sir, when a man goes about to alter the course of nature,—the case is very plain, you may as well arrest the chariot of the sun, or alter the eclipses of the moon; for, sir, this being of another nature, the nature of it is to be unnatural, you conceive me, sir?—therefore we must crave your absence, sir, for a few minutes, till we have debated this great affair.

SIR PATIENT. With all my heart, sir, since my case is so desperate, a few hours were not too much.

[Exit SIR PATIENT.]

SIR CREDULOUS. Now, sir, my service to you. . . . [Drinks.]

[They drink round the while.]

AMSTERDAM. Sir, my service to you, and to your good lady, sir.

LEYDEN. Again to you, sir, not forgetting your daughters: they are fine women, sir, let scandal do its worst. [Drinks.]

TURBOON. To our better trading, sir.

BRUNSWICK. *Faith it goes badly on, I had the weekly bill, and 'twas a very thin mortality; some of the better sort die indeed, that have good round fees to give.*

TURBOON. *Verily, I have not kill'd above my five or six this week.*

BRUNSWICK. *How, sir, kill'd?*

TURBOON. *Kill'd, sir! ever whilst you live, especially those who have the grand verole: for 'tis not for a man's credit to let the patient want an eye or a nose, or some other thing. I have kill'd ye my five or six dozen a week—but times are hard.*

BRUNSWICK. *I grant ye, sir, your poor for experiments and improvement of knowledge and to say truth, there ought to be such scavengers as we to sweep away the rubbish of the nation.*

[SIR CREDULOUS and FAT *seeming in Discourse.*]

SIR CREDULOUS. *Nay, and you talk of a beast, my service to you, sir—* [Drinks.] *Ay, I lost the finest beast of a mare in all Devonshire.*

FAT DOCTOR. *And I the finest spaniel, sir.*

[Here they all talk together. . . .]

TURBOON. *Pray what news is there stirring?*

BRUNSWICK. *Faith, sir, I am one of those fools that never regard whether Lewis or Philip have the better or worst.*

TURBOON. *Peace is a great blessing, sir, a very great blessing.*

BRUNSWICK. *You are i'th' right, sir, and so my service to you, sir.*

LEYDEN. *Well, sir, Stetin held out nobly, tho the gazettes are various.*

AMSTERDAM. *There's a world of men kill'd they say: why, what a shame 'tis so many thousands should die without the help of a physician.*

LEYDEN. *Hang 'em, they were poor rogues, and not worth our killing; my service to you, sir, they'll serve to fill up trenches.*

SIR CREDULOUS. *Spaniel, sir! no man breathing understands dogs and horses better than my self.*

FAT DOCTOR. *Your pardon for that, sir.*

SIR CREDULOUS. *For look ye, sir, I'll tell you the nature of dogs and horses.*

FAT DOCTOR. *So can my groom and dog-keeper; but what's this to th' purpose, sir?*

[Here they leave off.]

SIR CREDULOUS. *To th' purpose, sir! good Mr. Hedleburgh, do you understand, what's to th' purpose? You're a Dutch butter-ferkin, a kilderkin, a double jug.*

FAT DOCTOR. *You're an ignorant blockhead, sir.*

SIR CREDULOUS. *You lye, sir, and there I was with you again.*

AMSTERDAM. What, quarrelling, men of your gravity and profession.

SIR CREDULOUS. *That is to say, fools and knaves: pray, how long is't since you left toping and napping, for quacking, good brother cater-tray.—but let that pass, for I'll have my humour, and therefore will quarrel with no man, and so I drink.*

[Goes to fill again.]

BRUNSWICK.—*But, what's all this to the patient, gentlemen?*

SIR CREDULOUS. *Ay,—the wine's all out,—and quarrels apart, gentlemen, as you say, what do you think of our patient? for something I conceive necessary to be said for our fees.*

FAT DOCTOR. *I think that unless he follows our prescriptions he's a dead man.*

SIR CREDULOUS. Ay, sir, a dead man.

FAT DOCTOR. *Please you to write, sir, you seem the youngest doctor.*

[To AMSTERDAM.]

AMSTERDAM. Your pardon, sir, I conceive there may be younger doctors than I at the board.

SIR CREDULOUS. *A fine punctilio this, when a man lies a dying* [Aside.]—Sir, you shall excuse me, I have been a doctor this 7 years.

[They shove the pen and paper from one to the other.]

AMSTERDAM. *I commenc'd at Paris twenty years ago.*

LEYDEN. *And I at Leyden, almost as long since.*

FAT DOCTOR. *And I at Barcelona thirty.*

SIR CREDULOUS. And I at Padua, sir.

FAT DOCTOR. You at Padua?

SIR CREDULOUS. *Yes, sir, I at Padua; why what a pox do ye think I was never beyond sea?*

BRUNSWICK. *However, sir, you are the youngest doctor, and must write.*

SIR CREDULOUS. *I will not lose an inch of my dignity.*

FAT DOCTOR. Nor I.

AMSTERDAM. *Nor I.*

LEYDEN. Nor I.

[Put the paper from each other.]

BRUNSWICK. Death, what rascals are these?

SIR CREDULOUS. *Give me the pen—here's ado about your Padua and punctilios.*

[Sets himself to write.]

AMSTERDAM. *Every morning a dose of my pills Merda queorusticon, or the amicable pill.*

SIR CREDULOUS. Fasting?

LEYDEN. *Every hour sixscore drops of* adminicula vitae.

SIR CREDULOUS. *Fasting too?*

[SIR CREDULOUS *writes still.*]

FAT DOCTOR. *At night twelve cordial pills,* gallimofriticus.

TURBOON. *Let blood once a week, a glister once a day.*

BRUNSWICK. *Cry mercy, sir, you're a French man.—After his first sleep, threescore restorative pills, call'd cheatus redivivus.*

SIR CREDULOUS. *And lastly, fifteen spoonfuls of my aqua tetrachyma-gogon, as often as 'tis necessary; little or no breakfast, less dinner, and go supperless to bed.*

FAT DOCTOR. *Hum, your aqua tetrachymagogon?*

SIR CREDULOUS. *Yes, sir, my tetrachymagogon; for look ye do ye see sir, I cur'd the Arch-Duke of Strumbulo of a gondileero, of which he dy'd, with this very aqua tetrachymagogon.*

[Enter SIR PATIENT.]

SIR PATIENT. *Well, gentlemen, am I not an intruder?*

FAT DOCTOR. *Sir, we have duly consider'd the state of your body; and are now about the order and method you are to observe.*

BRUNSWICK. *Ay, this distemper will be the occasion of his death.*

SIR CREDULOUS. *Hold, brothers, I do not say the occasion of his death; but the occasional cause of his death.*

[SIR PATIENT *reads the Bill.*]

SIR PATIENT. *Why, here's no time allow'd for eating, gentlemen.*

AMSTERDAM. *Sir, we'll justify this prescription to the whole college.*

LEYDEN. *If he will not follow it, let him die.*

ALL. *Ay, let him die.*

The question of doctors' fees, considered so solemnly by Sir Credulous Easy and his colleagues, was treated rather irreverently by the dramatists. These even went so far as to affront professional honor with the accusation that the physician was in business primarily for gain:

ISABEL. *But he is a famous physician of Padua, and has retired himself on purpose to avoid patients.*

SOFTHEAD. *Then he is a fool and no physician; for the wise doctors never leave a patient whilst he has either breath in's body or money in's purse.*

LACY, Dumb Lady, I

TUCCA. *Quickly, you whorson egregious varlets; come forward. What? shall we sit all day upon you? You make no more haste, now, then* a beggar upon patt'ns: or a physitian to a patient that ha's no money, you pilchers.

JONSON, Poetaster, V, 3

Molière's caustic wit seeped through this joint in the armor also, and bit deep: "Since he is cloth'd like a physician, I had thought one must speak to him of money" (*La Jalousie du Barbouillé, I, 2*).

There are a host of other scurrilities, which would not be the better for classification. They range, in feeling, from Rinaldo's simile in Chapman's *All Fooles*:

> as fat
> As a phisician; and as giddy-headed,

III, 1

to Rhetius' torrent of vituperation in Ford's *The Lovers Melancholy* in Acts I and V:

> Mountebancks, empricks, quacksalvers, mineralists, wizards, alchimists, cast-apothecaries, old wives and barbers, are all suppositers to the right worshipfull doctor, as I take it.
>
> Some of yee are the head of your art, & the hornes too, but they come by nature; thou livest single for no other end, but that thou fearest to be a cuckold. . . .
>
> Thou art in thy religion an atheist, in thy condition a curre, in thy dyet an epicure, in thy lust a goate, in thy sleepe a hogge; thou tak'st upon thee the habit of a grave physition, but art indeed an impostrous emperike. Physicions are the bodies coblers, rather the botchers of mens bodies; as the one patches our tatterd clothes, so the other solders our diseased flesh. . . .
>
> Thar't an excellent fellow. Diabolo. O this lousie close-stoole empricks, that will undertake all cures, yet know not the causes of any disease. Dog leaches. By the foure elements I honor thee, could finde in my heart to turne knave, and bee thy flatterer.

They reach the height of humor in an old doctor's rules for a young practitioner to observe, as set forth by John Lacy in *The Dumb Lady*:

OTHENTICK. First, have always a grave, busie face, as if you were still in great care for some great persons health, though your meditations truly known are only imployed in casting where to eat that day: Secondly, be sure you keep the church strictly on Sundays; and i' th' middle o' th' sermon let your man fetch you out in great haste, as if 'twere to a patient; then have your small agent to hire forty porters a day to leave impertinent notes at your house, and let them knock as if 'twere upon life and death; these things the world takes notice of, and you'r cryed up for a man of great practice, and there's your business done. . . .

Be sure you ingratiate yourself with the bauds, pretending to cure the poor whores for charity, that brings good private work after it. Strike in with mid-wives too, that you may be in the counsel for by-blows, that secures a patient during life; and with apothecaries, and nurse-keepers go snips; but above all acquire great impudence, lest you be out of countenance at your own miscarriages.

V

It has been no trouble at all to scavenge the old plays for this crop of derogatory references to the medical men.[16] It has been far more difficult to gather a ragged nosegay of praise. Not many of the dramatists considered medicine an unmixed blessing, or believed

> . . . as the prince
> Of poets, Homer, sung long since,
> A skilful leech is better far
> Then half a hundred men of war.
>   BUTLER, Hudibras, Pt. I, Canto 2

Euphues, it is true, wrote to his friend Philalautus:

If lawe seeme loathsome unto thee, searche the secretes of phisicke, whereby thou maist know the hidden nature of hearbes, whereby thou maiste gather profite to thy purse, and pleasure to thy minde. What can be more exquisite in humaine affaires then

---

[16] There are numerous other squibs and skits: Brome, Court Beggar, I, 1 (Gabriel), Queen and Concubine, III, 1 (Poggio); Congreve, Way of the World, II (Witwoud); Beaumont and Fletcher, Monsieur Thomas, III, 1 (Thomas); Ford, Perkin Warbeck, V (Warbeck); Randolph, Aristippus (Aristippus); Rowley, All's Lost by Lust, II (Antonio); Shirley, Hide Park, I (Caroll), Wittie Faire One, II (Fowler); Vanbrugh, Aesop, Pt. I, V (Doris), Relapse, III, 2 (Berinthia); Webster, White Divel, II, 1 (Flamineo); Wycherley, Love in a Wood, V (Valentine).

for every fever bee it never so hot, for every palsey be it never so colde, for every infection be it never so straunge, to give a remedy? The olde verse standeth as yet in his olde vertue, "That Galen giveth goods, Justinian honors."

LYLY, *Euphues*, I, 251

Here, however, John Lyly was carried away in the flood of his own rhetoric. Two years later he changed his mind and the tenor of his advice: "Let thy practise be lawe, for the practise of phisicke is too base for so fyne a stomacke as thine" (*Euphues and his England*, II, 188).

"Three faces wears the doctor, when first sought, an angel's. . . ." In 1616, a time of health, Dekker wrote:

DOCTOR. *How now! where is he? will he meet me?*
SERVANT. *Meet you, sir, hee might have met with three fencers in this time, and have received lease hurt then by meeting one doctor of phisicke. . . .*

Honest Whore, Pt. I, IV

He had apparently forgotten the years of the plague, when in his fright he had apostrophized those same doctors of phisicke in *Newes from Graves-ende* (1604):

The Cure of the Plague

But for we see the army great
Of those whose charge it is to beat
This proud invader, and have skill
In all those weapons, that do kill
Such pestilent foes, we yeeld to them
The glory of that stratagem:
To whose oraculous voice repaire,
For they whose Delphick prophets are,
That teach dead bodies to respire,
By sacred Aesculapian fire:
We meane not those pied lunatickes,
Those bold fantastical empirickes,
Quack-salvers, mishrump Mountebancks,
That in one night grow up in rancks
And live by pecking phisickes crummes,
O hate these venemous broods, there comes

Worse sores from them, and more strange births
Then from ten plagues, or twentie deaths . . . .
                                        Plague Pamphlets, 102–103

And some years later, John Ford, whose plays are notable for
their acrimonious allusions to physicians, forgot his bitterness
long enough to pay a tribute to the profession which must have
been far commoner in real life than on the stage. Florio comforts
the ailing Annabelle: "Looke, I have brought you company;
here's one, a learned doctor, lately come from *Padua*, much skild
in physicke, and for that I see you have of late beene sickly, I
entreated this reverent man to visit you some time" ('*Tis Pitty
Shee's a Whore*, II).

The medical school at Padua was in especially good repute
throughout the century, as many dramatic allusions show. Caius,
Harvey, and Thomas Browne, among others, were graduates of
this famous university, and when Sir Credulous Easy, pitched
among graduates of Paris, Leyden, Heidelburg, and Barcelona,
determines to assert his place in the heirarchy, he silences them
all with "And I at *Padua*, sir."

The physician has not always held his present high place on
the social ladder, although at no time has he descended to the
surgeon's once base level. [Sir Richard Mead (1673–1754) was a
notable exception to this piece of dogmatism; Sir Richard Blackmore (c. 1655–1729) and Sir Samuel Garth (1661–1719) were,
perhaps, not Ed.] It is a soothing salve to the pride, therefore, to
read of some physicians whose medical degree was, after a fashion, equal to a patent of nobility:

MONY-LACKS. *I have it from the opinion of most learned doctors, rare*
    physitians, and one that dares call himselfe so.
BRITTLEWARE. *What doctor is he, a foole on horsebacke?*
MONY-LACKS. *Doctor Thou-Lord, you know him well enough.*
REBECCA. *Yes, we know Doctor Thou-Lord, though he knowes none*
    but lords and ladies, or their companions. And a fine conceited
    doctor he is, and as humorous I warrant yee; and will Thou and
    Thee the best lords that dares be acquainted with him; calls
    knights Jacke, Will, and Tom familiarly; and great ladies, Gills,
    and Sluts too, and they crosse him.
                                        BROME, *Sparagus Garden*, II, 2

There was something of the Doctor Thou-Lord in John Radcliffe (1650–1714), one of the wisest, wittiest, and most generous physicians of any age. Radcliffe was noted for "the coarseness of his wit, [and] the imprudent levity of conduct, in which it was his humour occasionally to indulge." [17] He Thou'd and Thee'd a good many lords, and even jested (more unwisely than unwittingly) with kings.

King William sent for Doctor Radcliffe to come to the Palace at Kensington. "In reply to some questions put by the physician, the king, shewing his swollen ankles, which formed a striking contrast to the rest of his emaciated body, exclaimed, 'Doctor, what think you of these?' 'Why truly,' said he, 'I would not have your majesty's two legs for your three kingdoms.' " [18]

In the allusions to physicians and physic there is often a bitter flavor which is lacking in references to another class of "scientific men." Three hundred-odd years ago—before *The Skeptical Chemist* (1661)—chemists and alchemists differed mainly in the prefix to their title. The Black Art and its practitioners came in for their just share of dramatic satire; but, whereas the medical satire is tinged with grisly humor, the alchemical pasquinades are full of patronizing contempt.

The alchemist was not a literary idol. The protagonist of Ben Jonson's play, *The Alchemist,* used the art only as a means to a knavish end. Perhaps a more characteristic popular reaction to alchemy is set forth in the following lines from a play by Middleton:

LADY CRESSINGHAM. *Good friend, I have a suit to you.*
CRESSINGHAM. *Deerest self, you most powerfully sway me.*
LADY CRESSINGHAM. *That you would give o're this fruitless, if I may not say this idle, study of alchimy; why half your house looks like a glass-house.*
SAUNDER. *And the smoke you make is a worse enemy to good housekeeping than tobacco.*
LADY CRESSINGHAM. *Should one of your glasses break, it might bring you to a dead palsie.*

[17] William Macmichael, *Lives of British Physicians* (London, 1830), p. 112.
[18] *Ibid.,* p. 133.

SAUNDER. *My Lord, your quicksilver has made all your more solid gold and silver flie in fume.*
CRESSINGHAM. *Ile be rul'd by you in any thing.*
LADY CRESSINGHAM. *Go Saunder, break all the glasses.*
Any thing for a Quiet Life, I, 1

The waste of precious metal was one of the covetous bystander's soundest objections to the practice of the art. Here we see Saunder's objection again:

RHODOPHIL. *. . . . And for the King, she haunts, and watches him so narrowly in a morning, that she prevents even the chymists who beset his chamber, to turn their mercury into his gold.*
DRYDEN, *Marriage A-La-Mode, I*

The popular conception of the type of man who became an adept in chemistry is pretty clearly evident from the plays. A credulous, poverty-stricken, half-cracked fellow, smelling of the furnace, emerges from a number of references like these:

MENDOZA. *Thou art very poore.*
MALEVOLE. *As Job, an alcumist, or a poet.*
MARSTON, *Malcontent*, III, 3

HORNER. *Doctor, thou wilt never make a good chymist, thou art so incredulous and impatient.*
WYCHERLEY, *Country-Wife*, I

JEREMY. *. . . . he's as mad as any projector, fanatick, chymist, lover, or poet in* Europe.
CONGREVE, *Love for Love*, IV

CLARISSA. *What in the name of dulness is the matter with you, Colonel? you are as studious as a crack'd chymist.*
VANBRUGH, *Confederacy*, II

The successive failures of the alchemist in his attempts at transmutation or projection provoked almost as many gibes from the dramatists as did his poverty and credulity. There is as little sympathy for a man doomed to perennial disappointment as there is bitterness against a rogue and imposter. Evidently, the alchemist was himself a self-deluded creature, rather than one who deluded others.

MRS. MARWOOD. . . . . Here comes the good lady, panting ripe; with a heart full of hope, and a head full of care, like any chymist upon the day of projection.

CONGREVE, *Way of the World,* III

SIR WILLIAM BELFOND. How long, like chymists, have I watch'd and toil'd? and in the minute when I expected to have seen projection, all is blown up in fumo.

SHADWELL, *Squire of Alsatia,* V

The odd obsession with alchemy did not make the adepts happy, one gathers. Disappointed in their experiments, threatened by their patrons, and withal mocked by the dramatists, many of them came to an end as bad as the following example:

[Mary Herbert, Countess of Pembroke] was a great chymist and spent yearly a great deale in that study. . . . She also gave an honourable yearly pension to . . . Boston, a good chmyist, a Salisbury man borne, who did undoe himselfe by studying the philosopher's stone, and she would have kept him but he would have all the gold to him selfe and so dyed I thinke in a goale.

AUBREY, *Brief Lives,* I, 311

At that, Mr. Boston's fate was not so cruel as it might have been, for there are cases on record in which the patron's disappointment demanded a harsher revenge. John Lyly tells one such lugubrious tale:

There came to a Duke in Italie, a large lubber and a beggarlie, saying hee had the Philosophers Stone, and that hee could make golde faster, then the Duke could spend it; the Duke askt him, why hee made none to maintaine himselfe? Because, quoth he, I could never get a secret place to worke in; for once I endevoured, and the Popes holinesse sent for me, whom if he had caught, I should have been a prentice to maintaine his pride. The Duke minding to make triall of his cunning, & eager of golde, set him to worke closely in a vault, where it was not knowen to his nearest servaunts. This alcumist, in short time consumed two thousande pound of the Dukes gold, and brought him halfe a ducket: whie (quoth the Duke) is this all? All quoth he my Lord, that I could make by art. Wel said the Duke, then shalt thou see my cunning: for I will boyle thee, straine thee, and then drie thee,

so that of a lubber, that weighed three hundred weight, I will at
last make a dram of knaves pouder. The Duke did it.
                                          Pappe with an Hatchett, III, 402

In Germany and Austria, until the early nineteenth century,
the military surgeons had not only to dress the wounded, but to
shave the officers as well. The early English surgeons were considerably better off than this, though even they were more at
home in a barbershop than in polite society. Nevertheless, the
surgeons had their Doctor Thou-Lords also; witness Mr. Serringe:

LOVELESS.—*Bear him up! Where's your wound?*

LORD FOPPINGTON. *Just thro' the guts.*

LOVELESS. *Call a surgeon there: unbutton him quickly.*

LORD FOPPINGTON. *Ay, pray make haste.*

                                    [Enter SERRINGE and SERVANT.]

SERVANT. *Here's Mr. Serringe, sir, was just going by the door.*

LORD FOPPINGTON. *He's the welcom'st man alive.*

SERRINGE. *Stand by, stand by, stand by. Pray, gentlemen stand by.*
    Lord have mercy upon us, did you never see a man run thro' the
    body before? Pray stand by.

LORD FOPPINGTON. *Ah, Mr. Serringe—I'm a dead man.*

SERRINGE. *A dead man, and I by—I shou'd laugh to see that, I'gad.*

LOVELESS. *Prithee don't stand prating, but look upon his wound.*

SERRINGE. *Why, what if I won't look upon his wound this hours, sir?*

LOVELESS. *Why then he'll bleed to death, sir.*

SERRINGE. *Why, then I'll fetch him to life again, sir.*

LOVELESS. *'Slife, he's run thro' the guts, I tell thee.*

SERRINGE. *Wou'd he were run thro' the heart, I shou'd get the more*
    credit by his cure. Now I hope you are satisfy'd?—Come, now let
    me come at him; now let me come at him. [Viewing his wound.]
    Oons, what a cash is here?—Why, sir, a man may drive a coach
    and six horses into your body.

LORD FOPPINGTON. *Ho—*

SERRINGE. *Why, what the devil, have you run the gentleman thro'*
    with a sythe—[Aside] *A little prick between the skin and the ribs,*
    that's all.

LOVELESS. *Let me see his wound.*

SERRINGE. *Then you shall dress it, sir; for if any body looks upon it, I*
    won't.

LOVELESS. *Why, thou art the veriest coxcomb I ever saw.*
SERRINGE. *Sir, I am not master of my trade for nothing.*
LORD FOPPINGTON. *Surgeon.*
SERRINGE. *Well, sir.*
LORD FOPPINGTON. *Is there any hopes?*
SERRINGE. *Hopes,—I can't tell—What are you willing to give for your cure?*
LORD FOPPINGTON. *Five hundred pounds with pleasure.*
SERRINGE. *Why, then, perhaps there may be hopes. . . .*

VANBRUGH, Relapse, II, 1

Said Loveless, summing up the situation, "He's fallen into the hands of a roguish surgeon, I perceive designs to frighten a little money out of him." Apparently it was a traditional part of the surgeon's trade to prolong or magnify his patients' cure. One Dardevill has also been wounded in a duel, and as he is lying in bed vociferously bemoaning his early demise he is asked to get up and dance:

DARDEVILL. *Dance, madam! I am dying.*
PHILLIS. *That's false, to my knowledge, madam: For the surgeon told me last dressing, it was so slight a wound, he had much ado to keep it from healing.*

OTWAY, Atheist, V

The surgeon made up for this little failing, however, in the possession of other sterling qualities. He was secret as the grave in his clients' interests, and to protect them he had no scruples in tampering with truth:

1 SURGEON. *When we cure gentlemen of foule diseases,*
They give us so much for the cure, and twice as much,
That we doe not blab on't.

WEBSTER, Devils Law-case, III, 2

QUACK. *I'll bring half the chirurgeons in town to swear it.*
PINCHWIFE. *They—they'll sweare a man that bled to death through his wounds died of an apoplexy.*

WYCHERLEY, Country-Wife, V

HONISUCKLE. *I beseech thee good Mistris Birdlime tel me who it was.*
BIRDLIME. *O God sir we are sworne to secrecy as wel as surgeons.*

DEKKER, West-ward Hoe, IV

But if surgeons were no better at holding their tongues than were the midwives, Dekker wrote these lines with tongue in cheek. Old Garrula, who tipples and chatters her way through Brome's *The Lovesick Court*, compliments herself on her ability to keep a tight mouth:

> And were I
> A woman to tongue, as most are of my calling
> (Though midwives ha' been held the best at secret
> Councel keeping) it had been out I fear.
>
> III, 1

And when Horner in *The Country-Wife* wishes to spread abroad a report of his eunuchism he bids the Quack tell "all the midwives you know, the orange wenches at the play-houses, the city husbands, and old fumbling keepers of this end of the town, for they'l be the readiest to report it." (I, 1).

Surgical satire, like its medical counterpart, often follows well-worn grooves. In one of these lies Sergeant Kite's promise to a potential recruit:

KITE. . . . Give me your hand—You are by trade either a butcher or a surgeon.
BUTCHER. True—I am a butcher.
KITE. And a surgeon you will be, the employments differ only in the name—He that can cut up an ox, may dissect a man; and the same dexterity that cracks a marrow-bone, will cut off a leg or an arm.

> FARQUHAR, Recruiting Officer, IV

But Lyly had denied this one hundred years before:

> For if the butcher should take upon him to cut the anatomy of a man bicause he hath skil in opening an oxe, he would prove himself a calfe: or if the horselech would adventure to minister a potion to a sick patient, in that he hath knowledge to give a drench to a diseased horse, he would make himselfe an asse.
>
> Euphues, I, 180

Dr. Drench was not to be tricked by terminology: "a drench is a potion, and a potion is a drench; only the distinction is, when you put it into a horn, then 'tis a drench for a horse; and when you put it into a vial-glass, 'tis a potion for a man . . ." (Lacy, *Dumb Lady*, I).

The mellifluous sound of Lyly's prose leads us back once more to the question of language and truth. The inventor of the euphuistic style was willing to sacrifice sense to sound; medical men sacrifice both sense and sound in the development of a new language which, in its more inspired moments, seems to possess neither. In their efforts to describe complicated disease processes by equally complicated words, physicians have become slaves to cant. For every new experience or idea the scientist coins a new term. The only justification for the procedure is that it demands less time and skill to invent a "portmanteau" word than to learn to use the inexhaustible reserves of the English language to compose a lucid description of the phenomenon. It is obvious, of course, that as science expands, more and more terms to describe the expansion may become necessary. But there is no need for scientific vocabularies to increase geometrically when a simple arithmetic progression would suffice. Since 1650 the official pharmacopoeias have contained fewer and fewer drugs, the medical lexicons more and more polysyllabic terms.

One wonders whether the use of these hard words is not a relic of the diabolism that once sought to drive out disease-demons by nauseous smells and ear-splitting noise. Massinger's pointed comment shows the futility of such therapeutic measures:

MACRINUS. *Physitians but torment him, his disease laughs at their gibrish language.* . . .

Virgin-Martir, IV

It is not strange that the dramatists, whose business was words, should realize that there are times when even the most recondite terms are without virtue. James Shirley wrote:

FERNANDO. *But there is more than your skill requir'd*
    To state a health, your recipes, perplex't
    With tough names, are but mockeries, and noise,
    Without some dew from Heaven, to mix and make 'em
    Thrive, in the application. . . .

The Brothers, IV

Shirley's thesis is illustrated by the fatal illness of Don Vincent, who was attended by two of the most eminent physicians in Madrid. They both agreed that the old man's humors were in a state of mutiny—orgasmos—but there all agreement ended. One declared that "orgasmos" meant a "fermentation of the humors," the other that it signified a "concoction." In a huff the younger and more knowledgeable physician withdrew from the case, and the poor patient promptly expired under the lancet-strokes of the victor. "Such was the final close of Signor Dom Vincent, who had lost his life because his physician did not know Greek." (Le Sage, *Gil Blas*, Bk. IV, Ch. 3).

There is a scene in Act IV in Middleton's *A Faire Quarrell* which, better than any sermon, emphasizes the need for salutary reform in the promiscuous use of medical gibberish. The Colonel, wounded in a duel, is discovered lying on a couch. As the attending surgeon is going out, the Colonel's sister enters. Cries she:

> Come hither, honest surgeon, and deale faithfully
> With a distressed virgin: what hope is there?
> SURGEON. Hope, Chillis was scapt miraculously lady.
> SISTER. Whats that sir.
> SURGEON. Cava Vena: I care but little for his wound 'ith orsophag, not thus much trust mee, but when they come to diaphragma once, the small intestines, or the Spynall medull, or i' th rootes of the emunctories of the noble parts, then straight I feare a syncope; the flankes retyring towards the backe, the urine bloody, the exrements purulent, and the colour pricking or pungent.
> SISTER. Alasse, I'me neer the better for this answer.
> SURGEON. Now I must tell you his principal Dolour lies i' th region of the liver, and theres both inflamation and turmefaction fear'd marry, I made him a quadrangular plumation, where I used sanguis draconis, by my faith, with powders incarnative, which I temperd with oyle of Hypericon, and other liquors mundificative.
> SISTER. Pox a your mundies figatives, I would they were all fired.
> SURGEON. But I purpose lady to make an other experiment at next dressing with a sarcotricke, medicament, made of Iris of Florence. Thus, (masticke,) calaphena, apoponax, sacrocolla.

SISTER. *Sacro-halter, what comfort is i' this to a poore gentlewoman: pray tell me in plaine tearmes what you thinke of him.*

SURGEON. *Marry in plaine tearmes I know not what to say to him, the wound I can assure you inclines to paralisme; and I find his body cacochymicke: being then in feare of fever and inflamation, I nourish him altogether with viands refrigeratives and give for potion the juyce of Savicola, dissolv'd with water corefolium: I could doe noe more lady, if his best guiguimos were dissevered.*

We know now why a common epithet was "a gibberish surgion" (Dekker, *Wonder of a Kingdome,* IV), and why Grimaldi said: "as far as I conjecture, the greatest danger of his wound, lies in the chirurgeon's hard words . . ." (Wilson, *Belphegor,* IV, 2).

Ben Jonson recognized the problem clearly. "Whom prove you the next canter?" he asks Peni-boy Senior.

PENI-BOY. *The doctor here, I will proceed with the learned.*
  When he discourseth of dissection,
  Or any point of anatomy: that hee tells you,
  Of vena cava, and of vena porta,
  The meseraicke, and the mesenterium,
  What does he else but cant? Or if he runne
  To his judiciall astrologie,
  And trowle the Trine, the Quartile, and the Sextile,
  Platicks aspect, and Partile, with his Hyleg
  Or Alchochoden, Cuspes, and Horroscope.
  Does he not cant? Who here does understand him? [19]
    Staple of Newes, IV, 3

There is really no incompatability between scientific description and simple writing. The responsibility for the development of medical cant lies with the men, not the material. They, like the surgeon above, "in plaine tearmes" know not what to say, or at least they have great difficulty in following it through their own ingenious verbal mazes.

Drs. Simmons and Fishbein in *The Art and Practice of Medi-*

[19] In Act IV, scene 2 of *The Bloody Brother* (4to, 1639) by J. B. F. (but ascribed to Fletcher) there is a sample of this astrological cant by a doctor. It is too incomprehensible to transcribe.

cal Writing [20] once devoted an entire chapter to medical jargon. In this they say, "The use of long, technical words when short, simple words would suffice is a serious fault in scientific literature." Just how serious a fault they prove from manuscripts submitted for their editorial approval.

Samuel Butler had words to describe this sort of language:

> A Babylonish dialect,
> Which learned pedants much affect.
> It was a particolour'd dress
> Of patch'd and pyball'd languages;
> 'Twas English cut on Greek and Latin,
> Like fustian heretofore on sattin.
> It had an odde promiscuous tone,
> As if h' had talk'd three parts in one.
> Which made some think, when he did gabble,
> Th' had heard three labourers of Babel;
> Or Cerberus himself pronounce
> A leash of languages at once.
> This he as volubly would vent,
> As if his stock would ne're be spent.
> And truly to support that charge
> He had supplies as vast and large.
> For he could coyn or counterfeit
> New words, with little or no wit:
> Words so debas'd and hard, no stone
> Was hard enough to touch them on.
> And when with hasty noise he spoke 'em,
> The ignorant for currant took 'em.
>
> Hudibras, Pt. I, Canto 1

The old annotator of Butler's poem could not resist the temptation to add a comment to the ninety-third line of the satire: [21]

A BABYLONISH, &c. *A confusion of languages, such as some of our modern vertuosi us'd to express themselves in.*

[20] Chicago, 1927, p. 41 *passim.*
[21] *Hudibras,* in Three Parts (London, 1726).

But the tense of the commentator's verb is incorrect. The problem has not lessened since the seventeenth century, nor are there signs that it will.[22]

[22] Dr. Edmund Andrews in an essay on "Medical Terminology," *Annals of Medical History*, X (1928), 180, asserts correctly that "Attempts to improve our medical English are beset with many pitfalls." To this philological medico, however, the coining of new words is not a problem! He writes:

"With the rather sudden expansion in scientific knowledge during the last century, there has occurred a corresponding increase in the vocabulary until at present it might almost be described as infinite. In literary circles, for some idiotic reason, it is not considered good form to use words not clearly recognized as standard English. Artificial limitations are thus applied to the language. New words cannot be coined freely. If they are coined they must at first be used between quotation marks and are looked at askance until they have gone through a rather painful process of naturalization. How different it is in German, for instance; they can freely combine any two or three roots and suffixes or prefixes of known import, and such new growths are encouraged instead of being frowned upon by the arbiters of good taste. Science fortunately follows the German example. Any one can make up any sort of a word, and if it fills a need, there is no objection."

No objection, indeed!

Epilogue

The follies of our forefathers are of greater importance to us than is the well-being of our posterity.
—James Stephens

It is a tribute to medicine and the medical man, not that they have both successfully withstood a devastating guerrilla attack on a wide-flung literary front, but that they have always been forces vital enough to inspire such treatment from dramatists whose first concern was not, after all, the pillorying of the physician. Whether the satirical mind of the playwrights agreed or not with current medical practice, the doctor went his blithe way, taking advantage of the *vis medicatrix naturae,* lending ailing bodies a sometimes enfeebling hand, and burying his mistakes.

The surgeon was paid a life annuity for a successful operation, and the physician wore three-pile velvet and received a hundred dollars as a consultation fee. As long as collections were good and a fair proportion of his patients survived, the doctor wore an impenetrable armor, and shafts of satire rebounded harmlessly into the air. After the seventeenth-century playgoer had laughed a stitch into his side at the antics of the medical men on the boards, he went home with his pain and immediately called in a physician who summoned a surgeon who charged him ten hard-earned shillings for letting him blood from a vein.

Appendix

ISAAC BICKERSTAFF AND THE POX

WHY A MORAL CATACLYSM OVERWHELMED ENGLAND BETWEEN 1700 and 1710 I cannot pretend to explain; the Reverend Jeremy Collier and his famous fulmination against the stage I regard as a symptom rather than a cause. That some far-reaching social revolution took place within those years is immediately evident to any student of the French Disease. Sir John Vanbrugh, the last of the Restoration playwrights (in feeling, at any rate), wrote from 1696 to 1705, and until the turn of the century he spiced his plays with pocky jokes and syphilitic innuendos worthy of Shadwell or Aphra Behn. In the prologue to his first play, *The Relapse*, Vanbrugh derided the ogling beaux who undertook to look a lady dead, and mourned

> . . . their fate,
> To think, that after victories so great,
> It should so often prove, their hard mishap,
> To sneak into a lane—and get a clap.

In the second part of *Æsop*, also published in 1697, one of these beaux describes the settlements he can make on a wife: "Why, if she be a very great heiress indeed, I believe I may settle—my self upon her for life, and my pox upon her children for ever."

Now this is the pox in the seventeenth-century manner: honest, unashamed, witty—and a shock to our habit of mealy-mouthed euphemism. But only a few years later we meet syphilis (no longer the pox) in essentially its modern dress: periphrastic, titillating, and delicately indecent. When we read No. 260 of *The Tatler*, and compare it with the quotations from Shakespeare to Farquhar, we realize that something more than literary styles had changed overnight. The moral outlook of the people had, in fact, shifted to a new position that would prevail for a long time to come.

The Tatler [No. 260]

Non cuicunque datum est habere Nasum. [Not everybody can have a nose.] Mart.

From *Tuesday Dec. 5.* to *Thursday Dec. 7.* 1710

From my own apartment, December 6.

We have a very learned and elaborate dissertation upon thumbs in *Montaigne's Essays,* and another upon ears in the *Tale of a Tub.* I am here going to write one upon noses, having chosen for my text the following verses out of *Hudibras:*

> So learned *Talicotius* from
> The brawny part of porter's bum
> Cut supplemental noses, which
> Lasted as long as parent breech:
> But when the date of nock was out,
> Off drop'd the sympathetick snout.
>
> Hudibras, Pt. i. canto i, line 281

Notwithstanding that there is nothing obscene in natural knowledge, and that I intend to give as little offense as may be to readers of a well-bred imagination, I must, for my own quiet, desire the criticks, (who in all times have been famous for good noses) to refrain from the lecture of this curious tract. These gentlemen were formerly marked out and distinguished by the little rhinocerical nose, which was always looked upon as an instrument of derision, and which they were used to cock, toss, or draw up in a contemptuous manner, upon reading the works of their ingenious contemporaries. It is not, therefore, for this generation of men that I write the present transaction,

> —*Minus aptus acutis*
> *Naribus horum Hominum—*
> [Less sensitive
> Than the noses of these men]

but for the sake of some of my philosophical friends in the Royal Society, who peruse discourses of this nature with a becoming gravity, and a desire of improving by them.

Many are the opinions of learned men concerning the rise of that fatal distemper which had always taken a particular pleasure in venting its spight upon the nose. I have seen a little burlesque poem in Italian that gives a very pleasant account of this matter. The fable of it runs thus: Mars, the god of war, having served during the siege of Naples in the shape of a French colonel, received a visit one night from Venus, the goddess of love, who had been always his professional mistress and admirer. The poem says, she came to him in the disguise of a suttling wench, with a bottle of brandy under her arm. Let that be as it will, he managed matters so well, that she went away big-bellied, and was at length brought to bed of a little Cupid. This boy, whether it were by reason of any bad food that his father had eaten during the siege, or of any particular malignity in the stars that reigned at his nativity, came into the world with a very sickly look, and crazy constitution. As soon as he was able to handle his bow, he made discoveries of a most perverse disposition. He dipped all his arrows in poison, that rotted every thing they touched; and what was more particular, aimed all his shafts at the nose, quite contrary to the practice of his elder brothers, who had made a humane heart their butt in all countries and ages. To break him of his roguish trick, his parents put him to school to Mercury, who did all he could to hinder him from demolishing the noses of mankind; but, in spight of education, the boy continued very unlucky; and, tho' his malice was a little softened by good instructions, he would very frequently let fly an envenomed arrow, and wound his votaries oftener in the nose than in the heart. Thus far the fable.

I need not tell my learned reader, that Correggio has drawn a Cupid taking his lesson from Mercury, conformable to this poem; nor that the poem it self was designed as a burlesque upon Fracastorius.

It was a little after this fatal siege of Naples that Talicotius began to practise in a town of Germany. He was the first clap doctor that I meet with in history, and a greater man in his age than our celebrated Dr. Wall. He saw his species extremely mutilated and disfigured by this new distemper that was crept into it; and therefore, in pursuance of a very seasonable invention, set up a manufacture of noses, having first got a patent that none should presume to make noses besides himself. His first patient was a great man of Portugal, who had done good services to his country, but in the midst of them unfortunately lost his nose. Talicotius grafted a new one on the remaining part of the gristle or cartilaginous substance, which would sneeze, smell, take snuff, pronounce the letters M. or N. and in short, do all the functions of a genuine or natural nose. There was however one misfortune in this experiment. The Portuguese's complexion was a little upon the subfusk, with very black eyes and dark eyebrows, and the nose being taken from a porter that had a white German skin, and cut out of those parts that are not exposed to the sun, it was very visible that the features of his face were not fellows. In a word, the *Comdè* resembled one of those maimed antique statutes that has often a modern nose of fresh marble glewed to a face of such yellow, ivory complexion as nothing can give but age. To remedy this particular for the future, the doctor got together a great collection of porters, men of all complexions, black, brown, fair, dark, sallow, pale, and ruddy; so that it was impossible for a patient of the most out-of-the-way colour not to find a nose to match it.

The doctor's house was now very much enlarged, and became a kind of college or rather hospital, for the fashionable cripples of both sexes that resorted to him from all parts of Europe. Over his door was fastened a large golden snout, not unlike that which is placed over the great gates at Brazen-Nose college in Oxford; and as it is usual for the learned in foreign universities to distinguish their houses by a Latin sentence, the doctor writ underneath this great golden proboscis two verses out of Ovid:

> Militat omnis Amans, habet & sua Castra Cupido. . . .
> [Every lover's a soldier, and Cupid has his camps.]

It is reported that Talicotius had at one time in his house twelve German counts, nineteen French marquisses, and a hundred Spanish cavaliers, besides one solitary English esquire, of whom more here-after. 'Tho the doctor had the monopoly of noses in his own hands, he is said not to have been unreasonable. Indeed if a man had occasion for a high Roman nose, he must go to the price of it. A carbuncle nose likewise bore an excessive rate: but for your ordinary short turned-up noses, of which there was the greatest consumption, they cost little or nothing; at least the purchasers thought so, who would have been content to have paid much dearer for them, rather than to have gone without them.

The sympathy betwixt the nose and its parent was very extraordinary. *Hudibras* has told us, that when the porter died, the nose dropped of course [*sic*] in which case it was always usual to return the nose, in order to have it interred with its first owner. The nose was likewise affected by the pain as well as death of the original proprietor. An eminent instance of this nature happened to three Spaniards, whose noses were all made out of the same piece of brawn. They found them one day shoot and swell extremely, upon which they sent to know how the porter did, and heard, upon enquiry, that the parent of the noses had been severely kicked the day before, and that the porter kept his bed on account of the bruises it had received. This was highly resented by the Spaniards, who found out the person that had used the porter so unmercifully, and treated him in the same manner as if the indignity had been done to their own noses. In this and several other cases it might be said, that the porters led the gentlemen by the nose.

On the other hand, if any thing went amiss with the nose, the porter felt the effect of it, insomuch that it was generally articled with the patient, that he should not only abstain from all his old courses, but should on no pretence whatsoever smell pepper, or eat mustard; on which occasion, the part where the incision had been made, was seized with unspeakable twinges and prickings.

The Englishman I before mentioned was so very irregular, and relapsed so frequently into the distemper which at first brought him to the learned Talicotius, that in the space of two years he wore out five noses, and by that means so tormented the porters, that if he would have given 500 l. for a nose, there was not one of them that would accommodate him. This young gentleman was born of honest parents, and passed his first years in fox-hunting; but accidentally quitting the woods, and coming up to London, he was so charmed with the beauties of the play-house, that he had not been in town two days before he got the misfortune which carried off this part of his face. He used to be called in Germany, The Englishman of Five Noses, and, The Gentleman that had thrice as many Noses as he had Ears: such was the raillery of those times.

I shall close this paper with an admonition to the young men of this town, which I think the more necessary, because I see several new fresh-coloured faces, that have made their first appearance in it this winter. I must therefore assure them, that the art of making noses is entirely lost; and, in the next place, beg them not to follow the example of our ordinary town rakes, who live as if there was a Talicotius to be met with at the corner of every street. Whatever young men may think, the nose is a very becoming part of the face, and a man makes but a very silly figure without it. But it is the nature of youth not to know the value of any thing till they have lost it. The general precept therefore I shall leave with them is, to regard every town-woman as a particular kind of siren, that has a design upon their noses; and that amidst her flatteries and allurements, they will fancy she speaks to 'em in that humorous phrase of old Plautus: *Ego tibi Faciem denasabo mordicùs.* "Keep your face out of my way, or I'll bite off your nose."

When the virtuous nineteenth-century editors came to reissue the *Tatler* papers, there was not much bowdlerizing left for them to do. Taliacotius was "the first clap doctor" Steele had met with in history. But "He was the first *love-doctor*" to that later editor to whom Steele's meretricious moralizing was still not delicate enough.

Bibliography

SPECIFIC EDITIONS CONSULTED

EARLIEST AVAILABLE TEXTS, FACSIMILE REPRODUCTIONS, REPRINTS, OR, in a few cases, standard modern editions have been used. Scientific and critical books and articles to which single or passing reference has been made are indicated in the footnotes and consequently are not repeated here.

Aubrey, John. *Brief Lives*, ed. Andrew Clark. 2 vols. Oxford, 1898.
———. *Miscellanies upon Various Subjects*. 4th ed. London, 1857.
Beaumont, Francis, and John Fletcher, ed. A. R. Waller. 10 vols. Cambridge, 1905–12. (Cambridge English Classics.)
Behn, Mrs. Aphra. *Plays, Histories and Novels*. 6 vols. London, 1871.
———. *The Ten Pleasures of Marriage*. New York, 1933.
B[etterton], T[homas]. *Love Will Find Out the Way*. London, 1661.
Brome, Richard. *Dramatic Works*, ed. John Pearson. 3 vols. London, 1873.
Brown, Thomas. *Letters from the Dead to the Living*. 2nd ed. London, 1702.
Browne, Sir Thomas. *The Works of Sir Thomas Browne*, ed. Geoffrey Keynes. 4 vols. 2nd ed. Chicago, 1964.
Buckingham, 2nd Duke of. *See* George Villiers.
Burton, Robert. *The Anatomy of Melancholy*, ed. Floyd Dell and P. Jordan-Smith. 2 vols. New York, 1927.
Butler, Samuel. *Hudibras*. Part I, London, 1662; Part II, London, 1663; Part III, London, 1678.
———. *Poetical Works*. 3 vols. Edinburgh, 1784.
Cervantes, Miguel de. *Don Quixote*. Ozell's revision of the translation of Peter Motteux. New York, 1930. (Modern Library.)
Chapman, George. *Comedies and Tragedies*. 3 vols. London, 1873.
Congreve, William. *Complete Plays*, ed. Alex. C. Ewald. London, n.d. (Mermaid Series.)
Coryat, Thomas. *Coryats Crudities*. . . . 2 vols. Glasgow, 1905.
Davenant, Sir William. *The Tempest*. New York, 1908. (The Bankside-Restoration Shakespeare.)
———. *The Unfortunate Lover*. London, 1643.
Day, John. *Works*, ed. A. H. Bullen. 7 pts. in 1 vol. London, 1881.

Dekker, Thomas. *The Dramatic Works of Thomas Dekker*, ed. R. H. Shepherd. 4 vols. London, 1873.

————. *North-ward Hoe*. London, 1914. (Tudor Facsimile Texts.)

————. *Plague Pamphlets of Thomas Dekker*, ed. F. P. Wilson. Oxford, 1925.

————. *West-ward Hoe*. London, 1914. (Tudor Facsimile Texts.)

Deloney, Thomas. *The Works of Thomas Deloney*, ed. F. O. Mann. Oxford, 1912.

Dover, John. *The Mall*. Reprinted in Vol. VIII of Dryden's *Works*, ed. Sir Walter Scott and George Saintsbury. Edinburgh, 1882–92.

Dryden, John. *Best Plays*, ed. George Saintsbury. 2 vols. London, n.d. (Mermaid Series.)

[————]. *The Mistaken Husband*. Reprinted in Vol. VIII of *Works*, ed. Sir Walter Scott and George Saintsbury. Edinburgh, 1882–92.

Duffett, Thomas. *The Mock-Tempest*. London, 1675.

————. *Psyche Debauch'd*. London, 1678.

————. *The Spanish Rogue*. London, 1674.

D'Urfey, Thomas. *A Fond Husband*. London, 1677.

————. *Love for Money*. London, 1691.

————. *Madam Fickle*. London, 1677.

————. *The Richmond Heiress*. London, 1693.

Earle, John. *Micro-cosmographie*, ed. E. Arber. London, 1868. (English Reprints, No. 12.)

Etherege, Sir George. *Dramatic Works*, ed. H. F. B. Brett-Smith. 2 vols. Boston, 1927.

Evelyn, John. *Diary*, ed. William Bray. 2 vols. London [1907]. (Everyman's Library.)

Farquhar, George. *Complete Works*, ed. C. A. Stonehill. 2 vols. Bloomsbury, 1930.

Field, Nathaniel. *Amends for Ladies*. London, 1639.

————. *A Woman is a Weathercocke*. London, 1612.

Fletcher, John. *See* Beaumont and Fletcher.

Ford, John. *Dramatic Works*. Vol. I, ed. W. Bang, Louvain, 1908. Vol. II, ed. H. De Voght, Louvain, 1927.

Greene, Robert. *The Carde of Fancie*. See *Shorter Novels*.

Heywood, Thomas. *The Dramatic Works of Thomas Heywood*, ed. R. H. Shepherd. 6 vols. London, 1874.

Jacke Drums Entertainement. London, 1601.

James I. *Daemonologie* and *Newes from Scotland*, ed. G. B. Harrison. London [1924]. (Bodley Head Quartos.)

Jonson, Ben. *The New Inne*. London, 1631.

————. *Workes*. London, 1616.

————. *Workes*. London, 1640.

Lacy, John. *The Dumb Lady*. London, 1672.

————. *The Old Troop*. London, 1672.

Le Sage, A. R. *Gil Blas of Santillane*, trans. Smollett, freely revised by B. H. Malkin. 2 vols. London [1928]. (Everyman's Library.)

Leanerd, John. *The Rambling Justice*. London, 1678.

Lyly, John. *Complete Works of John Lyly*, ed. R. W. Bond. 3 vols. Oxford, 1902.

Marlowe, Christopher. *Works*, ed. C. F. Tucker Brooke. Oxford [1925].

Marston, John. *The Plays of John Marston*, ed. H. H. Wood. 3 vols. Edinburgh, 1934–38.

Massinger, Philip. *Beleeve As Ye List*. London, 1907. (Tudor Facsimile Texts, Folio Series.)

――――. *The Roman Actor*. London, 1629.

――――. *The Virgin-Martir*. London, 1631.

Merry Devill of Edmonton, The. London, 1911. (Tudor Facsimile Texts.)

Middleton, Thomas. *The Changeling*. London, 1653.

――――. *A Faire Quarrell*. London, 1617.

――――. *The Roaring Girle*. London, 1914. (Tudor Facsimile Texts.)

――――. *Works*, ed. A. H. Bullen. 8 vols. London, 1885–86.

Molière [Jean-Baptiste Poquelin]. "The Flying Physician," trans. Herbert Silvette, *Medical Life*, 44 (New York, 1937), 342–348.

――――. *The Works of Mr. de Moliere*, trans. J. Ozell. 3 vols. London, 1714.

Nashe, Thomas. *The Unfortunate Traveller*, ed. H. F. B. Brett-Smith. Oxford, 1927. (Percy Reprints, No. 1.)

――――. *Works of Thomas Nashe*, ed. R. B. McKerrow. 5 vols. London, 1905.

Nero, The tragedy of. 2nd ed. London, 1633.

Otway, Thomas. *Best Plays*, ed. Roden Noel. London, n.d. (Mermaid Series.)

Pepys, Samuel. *Diary*, ed. Henry B. Wheatley. 10 vols. in 3. London, 1926.

Porter, Henry. *The Two Angry Women of Abington*. London, 1911. (Tudor Facsimile Texts.)

Rabelais, Francois. *Gargantua and Pantagruel*. London, 1927.

Randolph, Thomas. *Aristippus*. London, 1630.

――――. *The Muses Looking-Glasse*. London, 1643.

Ravenscroft, Edward. *The London Cuckolds*. London, 1682.

Rowley, William. *All's Lost by Lust and a Shoemaker, a Gentleman*, ed. C. W. Stork. Philadelphia, 1910.

Sedley, Sir Charles. *The Poetical and Dramatic Works of Sir Charles Sedley*, ed. V. de Sola Pinto. 2 vols. London, 1928.

Shadwell, Thomas. *Best Plays*, ed. George Saintsbury. London, n.d. (Mermaid Series.)

Shakespeare, William. *The Complete Works of Shakespeare*, ed. George Lyman Kittredge. Boston, 1936.

Shirley, James. *The Brothers*. London, 1652.

――――. *Hide Parke*. London, 1637.

――――. *The Triumph of Peace*. London, 1633.

――――. *The Wittie Faire One*. London, 1633.

Shorter Novels. Vol. I, *Elizabethan and Jacobean*. London, [1929]. (Everyman's Library.)

Steele, Richard. *See The Tatler.*

Suckling, Sir John. *The Works of Sir John Suckling in Prose and Verse,* ed. A. H. Thompson. London, 1910.

T[homas] B[etterton]. *Love Will Find Out the Way.* London, 1661.

Tatham, John. *The Rump.* London, 1660.

Tatler, The: The Lucubrations of Isaac Bickerstaff, Esq; revised and corrected by the author. . . . London, 1710?–12.

Tourneur, Cyril. *Works,* ed. A. Nicoll. London, n.d.

Vanbrugh, Sir John. *Complete Works,* ed. Bonamy Dobree and Geoffrey Webb. 4 vols. Bloomsbury, 1927.

Villiers, George. *The Rehearsal,* ed. E. Arber. London, 1868. (English Reprints, No. 10.)

Webster, John. *Complete Works,* ed. F. L. Lucas. 4 vols. Boston, 1928.

Wilson, John. *Belphegor.* London, 1691.

———. *The Cheats.* London, 1664.

Wisdome of Doctor Dodypoll, The. London, 1912. (Tudor Facsimile Texts.)

Wycherley, William. *Complete Plays,* ed. W. C. Ward. London, n.d. (Mermaid Series.)

Index

HERBERT SILVETTE has a literary and medical-scientific background that particularly suits him for writing *The Doctor on the Stage*. His education at the University of Virginia culminated in a doctoral degree in physiology, and during the course of his teaching career in medical schools he has written or collaborated in some one hundred and twenty papers in clinical pathology, biochemistry, physiology, pharmacology, immunology, and history of medicine. He is translator of Molière's *Le Médecin Volant* and an authority on Philemon Holland of Coventry, Doctor of Physicke (1552–1637). He is co-author of *Tobacco: Experimental and Clinical Studies* and the author of eight novels. He has been a Guggenheim Fellow and a Porter Fellow of the American Physiological Society and is currently Visiting Professor of Pharmacology at the Medical College of Virginia.

FRANCELIA BUTLER also earned a Ph.D. at the University of Virginia and is currently on the English staff at the University of Connecticut. Her books include *Cancer Through the Ages* and *The Strange Critical Fortunes of Shakespeare's Timon of Athens*, and she has written several articles in medical history and English literature.

The Doctor on the Stage

was designed by Helen Orton, whose ornamental drawings throughout reflect the light-hearted attitude toward seventeenth-century medicine that Herbert Silvette shares with the earlier dramatists.

The text is set in eleven-point Electra leaded two points, a type which the American typographer W. A. Dwiggins designed for the Linotype. When Electra became available in 1935, its companion italic (in response to Stanley Morison's notes "Toward an Ideal Italic") was differentiated from the roman only by its slant. *The handsome "oblique" italic is aptly employed in this volume to set off extracted material.* Dwiggins' later, more conventional cursive italic (in which the title is set above) is used here to distinguish certain words in the regular text.

The book was composed, printed on a paper manufactured by the S. D. Warren Company, and bound by Kingsport Press, Inc., Kingsport, Tennessee.

THE UNIVERSITY OF TENNESSEE PRESS